CHILD CUSTODY, VISITATION, AND SUPPORT IN FLORIDA

Edward A. Haman
Attorney at Law

SPHINX® PUBLISHING
AN IMPRINT OF SOURCEBOOKS, INC.®
NAPERVILLE, ILLINOIS
www.SphinxLegal.com

First Edition, 2002

Published by: **Sphinx® Publishing, An Imprint of Sourcebooks, Inc.®**

Naperville Office
P.O. Box 4410
Naperville, Illinois 60567-4410
630-961-3900
Fax: 630-961-2168
www.sourcebooks.com
wwwSphinxLegal.com

This publication is designed to provide accurate and authoritative information in regard to the subject matter covered. It is sold with the understanding that the publisher is not engaged in rendering legal, accounting, or other professional service. If legal advice or other expert assistance is required, the services of a competent professional person should be sought.

From a Declaration of Principles Jointly Adopted by a Committee of the American Bar Association and a Committee of Publishers and Associations

This product is not a substitute for legal advice.

Disclaimer required by Texas statutes.

Library of Congress Cataloging-in-Publication Data
Haman, Edward A.
Child custody, visitation, and support in Florida / Edward A. Haman.-- 1st ed.
p. cm. -- (Legal survival guides)
Includes index.
ISBN 1-57248-205-2 (alk. paper)
1. Custody of children--Florida--Popular works. 2. Visitation rights legislation--Florida--Popular works. I. Title. II. Series.
KFF104.6Z9 H36 2002
346.75901'73--dc21

2002026996

Printed and bound in the United States of America.

VHG Paperback — 10 9 8 7 6 5 4 3 2 1

Contents

USING SELF-HELP LAW BOOKS

Before using a self-help law book, you should realize the advantages and disadvantages of doing your own legal work and understand the challenges and diligence that this requires.

THE GROWING TREND

Rest assured that you won't be the first or only person handling your own legal matter. For example, in some states, more than seventy-five percent of divorces and other cases have at least one party representing him or herself. Because of the high cost of legal services, this is a major trend and many courts are struggling to make it easier for people to represent themselves. However, some courts are not happy with people who do not use attorneys and refuse to help them in any way. For some, the attitude is, "Go to the law library and figure it out for yourself."

We at Sphinx write and publish self-help law books to give people an alternative to the often complicated and confusing legal books found in most law libraries. We have made the explanations of the law as simple and easy to understand as possible. Of course, unlike an attorney advising an individual client, we cannot cover every conceivable possibility.

COST/VALUE ANALYSIS

Whenever you shop for a product or service, you are faced with various levels of quality and price. In deciding what product or service to buy, you make a cost/value analysis on the basis of your willingness to pay and the quality you desire.

When buying a car, you decide whether you want transportation, comfort, status, or sex appeal. Accordingly, you decide among such choices as a Neon, a Lincoln, a Rolls Royce, or a Porsche. Before making a decision, you usually weigh the merits of each option against the cost.

When you get a headache, you can take a pain reliever (such as aspirin) or visit a medical specialist for a neurological examination. Given this choice, most people, of course, take a pain reliever, since it costs only pennies; whereas a medical examination costs hundreds of dollars and takes a lot of time. This is usually a logical choice because it is rare to need anything more than a pain reliever for a headache. But in some cases, a headache may indicate a brain tumor and failing to see a specialist right away can result in complications. Should everyone with a headache go to a specialist? Of course not, but people treating their own illnesses must realize that they are betting on the basis of their cost/value analysis of the situation. They are taking the most logical option.

The same cost/value analysis must be made when deciding to do one's own legal work. Many legal situations are very straight forward, requiring a simple form and no complicated analysis. Anyone with a little intelligence and a book of instructions can handle the matter without outside help.

But there is always the chance that complications are involved that only an attorney would notice. To simplify the law into a book like this, several legal cases often must be condensed into a single sentence or paragraph. Otherwise, the book would be several hundred pages long and too complicated for most people. However, this simplification necessarily leaves out many details and nuances that would apply to special or unusual situations. Also, there are many ways to interpret most legal questions. Your case may come before a judge who disagrees with the analysis of our authors.

Therefore, in deciding to use a self-help law book and to do your own legal work, you must realize that you are making a cost/value analysis. You have decided that the money you will save in doing it yourself outweighs the chance that your case will not turn out to your satisfaction. Most people handling their own simple legal matters never have a problem, but occasionally people find that it ended up costing them more to have an attorney straighten out the situation than it would have if they had hired an attorney in the beginning. Keep this in mind if you decide to handle your own case, and be sure to consult an attorney if you feel you might need further guidance.

Local Rules

The next thing to remember is that a book that covers the law for the entire nation, or even for an entire state, cannot possibly include every procedural difference of every county court. Whenever possible, we provide the exact form needed; however, in some areas, each county, or even each judge, may require unique forms and procedures. In our *state* books, our forms usually cover the majority of counties in the state, or provide examples of the type of form that will be required. In our *national* books, our forms are sometimes even more general in nature but are designed to give a good idea of the type of form that will be needed in most locations. Nonetheless, keep in mind that your *state*, county, or judge may have a requirement, or use a form, that is not included in this book.

You should not necessarily expect to be able to get all of the information and resources you need solely from within the pages of this book. This book will serve as your guide, giving you specific information whenever possible and helping you to find out what else you will need to know. This is just like if you decided to build your own backyard deck. You might purchase a book on how to build decks. However, such a book would not include the building codes and permit requirements of every city, town, county, and township in the nation; nor would it include the lumber, nails, saws, hammers, and other materials and tools you would need to actually build the deck. You would use the book as your guide, and then do some work and research involving such matters as whether you need a permit of some kind, what type and grade of wood are available in your area, whether to use hand tools or power tools, and how to use those tools.

Before using the forms in a book like this, you should check with your court clerk to see if there are any local rules of which you should be aware, or local forms you will need to use. Often, such forms will require the same information as the forms in the book but are merely laid out differently, use slightly different language, or use different color paper so the clerks can easily find them. They will sometimes require additional information.

Changes in the Law

Besides being subject to state and local rules and practices, the law is subject to change at any time. The courts and the legislatures of all fifty states are constantly revising the laws. It is possible that while you are reading this book, some aspect of the law is being changed or a court is interpreting a law in a different way. You should always check the most recent statutes, rules and regulations to see what, if any changes have been made.

In most cases, the change will be of minimal significance. A form will be redesigned, additional information will be required, or a waiting period will be extended. As a result, you might need to revise a form, file an extra form, or wait out a longer time period; these types of changes will not usually affect the outcome of your case. On the other hand, sometimes a major part of the law is changed, the entire law in a particular area is rewritten, or a case that was the basis of a central legal point is overruled. In such instances, your entire ability to pursue your case may be impaired.

To help you with local requirements and changes in the law, be sure to read the section in Chapter 3 on "Legal Research."

Again, you should weigh the value of your case against the cost of an attorney and make a decision as to what you believe is in your best interest.

INTRODUCTION

This book is designed to help you understand the law in Florida regarding child custody, visitation, and support. It will enable you to pursue your rights through the legal system without hiring a lawyer. Even if you do hire a lawyer, this book will help you to work with him or her more effectively, which can also reduce the legal fee.

This book covers the law, forms, and procedures applicable to both married and unmarried parents. If you are married, this book explains obtaining custody, visitation, and support outside of the divorce process. It also covers changing custody, visitation, or child support, orders in a final judgment of divorce. This book is *not* a guide to obtaining a divorce, although the legal principles discussed do apply to divorces. If you are not married, this book covers establishing paternity, and obtaining custody, visitation, and child support orders as part of the paternity process.

This is a practical guide to get you through "the system" as easily as possible. The emphasis is on practical information in plain English. Legal jargon has been kept to a minimum. For ease of understanding, this book uses the terms child and children interchangeably. Also, as the discussion may involve spouses, ex-spouses, or parents who have never been married to each other, this book will often refer to the parents, the other parent, or the other party.

Please keep in mind that different judges and courts in different counties may have their own particular procedures, forms, or ways of doing things. The court clerk's office can often tell you if they have any special forms, procedures, or other unique requirements. Court clerks cannot give legal advice, but they can tell you what their court or judges require.

The first three chapters of this book will give you an overview of the law and the legal system, and help you decide if you want an attorney. If you decide to hire a lawyer, Chapter 2 will also give you some tips on how to find and work with a lawyer. Chapters 4, 5, and 6 will give you information about court procedures and forms that apply to all types of cases. Chapter 7 covers the law, forms, and procedures relating to establishing paternity. Chapters 8 through 10 will give more details about custody, visitation, and child support. Chapters 11 through 13 explain how to go about requesting a change in custody, visitation, and child support, if you are already under a court order. Chapter 14 discusses enforcing an order for custody, visitation, or child support if the other party is not complying with the existing order. You will also find a glossary of common legal terms, following Chapter 14.

There are three appendices to this book. Appendix A contains selected portions of the Florida law and court rules dealing with establishing paternity, custody, visitation, and child support. Appendix B contains worksheets to help you keep organized.

Appendix C contains the forms you will complete and file with the court. Instructions for completing these forms are found throughout this book. You will not use every form in Appendix C. This book will guide you in determining which forms you will need and how to complete them. (Chapter 4 provides important general information regarding the preparation and use of legal forms.)

An Overview of Custody, Visitation, and Child Support

1

This chapter will give you a general overview of the law and the legal procedures related to establishing paternity, custody, visitation, and support. Each of these areas will be explained in much greater detail in later chapters, however, it will be helpful if you first understand some of the basics and how these areas relate to each other.

Paternity

There are several ways in which *paternity* is determined. How paternity is determined in a particular situation will depend upon whether the parents are married. If they are not married, whether the parents are in agreement about paternity is the issue.

The most basic way paternity is determined is when a couple has a child, they are listed as the parents on the child's birth certificate. If a couple is married and the wife gives birth, the law presumes that the husband is the father. No legal document or court proceeding is required to declare the husband to be the father. If the couple is not married, both must sign a form indicating their consent to have the father listed on the initial birth certificate.

If a child is born out of wedlock and the father is not listed on the initial birth certificate, there are two ways to establish who is the father and have him listed on an amended birth certificate. The first way is by both parents signing a legal document, called an ACKNOWLEDGMENT OF PATERNITY (also called a *statement of paternity*), which allows an amended birth certificate to be issued listing the father's name. (see form 47, p.302.) The second way is for either the mother or the father to file a lawsuit to have a court determine paternity.

ACKNOWLEDGING PATERNITY

If a father of a child born out of wedlock wants to legally establish himself as the father, he can acknowledge his paternity by signing a document commonly called an **ACKNOWLEDGMENT OF PATERNITY**. (see form 47, p.302.) This document is sent to the Florida Bureau of Vital Statistics, which will then issue a revised birth certificate listing him as the father. Chapter 7 will provide more details about what is required for an **ACKNOWLEDGMENT OF PATERNITY** to be valid, how to complete the form, and the legal rights and obligations which result from the use of the form.

PATERNITY LAWSUITS

Generally, if either parent refuses to sign the necessary document to establish paternity, the other parent can file a lawsuit seeking to have paternity legally determined.

NOTE: *Even if paternity has been established by some other means, a paternity suit may be used to resolve disputes regarding custody, visitation, or child support.*

The court will order some type of scientific testing, and will make a determination based on the test results and any other evidence produced by the parties. If the court determines the man to be the father, the court then has the authority to make orders regarding custody, visitation, and child support. There are some circumstances in which a lawsuit to determine paternity may not be pursued, which will be explained in Chapter 7.

CUSTODY AND VISITATION

The issue of child custody most often arises in divorce cases, however, custody can also become an issue if married parents separate from each other, or in connection with a lawsuit to determine paternity. The terms *custody* and *visitation* are still commonly used by lawyers and judges, however, Florida law uses more recently developed terms and concepts. These are *parental responsibility*, which refers to who has the right to make major decisions about the child's welfare; and *primary residence*, which refers to where the child will live a majority of the time.

Traditionally, one parent ended up with *custody*, which meant the child lived with that parent a majority of the time, and that parent was primarily responsible for decision-making. The other parent had *visitation rights*. Today, the law begins by assuming that both parents should have a say in decision making, and both parents should have frequent contact with the child. The judge must have a very good reason for not ordering joint decision making, which is called *shared parental responsibility*. In the case where one parent is denied decision making ability, the other parent has *sole parental responsibility*.

Also, rather than saying one parent has custody, and the other has visitation; the law today speaks in terms of one parent being the child's *primary residential parent*, and the other parent being the child's *secondary residential parent*. Any time custody becomes an issue, the court will apply certain criteria set forth in the Florida Statutes to determine the matters of parental responsibility and primary residence.

Married Parents

If the child's parents are married to each other, the most common way that custody is resolved is through a divorce. In Florida, a divorce is called a *dissolution of marriage*. Under Florida law, married parents each have equal rights to the custody of their child. This may only be changed by an order from a judge. Once parents separate, either may ask for custody in their petition for dissolution of marriage. Either may also file a motion to seek *temporary custody* or *temporary visitation* while the dissolution of marriage case is pending. Although this book does not cover filing for dissolution of marriage, it does cover how to seek a change in custody after a final judgment of dissolution of marriage has been entered. (see Chapter 11, p.109.)

Sometimes married parents separate, but for religious or other reasons, they don't want to file for dissolution of marriage. This can create a custody problem. The Florida legislature has established a way for separated parents to seek child support, through a court procedure for support unconnected with dissolution of marriage. The primary focus of this court procedure is to obtain financial support, not to seek custody. However, it is possible to request custody in a case seeking child support unconnected with dissolution of marriage. This procedure will be discussed further in Chapter 10.

Unmarried Parents

If the child's parents are not married to each other, one of them will usually need to file a lawsuit for paternity in order to seek a custody order. While Florida law does provide that a child's parents have equal rights to custody, a man who has not been legally established as a parent does not have any such custody rights. Even if paternity has been legally established, only a court can resolve any dispute about custody. A paternity case can be brought to determine custody issues, regardless of whether paternity has been established by some other means. Paternity cases are discussed more fully in Chapter 7.

Child Support

As a general rule, both parents of a child have an obligation to contribute toward the support of their child. For the typical couple who are married and living together as a family unit, the support of their children is worked out between them, with no intervention of a court. This is often also the case when unmarried parents live together as a family unit. It's when the parents are living apart and have a disagreement about how much each should be contributing that they typically turn to the court.

If married parents file for dissolution of marriage, either parent can ask the court to order the other to pay child support. Either may also file a motion to seek *temporary child support* while the dissolution of marriage case is pending. Chapter 13 discusses how to seek a change in child support after a final judgment of dissolution of marriage has been entered.

Sometimes married parents separate, but for religious or other reasons they don't want to file for dissolution of marriage. One parent may abandon the other parent and the child, and stop contributing to their financial support. The Florida legislature has established a way for separated parents to seek child support, through a court procedure for support unconnected with a dissolution of marriage. This procedure will be explained in more detail in Chapter 10.

If a child is born out of wedlock, either parent can file a paternity case to ask the court to order the other parent to pay child support. Even if paternity has been legally established, any dispute about child support can only be resolved by a court. In a paternity case, the amount of child support is determined by using the guidelines set forth in the law governing child support in a dissolution of marriage case.

Lawyers 2

This chapter will help you to determine whether you want an attorney, and if so, how to go about hiring and working with one. Whether you need an attorney will depend upon many factors, such as how comfortable you feel handling the matter yourself, whether your situation is more complicated than usual, how much opposition you get from the other parent, and whether the other parent has an attorney. It may also be advisable to hire an attorney if you encounter a judge with a hostile attitude. A very general rule is that you should consider hiring an attorney whenever you reach a point where you no longer feel comfortable representing yourself. This point will vary greatly with each person, so there is no easy way to be more definite.

Generally, there are no appointed attorneys in cases involving custody, visitation, or support; so if you want an attorney you will have to hire one. One exception is if you are seeking public assistance for yourself or your child. In such cases, state government attorneys may be able to pursue your case in relation to establishing paternity and seeking child support.

Deciding if You Want a Lawyer

One of the first questions to consider, and most likely the reason you are reading this book, is: "How much will an attorney cost?" Lawyers usually charge an hourly rate ranging from about $75 to $300 per hour. Most new (and therefore less experienced) attorneys would be quite capable of handling a typical case. However, if your situation becomes more complicated, you would probably prefer a more experienced lawyer.

Advantages of Having a Lawyer

Some advantages to having a lawyer include:

- *Judges and other attorneys may take you more seriously.* Most judges prefer both parties to have attorneys. They believe this helps the case more in a more orderly fashion. Persons representing themselves very often waste a lot of time on matters which have absolutely no bearing on the outcome of the case.
- *A lawyer will serve as a "buffer" between you and the other parent.* This can speed things up by reducing the chance for emotions to take control.
- *Attorneys prefer to deal with other attorneys.* This is true for the same reasons listed above.
- *You can let your lawyer worry about all of the details.* By having an attorney, you need only become generally familiar with the contents of this book.
- *Lawyers provide professional assistance with problems.* In the event your case is complicated, or suddenly becomes complicated, it is an advantage to have an attorney who is familiar with your case. It can also be comforting to have a lawyer to turn to for advice, emotional support, and to get your questions answered.

Advantages to Representing Yourself

On the other hand, there are also advantages to representing yourself, such as:

- *You save the cost of a lawyer.*
- *Sometimes judges are more sympathetic toward a person not represented by an attorney.* This may result in the unrepresented person being allowed a certain amount of leeway with the procedural rules (but not with poor conduct).
- *The procedures may be faster.* In regards to lawyers, two of the most frequent complaints received by the bar association involve delay in completing the case and failure to return phone calls. Most lawyers have a heavy caseload, which sometimes results in cases being neglected for various periods of time (usually until the client calls or some deadline is approaching). If you are following the progress of your own case, you'll be able to push it along the system diligently.
- *Selecting an attorney is not easy.* As the next section of this chapter shows, it is difficult to know whether you are selecting an attorney with whom you will be happy. There are numerous "horror stories" of attorneys getting $1,000 in advance, using it up without any significant progress being made, and demanding more money to continue. This problem will be discussed in more detail later in this chapter.

Middle Ground

As a compromise, you may want to look for an attorney who will be willing to accept an hourly fee to answer your questions and give you help as you need it, without formally becoming your attorney in court. This way, you will save some legal costs, but still get some professional assistance.

SELECTING A LAWYER

Selecting a lawyer is a two-step process. First, you need to find an attorney to make an appointment with. Second, you need to have the meeting and decide if you want to hire that attorney.

FINDING LAWYERS

There are several ways to find a lawyer:

- *Check with the attorney who handled another legal matter for you.* If you are seeking to change some aspect of your divorce judgment, you may want to use the same attorney who represented you in the divorce.
- *Ask a friend.* A common, and frequently the best, way to find a lawyer is to ask someone you know to recommend one to you. This is especially helpful if the lawyer represented your friend in a divorce or other family law matter.
- *Call a lawyer referral service.* You can find one by looking in the Yellow Pages phone directory under "Attorney Referral Services" or "Attorneys." This is a service, usually operated by a bar association, which is designed to match a client with an attorney handling cases in the area of the law the client needs. The referral service does not guarantee the quality or work, nor the level of experience or ability, of the attorney. Finding a lawyer this way will at least connect you with one who is interested in family law matters and probably has some experience in this area. There are also private lawyer referral services.
- *Check the Yellow Pages under the heading for "Attorneys."* Many of the lawyer and law firms will place display ads indicating their areas of practice. Look for lawyers or firms which indicate they practice in areas such as "divorce," "family law," or "domestic relations." Your Yellow Pages may also have separate categories for firms that practice in certain areas.
- Ask another lawyer. If you have used the services of an attorney for some other matter (such as a real estate closing, traffic ticket, or will), you may want to call and ask for a referral to an attorney whose ability in the area of family law is respected.

EVALUATING A LAWYER

From your search, you should select a few (maybe three to five) lawyers worthy of further consideration. Your first step is to call each attorney's office. Explain what type of case you have (paternity, custody, modification of child support, etc.), and ask the following questions:

- Does the attorney (or law firm) handle this type of case?
- How much can you expect it to cost?
- Is there any charge for the initial consultation?
- How soon can you get an appointment?

If you like the answers you get, ask if you can speak to the attorney. Some offices will permit this, but others will require you to make an appointment. Make the appointment if that is what is required. Once you get in contact with the attorney (either on the phone or at the appointment), ask the following questions:

- How much will it cost?
- How will the fee be paid?
- Does the lawyer use a written fee agreement? (Make sure he or she does, since you want it clearly established how the fee will be determined and how payment will be made.)
- How long has the attorney been in practice?
- How long has the attorney been in practice in Florida?
- What percentage of the attorney's cases involve divorce or other family law matters? (Don't expect an exact answer, but you should be able to get a rough estimate that is at least 20% — the higher the better. You want an attorney who has significant experience in the area, not one who only handles a family law case occasionally.)
- How long will it take? (Again, don't expect an exact answer, but the attorney should be able to give you an average or a range, and discuss things that may make a difference.)

If you get acceptable answers to those questions, it's time to ask yourself the following questions about the lawyer:

- Do I feel comfortable talking to the lawyer?
- Is the lawyer friendly toward me?
- Does the lawyer seem confident in himself or herself?
- Does the lawyer seem to be straightforward with me, and able to explain things so that I understand?

If you get satisfactory answers to these questions, you probably have a lawyer with whom you will be able to work. Most clients are happiest with an attorney who makes them feel comfortable, is friendly, and is able to explain the law and procedures.

Working with a Lawyer

In general, you will work best with your attorney if you keep an open, honest and friendly attitude. You should also consider the following suggestions.

Get a Fee Agreement

Lawyers are usually the first to tell you: "Get it in writing." This should especially apply to your agreement with your lawyer. Many lawyers do have a standard *fee agreement*, which includes such things as the hourly fee to be charged, what is included in the fee and what is extra, and how the fee is to be billed and paid. Your fee agreement should also have a statement as to exactly what the lawyer is to do and when.

Example: Suppose that you are to give the lawyer $1,000 in advance. At the very least, your agreement should provide that the initial $1,000 includes the preparation and filing of a petition to modify your divorce judgment and proper service of the papers upon your ex-spouse. This will avoid a situation which is all too common: the lawyer makes several phone calls to your ex-spouse in order to try to get him or her to agree to a modification, then tells you that he has used up the $1,000 and wants another $1,000 before he will file the Petition.

Ask Questions

If you want to know something or if you do not understand something, ask your attorney. If you do not understand the answer, tell your attorney you do not understand and ask him or her to explain it again. There are many points of law that many lawyers do not fully understand, so you should not be embarrassed to ask questions. Many people who say they had a bad experience with a lawyer either did not ask enough questions or had a lawyer who would not take the time to explain things to them. If your lawyer is not taking the time to explain what he or she is doing, it may be time to look for a new lawyer.

Give Complete Information

It is very important to give your lawyer complete information. Anything you tell your attorney is confidential: an attorney can lose his or her license to practice if he or she reveals information without your permission. Do not hold back. Tell your lawyer everything, even if it does not seem important to you. There are many things which seem unimportant to the average person but can change the outcome of a case. Also, do not hold something back because you are afraid it will hurt your case. It will definitely hurt your case if your lawyer does not find out about it until he or she hears it in court from the other party's attorney. But if he or she knows in advance, he or she can plan to eliminate or reduce damage to your case.

Accept Reality

Listen to what your lawyer tells you about the law and the system and accept it. It will do you no good to argue because the law or the system does not work the way you think it should. For example, if your lawyer tells you that the judge cannot hear your case for two weeks, do not try demanding that he set a hearing tomorrow. By refusing to accept reality, you are only setting yourself up for disappointment. And remember: It is not your attorney's fault that the system is not perfect or that the law does not say what you would like it to say.

Be Patient

Being patient applies to being patient with the system (which is often slow, as we discussed earlier), as well as with your attorney. Don't expect your lawyer to return your phone call within an hour. He may not be able to return it the same day either. Most lawyers are very busy and overworked, and can't make each client feel as if he or she is the only client.

Talk to the Secretary

Your lawyer's secretary can be a valuable source of information. So be friendly and get to know him or her. The secretary can often answer your questions—and you will not get billed for the secretary's time.

Let Your Attorney Handle the Other Party

It is part of your lawyer's job to communicate with the other party, or his or her lawyer. Let your lawyer do his or her job. Many lawyers have had clients lose or damage their cases when the client decides to say or do something on his or her own. Letting your attorney handle communication also helps reduce your stress in the event of arguments.

Be On Time

Be sure to be on time for appointments with your lawyer and to court hearings. Plan on getting to court hearings at least fifteen minutes early.

Keep Your Case Moving

Keep your case moving. Many lawyers operate on the old principle of "The squeaking wheel gets the oil." Work on a case tends to get put off until a deadline is near, an emergency develops, or the client calls. There is a very good reason for this. Many attorneys are competing for clients, and the high cost of office overhead. Many lawyers find it necessary to take more cases than can be effectively handled in order to make an acceptable living. That is why many attorneys work 65 hours a week or more. Your task is to become a squeaking wheel that does not squeak too much. Whenever you talk to your lawyer ask the following questions:

- What is the next step?
- When do you expect it to be done?
- When should I talk to you next?

If you do not hear from the lawyer when you expect, call him or her the following day. Do not remind him or her that he or she did not call–just ask how things are going.

How to Save Money

Of course, you do not want to spend unnecessary money for an attorney. Here are a few things you can do to avoid excess legal fees:

- Do not make unnecessary phone calls to your lawyer.
- Give information to the secretary whenever possible.
- Direct your question to the secretary first. He or she will refer it to the attorney if he or she cannot answer it.
- Plan your phone calls so you can get to the point, and take less of your attorney's time.
- Do some "leg work" yourself. Pick up and deliver papers, for example. Ask your attorney what you can do to assist with your case.
- Be prepared for appointments. Have all related papers with you, plan your visit to get to the point, and make an outline of what you want to discuss and what questions you want to ask.

Paying Your Lawyer

Pay your attorney bill when it is due. No client gets prompt attention like a client who pays his lawyer on time.

Firing Your Lawyer

If you do not think your lawyer is doing a good job or you lose faith in your lawyer, it is time to fire your lawyer. It is a good idea to discuss your feelings with the lawyer and give him or her a chance to make you a happy client again. If this does not work, fire the lawyer. This is as simple as sending your attorney a letter saying: "This is to notify you that I am discharging you as my attorney." You should expect to pay for the services that have been provided (unless you are disputing that your attorney is entitled to payment).

Your attorney should give you his or her file on your case, or a copy of that file, so you can take it to another lawyer or use it yourself. If the lawyer refuses to give you the file for any reason, threaten to complain to the judge and to The Florida Bar. If the lawyer still refuses, send a written complaint to the judge and file a grievance with The Florida Bar.

THE LEGAL SYSTEM 3

This chapter will give you basic information about the legal system, both generally and in relation to family law. It will also explain how to find other sources of information. Regardless of whether your case involves paternity, custody, visitation, or support, the information in this chapter will apply to you.

THE FLORIDA COURT SYSTEM

There are four levels in the Florida state court system: County Court, Circuit Court, District Court of Appeal, and Florida Supreme Court. The first two are commonly referred to as *trial courts*, because they are where cases are initially heard and decided. The second two are called *appellate courts*, because they only hear appeals of cases that have already been decided in one of the trial courts. All of the types of cases discussed in this book will be filed in Circuit Court. The state of Florida is divided into twenty circuits, each covering one or more counties as follows:

Circuit Number	**Florida Counties**
First	Escambia, Okaloosa, Santa Rosa, Walton
Second	Franklin, Gadsden, Jefferson, Leon, Liberty, Wakulla
Third	Columbia, Dixie, Hamilton, Lafayette, Madison, Suwanee, Taylor
Fourth	Clay, Duval, Nassau
Fifth	Hernando, Lake, Marion, Citrus, Sumter

Circuit Number	Florida Counties
Sixth	Pasco, Pinellas
Seventh	Flagler, Putnam, St. Johns, Volusia
Eighth	Alachua, Baker, Bradford, Gilchrist, Levy, Union
Ninth	Orange, Osceola
Tenth	Hardee, Highlands, Polk
Eleventh	Dade
Twelfth	DeSoto, Manatee, Sarasota
Thirteenth	Hillsborough
Fourteenth	Bay, Calhoun, Gulf, Holmes, Jackson, Washington
Fifteenth	Palm Beach
Sixteenth	Monroe
Seventeenth	Broward
Eighteenth	Brevard, Seminole
Nineteenth	Indian River, Martin, Okeechobee, St. Lucie
Twentieth	Charlotte, Collier, Glades, Hendry, Lee

Which circuit you will file your case in will depend upon the type of case you are filing, where you live, and where the other party lives. This will be discussed in more detail in later chapters.

Theory versus Reality

Our legal system is a system of rules. There are basically three types of rules:

1. *Rules of Law*: These are the basic substance of the law, such as a law telling a judge how to calculate child support.
2. *Rules of Procedure*: These outline how matters are to be handled in the courts, such as requiring court papers to be in a certain form filed within a certain time.
3. *Rules of Evidence*: These set forth the manner in which facts are to be proven.

The theory is that these rules allow each side to present the evidence that is most favorable to that side, and an independent person or persons (the judge or jury) will be able to figure out the truth. Legal principles will be applied to that "truth" which will give a fair resolution of the dispute. These legal principles are supposed to be relatively unchanging so we can all know what will happen in any given situation, and can plan our lives accordingly. This will provide order and predictability to our society.

Any changes in the legal principles are supposed to occur slowly, so that the expected behavior in our society is not confusing from day to day. Unfortunately, the system does not really work this way. What follows are a few of the problems in the real legal system.

The Law Changes Constantly

Each year, new laws are passed by the Florida Legislature, appeals courts make new rulings that interpret both the new laws and the old, and the Florida Supreme Court and some of the Circuit Courts change their forms and rules.

The System is not Perfect

Contrary to how it may seem, legal rules are attempts to make the system as fair and just as possible. Unfortunately, these attempts have resulted in a complex set of rules. Sometimes in a certain situation, the rules do not give a fair result. Also, judges can make bad decisions and people can lie.

The System is Slow

Even lawyers get frustrated at how long it can take to complete a case (especially if they do not get paid until it is done). Whatever your situation, things will take longer than you expect. Patience is required to get through the system with a minimum of stress. Be calm and courteous.

Judges do not always Follow the Rules

This is a shocking discovery for many young lawyers. After spending three years in law school learning legal theory, countless hours preparing for a hearing, and having the law on your side, you find that the judge is not going to pay any attention to legal theories and the law. Many judges make a decision simply based upon what they think seems fair under the circumstances. Unfortunately, what "seems fair" to a particular judge may depend upon his or her personal ideals and philosophy.

No Two Cases are Alike

Just because your friend's case went a certain way does not mean yours will have the same result. The judge can make a difference, and more often than not, the circumstances will alter the outcome. Just because your co-worker makes the same income as you and has the same number of children, you can't assume you will be ordered to pay the same amount of child support. There are usually other circumstances your co-worker doesn't tell you about and possible doesn't understand.

Half of the People Lose

Remember, there are two sides to every legal issue, and there is usually only one winner. Do not expect to have every detail go your way.

Counseling, Mediation, and Parenting Classes

There is a growing trend throughout the nation to encourage or require parties in legal disputes to try to resolve their disagreements outside of the courtroom. In the area of family law, this includes marriage counseling and *mediation*. In some states, including Florida, parents are often required to take some type of course to help them minimize—or at least understand—the traumatic effects experienced by children of a broken relationship.

Counseling

Under Florida law, judges have the authority to order a married couple to undergo marriage counseling prior to granting a divorce. The hope here is that the couple can resolve their differences and avoid a divorce. Most judges will only order counseling when it appears that there is a real chance that counseling will work. Such counseling may not be ordered in cases where the parents are not married.

Mediation

The courts in Florida also have the authority to order a couple into mediation to try to reach an agreement. In meditation, the goal is not to avoid a divorce, but to get the couple to agree to the terms of divorce and thereby avoid a trial. A mediator is appointed by the court. The mediator's job is to help the couple reach an agreement on the issues of custody, visitation, child support, and (in a divorce) property division. The mediator will meet with the parties, sometimes together and other times separately. He or she will listen to what each party wants, propose compromises, and try to work out a settlement that is satisfactory to both parties. The mediator does not make decisions or issue orders. If mediation is not successful, the parties will proceed to a trial before the court.

Parenting Classes

The courts in some Florida counties require the parents to attend a program to make them aware of the effects on their children, and help them deal with those effects. These programs are called various names in different counties. When you file your case, the court clerk will tell you if any such classes are required. You may also find brochures on these classes or programs at the clerk's office. If your county does require that you attend such a program, you will not be allowed to proceed with your case until you have completed the program.

Legal Research

This book is designed so that you do not need to do legal research in most cases. However, if you need or want to find out more about the law regarding custody, visitation, and support, this section will give you some guidance.

Law Libraries

You may be able to find basic legal information, most commonly a copy of the Florida Statutes, at your local public library. But if they do not have the most current copy, or if you need more information, you will need to visit a law library. Each county has a law library connected with the Circuit Court, so you can ask the court clerk where the law library is located. Also, law schools have law libraries, which are often open to the public. Do not be afraid to ask the law librarian for assistance. They cannot give you legal advice, but they can show you where the books are located.

Online Research

If you have access to the Internet, you can obtain a lot of legal information online. The Florida Statutes can be found at:

www.leg.state.fl.us/statutes/index.cfm?Mode=ViewStatutes&Submenu=1

The Florida Rules of Court, the Florida Supreme Court approved forms, and other information, can be found at the Florida Supreme Court website:

http://www.flcourts.org

Another source of legal information is: **http://www.findlaw.com.** To obtain Florida information, click on "US State Resources"; then scroll down to and click on "Florida." This will bring you to a page with listings for various sources. Clicking on "Primary Materials-Cases, Codes and Regulations," then clicking on "State Code," will bring you to the Florida Statutes site listed above. You can then click on the chapter of the Florida Statutes you want to see.

Florida Statutes

The main source of information on Florida laws relating to paternity, custody, visitation, and support are the *Florida Statutes*. Laws relating to divorce, custody, visitation, and support are primarily found in Chapter 61 of the Florida Statutes. Laws relating to establishing paternity are primarily found in Chapter 742 of the Florida Statutes. Portions of these laws can be found in Appendix A of this book. At a law library you may also find a set of books titled *Florida Statutes Annotated*, which includes summaries of court opinions and other information about each section of the Florida Statutes.

Florida Rules of Court

The *Florida Rules of Court* are the rules that are applied in the various courts in Florida. They also contain approved forms and instructions. These rules deal mainly with forms and procedures. You will be primarily concerned with the "Family Law

Rules of Procedure" and "Rules of Civil Procedure." Many of the approved forms are reproduced in Appendix C of this book.

FLORIDA DIGEST

The *Florida Digest* is a set of books containing short summaries of court opinions. It also tells you where you can find the court's written opinion. The information in the digest is arranged alphabetically by subject, and there is also an index.

SOUTHERN REPORTER

The *Southern Reporter* is a set of books which contain the full written opinions of the appeals courts. There are two sets, or series, of the reporter; the older cases being found in the *Southern Reporter* (abbreviated "So."), and the newer cases being found in the *Southern Reporter, Second Series* (abbreviated "So.2d"). For example, if the Florida Digest refers you to "*Smith v. Smith*, 149 So.2d 721 (1994)," this tells you that the case of *Smith v. Smith* can be found by going to Volume 149 of the *Southern Reporter, Second Series*, and turning to Page 721. The number in parentheses is the year the case was decided. If all that is given in the year, it means the case is from the Florida Supreme Court. If you see a notation such as "(5 DCA 1996)" it means the case is from the Florida District Court of Appeals for the Fifth District (the first number) and was decided in 1996 (the second number).

FLORIDA JURISPRUDENCE

Florida Jurisprudence is a legal encyclopedia. You simply look up the subject you want ("Dissolution of Marriage," "Paternity," etc.) in alphabetical order, and it gives you a summary of the law on that subject. It will also refer you to specific court cases that can then be found in the *Southern Reporter.*

OTHER SOURCES

Other books you may want to ask for at the law library are:

Adoption, Paternity, and Other Florida Family Practice,
by the Florida Bar Continuing Legal Education

Florida Family Law Practice Manual,
by Gerald D. Schackow, Lexis Law Publishing

Florida Family Law - A Common Sense Approach,
by Seymour Benson, Lawyers Cooperative Publishing

Florida Family Law,
by Brenda M. Abrams, Matthew Bender (now LexisNexis)

Florida Dissolution of Marriage,
by the Florida Bar Continuing Legal Education

Florida Civil Trial Practice,
by the Florida Bar Continuing Legal Education

These will explain the law in great detail and provide additional forms if you need them.

4 Basic Forms and Procedures

This chapter will give you basic information about legal forms and the procedures to get your case started. Regardless of whether your case involves paternity, custody, visitation, or support; the information in this chapter will be necessary for you. Instructions for completing several essential forms are found in this chapter. Later chapters will frequently refer you back to these instructions.

Legal Forms

There is nothing magical about legal forms. They are simply a way of communicating information to the court. Most of the forms in Appendix C of this book follow forms approved by the Florida Supreme Court. Some of these "official" forms are poorly drafted, but their use is required in most counties. A few counties may have their own forms (which you must obtain from the court clerk), but they will be very similar to the forms in this book. Additional forms have been included in Appendix C to cover some common situations for which there are no Supreme Court forms. You will not need to use every form found in Appendix C. Later chapters of this book will help you determine which forms you will need for your situation.

The forms in this book are legally correct, however, one occasionally encounters a troublesome clerk or judge who is very particular about how he or she wants the forms. If you encounter any problem with the forms in this book being accepted by the clerk or judge, you can try one or more of the following:

- Ask the clerk or judge what is wrong with your form, then try to change it to suit the clerk or judge.

- Ask the clerk or judge if there is a Florida Supreme Court form or a local form available. If so, find out where you can obtain it, then get it and use it. The instructions in this book will still help you to fill it out.
- Consult a lawyer.

If you tear the forms out of this book, it suggested that you make photocopies of the forms, and keep the originals blank to use in case you make a mistake or need additional copies.

Typing Forms

Although the instructions in this book will often tell you to "type in" certain information, it is not absolutely necessary to use a typewriter. If typing is not possible, you can print the information required in the forms. Just be sure your handwriting can be easily read or the clerk may not accept your papers for filing.

> ***Warning:*** Some, if not all of the counties require the use of black ink on the forms. Therefore, whenever you sign a form, or if you write in the information instead of typing, be sure to use a pen with black ink.

Form Numbers and Titles

In most places in this book, each form is referred to by both the title of the form and a form number. Be sure to check the form number because some of the forms have similar titles. The form number is found at the top, outside corner of the first page of each form. Also, a list of forms, by both number and title, is found at the beginning of Appendix C. The only exception to using the form number will be when there is more than one form of a certain type and the explanation relates to all forms of that type. For example, there are several types of **Petition** forms. A statement about "the Petition" without a form number, means that it applies to whichever **Petition** form you are using.

NOTE: *There is a different form number at the bottom of each form. For example, the bottom of the form beginning on page 223 reads: "Florida Family Law Rules of Procedure Form 12.910(a), Summons: Personal Service on an Individual (9/00)." This is the form number assigned by the Florida Supreme Court in Rule 12.910(a) of the Florida Family Rules of Procedure. The designation "(9/00)" indicates the month and year that particular form was last revised; in this case it was September of 2000.*

Case Style

Most of the forms in Appendix C of this book have the same format at the top of the first page. This section of a legal form is called the *case style*. The case style tells the court in which the case is filed, the case number, and the names of the parties. If you are filing a new case, the court clerk will assign a case number when you file the first papers. If you are filing papers in an existing case, such as to modify custody or support, you will use the case style from the previous papers filed. The case style section of each form will be completed as follows:

- The blank space in the first line of the case style is for the number of the judicial circuit in which your case will be filed. For a new case, you can look in the phone book or call the court clerk's office to find out your court's circuit number. If you are filing papers in a case that has already been commenced, fill in the same information as in the other papers.
- The blank in the second line is for the name of the county in which the case is filed.
- If you are filing a new case, the court clerk will give you the case number at the time your papers are accepted for filing. Some circuits also use a division designation to indicate the judge assigned to the case. If so, the court clerk will give you this information also. If you are filing papers in a case that has already been commenced, fill in the same case number and divisions information as in the other papers.
- If you are filing a new case, type in your name on the line marked "Petitioner," and the other party's name on the line marked "Respondent." Do not use nicknames or shortened versions of names. Use full legal names as they appear on birth certificates or marriage licenses. If you are filing papers in a case that has already been commenced, fill in the names as they appear in the other papers.

When completed, the case style should look something like the following example:

IN THE CIRCUIT COURT OF THE___THIRTEENTH___JUDICIAL CIRCUIT

IN AND FOR___HILLSBOROUGH___COUNTY, FLORIDA

Case No.: ___02-19028___

Division:___F___

Rhett Butler___,
Petitioner,

and

Scarlett O'Hara Butler___,
Respondent.

SIGNATURES AND NOTARIES

At the end of each form there will be a place for you to sign your name, and type in your name, address, and phone numbers. Space is provided for a "Fax Number," but this can be left blank if there is no fax machine available to you. Your signature must be *notarized* on certain forms, in which case there will be a space for the *notary public* or a deputy court clerk to complete.

Assistance from Nonlawyers

At the very end of most forms, there will be a section beginning with the words "If a nonlawyer," which must be completed by someone who is not a lawyer, but who helps another person complete the form. This is primarily used by paralegals. If you are filling out your own papers, you do not need to be concerned with this section of the form and should leave it blank.

Filing with the Court Clerk

This section will explain basic filing procedures, and discuss a few forms that will need to be filed in most cases. More specific information for the type of case you are filing will be presented in later chapters.

Filing Procedures

Later chapters of this book will guide you in figuring out which forms you will need to file. Once you have determined which forms you need to get started, and have them prepared, it is time to file them with the court clerk. First, make at least three copies of each form (the original for the clerk, one copy for yourself, one for the other party, and one extra copy just in case the clerk asks for two copies or you decide to hire an attorney later).

Filing is actually about as simple as making a bank deposit, although the following information will make things go more smoothly. Call the clerk's office. You can find the phone number under the county government section of your phone directory. Ask the clerk the following questions (along with any other questions you have, such as where the clerk's office is located and what are their hours):

- How much is the filing fee for the type of case or petition you will be filing?
- Does the court have any special forms (other than the Supreme Court forms) that need to be filed? (If there are special forms that do not appear in this book, you will need to go to the clerk's office and pick them up. There may be a fee for such forms.)
- How many copies of the forms do you need to file with the clerk?

Next, take your forms to the clerk's office. The clerk's office handles many different types of cases, so be sure to look for signs that tell you which office or window to go to. You should be looking for signs that say such things as "Family Court," "Family Division," "Filing," etc. If it's too confusing, ask someone where to file the type of case you are filing.

Once you have found the right place, simply hand the papers to the clerk and say, "I'd like to file this." The clerk will examine you papers, then do one of two things: either accept them for filing (and collect the filing fee or direct you to where to pay it), or point out something that is not correct or that is incomplete (such as you forgot to sign the form, or missed checking a space).

If you are told something is wrong, ask the clerk to explain what is wrong and how to correct the problem. It may be possible to correct the problem at the clerk's counter. Although clerks are not permitted to give legal advice, the types of problems they spot are usually very minor things that they can tell you how to correct. It is often possible to figure out how to correct the form from the way they explain what is wrong.

CIVIL COVER SHEET

Regardless of the type of case you are filing, you will need to file a CIVIL COVER SHEET. (see form 8, p.207.) This form is required by all courts for administrative purposes. To prepare the CIVIL COVER SHEET, follow the instructions in the chapter relating to the type of case you are filing.

NOTICE OF SOCIAL SECURITY NUMBER

If you are filing a petition to modify an existing judgment in a case where you have already provided your social security number, you do not need to be concerned with this section. Otherwise, you will need to file a NOTICE OF SOCIAL SECURITY NUMBER(S) (see form 6, p.203):

☛ Complete the case style portion of the form according to the instructions given on page 21.

☛ On the first line in the main paragraph, fill in your full name.

☛ On the second line in the main paragraph, fill in your social security number.

☛ On the third line in the main paragraph, fill in your date of birth.

☛ Check the line before paragraph 2, and fill in the name, birthdate, and social security number of each minor child who is the subject of this divorce, support, or paternity case.

☛ Do not sign your name on this form until you are before a notary public of a deputy court clerk.

☛ Fill in the date on the line indicated, and below the signature line, type in your name, address, and telephone information.

☛ Take this form to a notary public or to the court clerk's office. You will need to sign your name on the signature line before the notary or a deputy court clerk. The notary or clerk will complete the remainder of the form, and it will be ready for filing with the clerk.

NOTICE OF CURRENT ADDRESS

Regardless of the type of case you are filing, you should file a **NOTICE OF CURRENT ADDRESS** (see form 22, p.237):

- Complete the case style portion of the form according to the instructions given on page 21.
- In the first paragraph, fill in your full name, current address, telephone number, and fax number (if you have one), on the lines indicated.
- In the third paragraph, check the appropriate space to indicate how you provided the other party with a copy of this form, and fill in the date you did so.
- Under the heading "Other party or his/her attorney," fill in the name, address, and fax number (if any) of the other party or his or her attorney. If the other party does not have an attorney, a copy must be provided to the other party. If the other party does have an attorney, the copy should be sent to the attorney instead.
- Take this form with you when you file your initial papers, and sign it before the deputy court clerk (as an option, you can also sign it before a notary public before you take it for filing). At the time you sign it, fill in the date where indicated, and sign your name on the line marked "Signature of Party."

The notary or deputy clerk will fill in the bottom portion of the form.

WHEN YOU CANNOT AFFORD COURT COSTS

If you cannot afford to pay the filing fee or other court costs, you will need to file an **AFFIDAVIT OF INDIGENCY**. (see form 1, p.173.) In order to qualify for a waiver of the filing fee, you must be *indigent*. If you are indigent, your income is probably low enough for you to qualify for public assistance (welfare).

> ***Warning:*** If you decide to use this form, you will probably be asked for more information to prove that you meet the requirements for being declared indigent. Before you file this form, you may want to see if the court clerk will give you any information on what is required to be declared indigent. You should also be aware that you can be held in contempt of court for giving false information on this form or in court.

AFFIDAVIT OF INDIGENCY

To complete the **AFFIDAVIT OF INDIGENCY** (form 1):

- Complete the case style portion of the form according to the instructions on page 21.
- In the first paragraph, type in your name.

- If you are on public assistance, place an "X" on the line before paragraph "a." Then type in the amount of assistance you receive, the period it represents (week, month, etc.), and your public assistance case number. If you are on public assistance, you do not need to complete paragraph "b."
- If you are not on public assistance, you will need to check paragraph "b." Be sure that you have filed a **Family Law Financial Affidavit (Short Form)** (see form 2, p.175) or be sure to file it along with form 1.
- Complete the certificate of service section, and type in your name, address, and telephone information under the line marked "Signature of Party." Do not sign your name until you are before a notary public or a deputy court clerk.

Take this form to a notary public, or to the deputy court clerk, and sign it before the notary or clerk. The notary or clerk will complete the remainder of the form, and it can then be filed.

If the judge approves your **Affidavit of Indigency**, he or she will issue an order declaring you indigent and waiving filing fees and other court costs. You will need to show a copy of this order to the court clerk so that you will be allowed to file your other papers without paying the filing fee.

You will also need to provide a copy of this order to the sheriff's office if you need to have the other party served with papers without paying the service fee. However, if you need to publish a **Notice of Action** in a newspaper, you will still need to pay the newspaper's fee. (see form 20, p.235.) The waiver of fees only applies to fees charged by government agencies such as the court and the sheriff's office. Private persons or companies are not required to provide you with free services.

5 Notice Requirements and Defaults

In order to have any type of case heard by a court, it is necessary to notify the other party that you have begun a court proceeding. Once this is done, you will need to provide the other party with copies of all documents you file with the court, and notify the court that you have done so. This chapter will explain the various methods of providing the required notices, including when each type is to be used and the forms needed. This chapter will also discuss what to do if the other party does not respond to the papers you file.

Regardless of whether your case involves paternity, custody, visitation, or support; the information in this chapter will be necessary for you. Instructions for completing many essential forms are found in this chapter. Later chapters will frequently refer you back to these forms and instructions.

Personal Service

The best way to notify the other party that you have begun a legal proceeding is by *personal service*. This means the sheriff delivers a copy of your court papers to the other party. You must use personal service if you are filing a new case, such as to establish paternity, or to seek support or custody when you are not married to the other party. If you are filing papers to change an order in an existing case, you must use personal service if you are seeking to get child support when none was awarded in your divorce judgment.

Even if personal service is not required, it is the best way to prove to the judge that the other party actually received notice of the court proceeding. In addition to a copy of your **Petition**, there are several other forms you will need to prepare and file. The particular type of PETITION you need will be discussed in later chapters. The following information will help you complete the other forms you will need.

SUMMONS: PERSONAL SERVICE ON AN INDIVIDUAL

The PETITION will be delivered along with a Summons. Check with your court clerk to see if the clerk will prepare the Summons or if you will need to prepare one. If you need to prepare it, use the SUMMONS: PERSONAL SERVICE ON AN INDIVIDUAL (see form 15, p.223):

- Complete the top portion of the form according to the instructions on page 21.
- Type the other party's name and an address where he or she can be found (preferably during the day) on the first two lines (just above the word "Important"). The address you give is where the sheriff will first try to find the other party, so be as certain as possible that it is a good address.
- Type in the street address of the courthouse on the line in the first paragraph below the word "Important."
- Type in your name and mailing address on the lines in the third paragraph, after the words "(Name and address of the party serving the Summons)."
- Go to the court clerk's office and have the clerk date and sign the Summons at the bottom of the third page.

After the clerk signs the Summons, you will need to deliver or mail to the sheriff the original and one copy of the Summons, a copy of your PETITION and whatever papers you file along with the PETITION (such as your FAMILY LAW FINANCIAL AFFIDAVIT, UNIFORM CHILD CUSTODY JURISDICTION ACT AFFIDAVIT, etc.). The sheriff will deliver these papers to the other party and then file a paper with the court verifying the date and time the papers were *served* (delivered).

PROCESS SERVICE MEMORANDUM

To assist the sheriff, you should also complete the PROCESS SERVICE MEMORANDUM (see form 16, p.226), which is self-explanatory. On form 16 there is a space to give any special instructions, such as the hours of the day the other party will most likely be at the place you intend for him or her to be served, or alternate addresses such as his or her work address.

Service by Mail

Under a few very specific circumstances, you may be able to notify the other party by mail instead of by personal service. You may notify the other party by mail only if both of the following apply:

1. You are filing papers to change an order in an existing case.
2. You are not seeking to get child support when none was awarded in the original order.

Mailing

For service by mail you will send the other party a copy of your **Petition**, Summons, and any other papers you file with them, using *certified mail, return receipt requested.* This is where the mailman has the other party or someone in his or her home, sign a green card showing the date the mail was received. This card will be mailed back to you, and will be your proof to the judge that the other party was notified of your **Petition**. This is probably the best method of service if the other party lives in another state, although you could contact the sheriff where the other party lives and arrange for personal service.

Certificate of Service

After mailing the **Petition** and other papers, you will need to file a **Certificate of Service**. (see form 21, p.236.) You will also prepare and file a **Certificate of Service** every time you send copies of legal papers to the other party. Follow these instructions to complete the **Certificate of Service**:

- ☛ Complete the top portion of the form according to the instructions on page 21.
- ☛ Type in the name of each form you sent to the other party on the line in the main paragraph, which begins "I certify that a copy." (Such as "Supplemental Petition for Modification of Child Support and Family Law Financial Affidavit.")
- ☛ Check the appropriate space for the manner in which you sent or delivered the forms. For service by mail, check the space for "mailed." Notice that you may also personally hand deliver the forms, but this will not give you any proof that the other party received them, as will a green certified mail return receipt card. (Of course, you could always take a friend to be a witness, or have the friend deliver the papers and then complete the **Certificate of Service** form.)
- ☛ Type in the date the papers were mailed or delivered on the line after the word "(date)."
- ☛ Type in the name, address, and telephone number for the other party or attorney (whichever you mailed the papers to), on the lines below the words "Other party or his/her attorney."

- ☛ The person mailing or delivering the papers must sign on the line marked "Signature of party," and that person's name, address, and telephone number must be typed in below that line. Once completed, this form is to be filed with the court clerk.

Warning: If you mail your Petition, you must send it to the other party; not to his or her attorney. You can't assume the lawyer who represented the other party in the original case is still representing him or her. You can only send the papers to the lawyer after the other party has received the Petition and has advised you that he or she has a lawyer.

Service by Publication

If you do not know where the other party is and cannot find him or her, you will need to use *service by publication*. As a practical matter, this will probably not be used to seek an increase in child support. If you do not know where the other party is, you probably are not receiving the child support as required by the current order. In such a case you would probably be better off trying to go through your local Child Support Enforcement Office to locate the other party, and worry about an increase later.

If you are no longer financially able to pay the amount of child support required by the current order, you need to file a Petition immediately. Even if you have not been paying because there is no address to which to send the payments, child support *arrearages* will keep growing, so do not wait.

NOTE: *Service by publication is one of the more complicated procedures in the legal system. Follow the steps listed below very carefully.*

The Diligent Search

The court will only permit publication when you cannot locate the other party. This includes the situation where the sheriff has tried several times to personally serve the other party, but it appears that the other party is hiding to avoid being served. First, you will need to show that you cannot locate the other party by telling the court what you have done to try to find him or her.

To get an idea of what is expected of such a search, read the items in paragraph 1 of the Affidavit of Diligent Search and Inquiry. (see form 19, p.232.) You should try all of the items listed in form 19 that you believe might lead you to find the other party. Some of these will apply to everyone, while others will only be used if they would apply to the other party in your case.

Example: You know that the other party has never engaged in a job which might be under a union, or that is subject to any kind of professional or occupational licensing. In this situation, you would not be expected to make that kind of a search.

If you do come up with a current address in Florida, go back to personal service by the sheriff (or service by mail, if appropriate). If not, continue with this procedure.

PREPARING AND FILING COURT PAPERS

Once you have completed your search, you need to notify the court. This is done by filing the AFFIDAVIT OF DILIGENT SEARCH AND INQUIRY. (see form 19, p.232.) This form tells the court what you have done to try to locate the other party, and asks permission to publish your notice. Follow the instructions below to complete the AFFIDAVIT OF DILIGENT SEARCH AND INQUIRY:

- Complete the top portion of the form according to the instructions on page 21.
- Type your name in the blank in the first (unnumbered) paragraph.
- In paragraph 1, check the space for "Petitioner" or "Respondent," whichever applies to the other party. Next, check the line before all of the items that you used in your search for the other party. There are numerous spaces for you to check a space for "Petitioner" or "Respondent," whichever applies to the other party. If you can't locate the other party, you will need to check with the various branches of the armed services to find out if the other party is in the military service. This will require you to use the MEMORANDUM FOR CERTIFICATE OF MILITARY SERVICE. (see form 17, p.229.) The last item is for you to add anything that was not covered by the other items.
- In paragraph 2, check the appropriate space for "Petitioner" or "Respondent," whichever applies to the other party, and check the appropriate space to indicate if you know the other party's age (if you do know, fill in his or her age on the line indicated).
- In paragraph 3, you will need to select one of the three optional paragraphs, and check the appropriate spaces for "Petitioner" or "Respondent," whichever applies to the other party. If you have located the other party and he or she lives outside of Florida, you will need to fill in his or her address on the line in paragraph "b."
- Take the form to a notary public and sign your name before the notary on the line marked "Signature of Party."

You will also prepare a NOTICE OF ACTION. (see form 20, p.235):

- ☛ Type the other party's name after the word "TO:"
- ☛ Type your name and address in the blanks in the first paragraph. Leave the other spaces blank, as they are for the court clerk to complete.
- ☛ Take the original AFFIDAVIT OF DILIGENT SEARCH AND INQUIRY (form 19), and the original and two copies of the NOTICE OF ACTION (form 20), to the court clerk.

The clerk will fill in the remaining blanks on the NOTICE OF ACTION, and return two copies to you. If the clerk finds any errors in your papers, he or she will notify you as to what needs to be corrected. You may need to provide the clerk with a self-addressed, stamped envelope when you deliver your NOTICE OF ACTION.

PUBLISHING

After the clerk completes the NOTICE OF ACTION (form 20), you need to have a newspaper publish it. Check the Yellow Pages listings under "Newspapers," and call several of the smaller ones in your county (making sure it is in the same county as the court). Ask if the newspaper is approved by the court for legal announcements. If it is, ask: "How much do you charge to publish a NOTICE OF ACTION not involving property?" You want the cheapest newspaper. Most areas have a newspaper that specializes in publishing legal announcements at a much cheaper rate than the regular daily newspapers. If you look around the courthouse, you may find a copy or a newsstand for this newspaper.

Once you find the newspaper you want, send them a copy of the NOTICE OF ACTION (form 20), along with a check for the publication fee and a cover letter stating:

Enclosed is a NOTICE OF ACTION for publication as required by law. Please take notice of the return date in the NOTICE OF ACTION, and ensure that the dates of publication meet the legal requirement that the return date be "not less then twenty-eight nor more than sixty days after the first publication." If you cannot comply with this requirement, please notify me immediately, so I can obtain an amended NOTICE OF ACTION.

The NOTICE OF ACTION will be published once a week for four weeks. Get a copy of the newspaper the first time the NOTICE OF ACTION will appear, and check to be sure it was printed correctly. If you find an error, notify the newspaper immediately.

Look at the date the clerk put in the blank space in the main paragraph of the NOTICE OF ACTION. You must make sure that this date is at least twenty-eight days after the date the newspaper first published the NOTICE OF ACTION. Also make sure it is no more than sixty days after the date of the first publication. If these requirements are not met, notify the newspaper of their mistake. Remind them of your cover letter if necessary. You will also need to prepare a new NOTICE OF ACTION for the clerk to sign, and go through the publishing process again. If the newspaper made the mistake, they should not charge you for the second publication.

As indicated in the NOTICE OF ACTION, the other party has until a certain date to respond. If the other party responds to the NOTICE OF ACTION published in the newspaper, proceed with setting a *hearing date*. (See the section in this chapter on "Setting a Court Date.") If the other party does not respond by the date indicated in the NOTICE OF ACTION, proceed with seeking a *default* as described later in this chapter.

THE OTHER PARENT AND MILITARY SERVICE

Special problems can arise if the other party is in the military service. To determine whether this may be a problem, and to satisfy the judge that it is not a problem, one or more forms may be needed. These will be discussed in this section.

MEMORANDUM FOR CERTIFICATION OF MILITARY SERVICE

If you do not know whether the other party is in the military service, you will need to complete the MEMORANDUM FOR CERTIFICATE OF MILITARY SERVICE (see form 17, p.228):

- Complete the top portion of the form according to the instructions on page 21.
- Type the other party's name and social security number on the lines marked "{Name of Party About Whom Information Is Requested}" and "{Party's Social Security Number}."
- Make six copies of the form, one for each branch of the service listed on the form after the word "To." On each copy, check a different space for each service branch.
- Make a telephone call to each branch at the numbers listed below, and ask how much is the search fee and how the check should be made out.

Coast Guard:	202-267-1340	Marine Corps:	703-784-3941
Air Force:	210-652-5775	Surgeon Gen.:	301-594-2963
Navy:	703-614-5022 or 703-614-9221	Army:	703-325-3732

- Fill in the amount of the search fee on the line in the main paragraph of the form. Be sure that the amount you fill in is the correct amount for the branch of service checked on the particular copy of the form.

- Sign your name on the line marked "Signature of Party Requesting Information," and fill in your name, address, and telephone numbers on the lines below the signature line.
- Mail one copy of the form to each branch of the service, along with a check for the required amount and a self-addressed, stamped envelope.

Each branch will check its records, and mail you a notice as to whether the other party is in that branch. These notices should be filed with the court clerk. If the other party is in military service, his or her address will be provided. If the other party is in military service, but will not cooperate in reaching an agreement to resolve the case, you should contact an attorney. Federal laws designed to protect service personnel while overseas can create special problems, and you will need a lawyer to help you.

NONMILITARY AFFIDAVIT

If the other party is not in military service (and will not quickly reach an agreement with you), you will need to complete the **NONMILITARY AFFIDAVIT** (see form 18, p.230):

- Complete the top portion of the form according to the instructions on page 21.
- Type your name in the blank space in the first (unnumbered) paragraph.
- Check either paragraph 1 or 2, whichever applies, and check the space for "Petitioner" or "Respondent," whichever applies to the other party.
- Take the form to a notary public, and sign it before the notary on the line marked "Signature of Party," then fill in your name, address, and telephone numbers on the lines below the signature line.

Call the court clerk and ask when the **NONMILITARY AFFIDAVIT** needs to be filed. Some courts require that it not be signed too far in advance because they want the information to be fairly current. Some courts require that the notary public's date on the **NONMILITARY AFFIDAVIT** be within a certain number of days before filing a **MOTION FOR DEFAULT**. (see form 29, p.248.)

NOTE: *Some courts require that the notary public's date on the* ***NONMILITARY AFFIDAVIT*** *be within a certain number of days before the final hearing.*

DEFAULT

You must give the other party at least twenty days to respond to your Petition. If the other party does not file a respond by the twentieth day, he or she is in *default*. This allows you to proceed with your case. A response must be in writing and must be filed with the court clerk. If you receive a response but the other party does not file a copy with the court clerk, you need to make a copy and file it.

You may set a hearing date once the other party files a response or after the twenty-day period, whichever occurs first. Depending upon which method of service you use, count twenty days from the date the other party is personally served by the sheriff (check the sheriff's affidavit of service for the date), or from the date the other party signed the green return receipt card for certified mail. For service by publication, use the date filled in on the NOTICE OF ACTION.

MOTION FOR DEFAULT

If the other party does not respond within twenty days, you will need to notify the court clerk that a response has not been filed, and ask the clerk to formally enter the default in the court file. To accomplish this, you need to complete a **MOTION FOR DEFAULT** (see form 29, p.248):

- ☛ Complete the top portion of the form according to the instructions on page 21.
- ☛ In the main paragraph, check the appropriate space for "Petitioner" or "Respondent," whichever applies to the other party.
- ☛ In the second paragraph, check one item to indicate how you sent a copy of this form to the other party, and fill in the date it was delivered or sent.
- ☛ On the lines below the words: "Other party or his/her attorney," fill in the other party's name and address, and fax number if you sent a copy of this form by fax (this should be the other party's last known address, which will probably be the address where he or she was served by the sheriff). If the other party has an attorney, fill in the attorney's name and address. You will send or deliver a copy to the attorney instead of to the other party.
- ☛ Fill in the date, sign your name on the line marked "Signature of Petitioner," and type in your name, address, and telephone and fax numbers on the lines below your signature.
- ☛ Take this form to the court clerk for filing.

DEFAULT

The **DEFAULT** is the form the court clerk will sign to officially declare that the other party is in default (see form 30, p.249):

- ☛ Complete the top portion of the form according to the instructions on page 21.
- ☛ In the main paragraph, check the appropriate space for "Petitioner" or "Respondent," whichever applies to the other party. Leave the date line above the word "SEAL" and the clerk's signature line blank; the clerk will fill these in later.
- ☛ On the lines below the words "Other party or his/her attorney," fill in the other party's name and address, and fax number if you sent a copy of this form by fax.

- ☛ Type in your name, address, and telephone numbers on the lines below the line marked "Signature of Party."
- ☛ Make one copy of this form for yourself, and one copy for the other party. Take this form (and the copies) to the clerk, along with the MOTION FOR DEFAULT (form 29). The clerk will review these forms, check the court file to be sure that the required time has expired and that no response has been filed by the other party, and will date and sign the DEFAULT (form 30). Have the clerk date and stamp the copies.

NOTE: *While you are at the clerk's counter, complete the certificate of service section by checking the space to indicate how you will get a copy to the other party (usually by mailing a copy). Fill in the date, and sign on the line marked "Signature of Party." Make sure that you send one copy to the other party (or his or her attorney) in the manner you indicated on the form.*

6 Trials and Hearings

This chapter will give you basic information relating to hearings and trials. Regardless of whether your case involves paternity, custody, visitation, or support; the information in this chapter will be necessary for you. Instructions for completing many essential forms are found in this chapter. Later chapters will frequently refer you back to these forms and instructions.

There are many things that you may need to do to prepare for your hearing. These include setting a court date, sending out hearing notices, interviewing any witnesses you intend to call, sending out subpoenas for witnesses and documents, arranging for your children to testify, becoming familiar with courtroom proceedings and some of the basic rules of evidence, preparing the questions you will ask, and determining the order in which to present the various parts of your case so it all makes sense to the judge. These basic matters will be discussed in this chapter. More will be discussed about particular types of cases in later chapters.

Setting a Court Date

The terms *trial* and *hearing* are often used interchangeably. A trial is actually a particular type of hearing. Both terms refer to a formal proceeding before someone who will decide a legal matter. Issues in dispute in a lawsuit may be presented to a judge, or an attorney designated by the court to hear certain matters. Such attorneys are given the title of *general master* or *hearing officer*. The decision of a general master or hearing officer is usually not final, as it must be approved by a judge. Generally, the term *hearing* relates to any matter heard by a general master or hearing officer, as well as any preliminary matter heard by a judge. The term *trial* refers to a hearing before a judge, that will resolve all of the issues in the case.

Once the other party files a response, or fails to respond and a default is entered, you need to get a hearing date. Getting a hearing date set is a simple matter. Call the secretary (or judicial assistant) of the judge assigned to your case. (If you do not know which judge, call the court clerk, give the clerk your case number, and ask for the name and phone number of the judge assigned to your case.) Usually the judge's phone number can be found in the government section of your phone book. Tell the secretary what type of PETITION you've filed, and that you need to set a hearing date.

The secretary may ask you how long the hearing will take. The answer will depend upon the type of PETITION you filed. A PETITION to establish paternity may take several hours if witnesses are to be called, especially if there are expert witnesses who will explain the results of scientific testing. For a custody dispute, there are frequently several witnesses for both parties, which can result in a hearing anywhere from a couple of hours to several days. A simple PETITION for change child support may only require ten minutes if all necessary financial information has been provided by both parties. More about the length of time for a hearing will be discussed in later chapters.

It is a good idea to ask for the most amount of time you think it will take. If you don't finish the hearing in the time allotted, it may be several weeks before you can get another hearing date to finish. A general guideline would be to allow about twenty to thirty minutes for each witness. Of course this amount of time can easily double or triple if an attorney is questioning the witness. And do not forget to figure in the number of witnesses the other party may bring.

The secretary will give you a date and time for the hearing, but you will also need to know where the hearing will take place. Ask the secretary for the location. You will need to know the street address of the courthouse, as well as the room number, floor, or other location within the building. All of this information will need to be included in the hearing notices, which are explained in the following section.

TRIAL OR HEARING NOTICES

Depending upon your county, there are various ways of getting a hearing set. In some counties, you can call the judge's secretary or the court clerk and get a hearing date, then send the other party a NOTICE OF HEARING (GENERAL). (see form 31, p.250.) In other counties, you will need to file a NOTICE FOR TRIAL (see form 32, p.252) before you can get a hearing scheduled. In still other counties, you will first need to file a MOTION TO SET FINAL HEARING/TRIAL (see form 27, p.246) and submit an ORDER SETTING MATTER FOR FINAL HEARING or for STATUS CONFERENCE (see form 28, p.247).

The judge will complete the order and return it to you. You can then send the other party the proper NOTICE OF HEARING form. In still other counties, your case may be referred to a *hearing officer* or a *general master*, who is an attorney that will hear your case and make a recommendation to the judge.

If a general master will be used, the court will notify you either by sending you an order, or asking you to prepare and submit an order. If you need to prepare the order, you will complete the ORDER OF REFERRAL TO GENERAL MASTER. (see form 24, p.240.) You will then arrange a hearing date and time with the general master's office, and send the other party a NOTICE OF HEARING BEFORE GENERAL MASTER. (see form 25, p.242.) If your case will be heard by a *child support enforcement hearing officer*, you will use the NOTICE OF HEARING (CHILD SUPPORT ENFORCEMENT OFFICER). (see form 26, p.244.) Following are instructions to help you complete each of these forms.

NOTICE OF HEARING

To complete the NOTICE OF HEARING (GENERAL) (see form 31, p.250) or the NOTICE OF HEARING (CHILD SUPPORT ENFORCEMENT OFFICER) (see form 26, p.244):

- Complete the top portion of the form according to the instructions on page 21.
- Type in the other party's name and address after the word "TO:"
- Complete the main paragraph by typing in the information relating to when and when the hearing will be held.

Example: There will be a hearing before Judge {name}__Barry D. Hatchett______,
on {date}__October 23____, 2002 , at {time} 9:00 a.m. , in Room 245
of the__Hillsborough County__Courthouse, on the following issues:
modification of child support__.

- On form 26, you will insert the name of the hearing officer instead of the judge.
- After you have scheduled a hearing date, fill in the amount of time you reserved for the hearing.
- Call the court clerk to obtain the information you need to complete the section of the form relating to the Americans with Disabilities Act.
- Complete the certificate of service section at the bottom of the first page of the form, indicating how and when you sent or delivered a copy of the form to the other party; and fill in the other party's name, address, and telephone information. If the other party has an attorney, you will send or deliver a copy to the attorney, and fill in the attorney's name, address, and telephone information.

- At the top of the second page, fill in the date, and sign your name on the line marked "Signature of Party." Type in your name, address, and telephone information on the lines indicated.

- Make three copies of the NOTICE OF HEARING and mail one copy to the other party (or attorney). If you are seeking child support, or to change child support, also send a blank FAMILY LAW FINANCIAL AFFIDAVIT (see form 2, p.175; or form 3, p.182). File the original NOTICE OF HEARING with the court clerk, and keep two copies for yourself.

MOTION TO SET FINAL HEARING/TRIAL

To complete the **MOTION TO SET FINAL HEARING/TRIAL** (see form 27, p.246):

- Fill in the top portion of the form according to the instructions on page 21.

- Check the appropriate boxes.

- Type in how long you expect the hearing will take in paragraph "2," complete the certificate of service section, and fill in your name, address, and telephone information.

- Sign the form and file it with the clerk.

ORDER SETTING MATTER FOR FINAL HEARING OR STATUS CONFERENCE

When you file the **MOTION TO SET FINAL HEARING/TRIAL** (form 27), you will also need to complete the top portion of the **ORDER SETTING MATTER FOR FINAL HEARING OR STATUS CONFERENCE**. (see form 28, p.247), and leave it with the court clerk (along with two extra copies to be returned to you). The clerk or judge will then fill in the rest of the form, and return a copy of form 28 to you.

If your case is contested, the judge may set it for trial, or may first schedule a *status conference* where you and the other party will sit down with the judge for a few minutes to make it clear to everyone what issues the judge needs to determine at the trial. Your next step will be to notify the other party of the hearing or status conference by sending him or her a copy of the **ORDER SETTING MATTER FOR FINAL HEARING OR STATUS CONFERENCE**.(see form 28, p.247.) You will also need to prepare and file a **CERTIFICATE OF SERVICE** (form 21) listing the **ORDER SETTING MATTER FOR FINAL HEARING OR STATUS CONFERENCE** as the document served. (See the subsection of this chapter on "Notice of Hearing.")

MOTION FOR REFERRAL TO GENERAL MASTER

If your circuit court has a general master, either you or the other party may ask the judge to refer the case to the general master; or the judge may take the initiative and refer the case to the general master. The main reason for having a general master is to take some of the caseload off of the judge, and allow cases to be scheduled for hearing more quickly than the judge's docket backlog will allow. If you want your case referred to the general master, you will need to complete the **MOTION FOR REFERRAL TO GENERAL MASTER** (see form 23, p.239):

- Complete the top portion of the form according to the instructions on page 21.
- In the main paragraph, fill in your name and the issues that the general master will need to resolve (such as "Petitioner's request for custody and child support," or "Petitioner's request for a decrease in child support").
- Fill in the certificate of service section of the form, indicating how and when a copy of the form will be sent to the other party, and the other party's name, address, and telephone information. If the other party has an attorney, you will instead send or deliver a copy of the form to the attorney, and fill in the attorney's name, address, and telephone information.
- Fill in the date, and sign your name on the line marked "Signature of Party." Fill in your name, address, and telephone information on the lines below your signature.

Order of Referral to General Master

If the judge refers your case to a general master, you will need to complete the **Order of Referral to General Master** (see form 24, p.240), and submit it to the judge for his or her signature. Read the entire form carefully because it spells out your rights and provides other important information regarding referrals to general masters.

Follow these instructions to complete this form:

- Complete the top portion of the form according to the instructions on page 21.
- Fill in the name, address, and telephone number information for you and the other party on the second page of the form.
- Check with the judge's secretary or the court clerk to find out if you need to complete more of this form. If so, you will need to list the matters being referred to the general master in items 1 through 4 at the top of the form, type in the name of the general master in the first paragraph, and fill in any other information as instructed. (Or, the judge or clerk may fill in these items.)

Once signed by the judge, a copy of this order will be sent to you, the other party, and the general master. The general master will then schedule a hearing date.

Notice of Hearing Before General Master

Once the general master sets a hearing date, you will need to notify the other party by sending him or her a **Notice of Hearing Before General Master**. (see form 25, p.242.) This is very similar to form 26 and form 31. See the instructions for these forms on pages 244 and 250.

WITNESSES

In preparing your case you will need to determine the witnesses you may need to call to support your position, and think about who the other party may call to support his or her position. For matters involving support, in most cases witnesses are not called. Instead, the court will use the information provided by each party in the FAMILY LAW FINANCIAL AFFIDAVIT. The only time witnesses would be called is when one party wants to prove that the other has not given complete and accurate information in the FAMILY LAW FINANCIAL AFFIDAVIT. Witnesses are more likely to be called in cases to establish paternity, or dealing with the issue of custody. In general, you want to interview any witnesses you intend to use, to be sure the information they give will help you.

Warning: Do not ask a witness a question unless you already know what their answer will be. Later chapters will provide more information about witnesses for your particular type of case.

SUBPOENAS

To prepare for your hearing, you may need to have *subpoenas* issued. There are several types of subpoenas, so be sure you use the correct form.

SUBPOENAS TO GET INFORMATION BEFORE THE HEARING

If you are seeking to obtain a change in child support (including a change in support as part of a change in custody), the judge will require a FAMILY LAW FINANCIAL AFFIDAVIT from you, and one from the other party. (see form 2, p.175 or form 3, p.182.) You may have to try to get the information yourself if the other party has indicated that he or she will not cooperate and provide a FAMILY LAW FINANCIAL AFFIDAVIT, or if you believe the other party may not provide complete and accurate information.

You can go to the hearing and tell the judge that the other party will not cooperate, but the judge may just issue an order requiring the other party to provide information, and continue the hearing until a later date. You can tell the judge that the other party has provided false or incomplete information, but you will then need acceptable documentation to prove it. In either case, it will speed things up if you are able to get the information yourself and have it available at the hearing. This will require you to get a subpoena issued.

> ***Warning:*** Before you send a subpoena to the other party's employer, bank, stock broker, accountant, etc., you need to let the other party know what you are about to do. The thought that you are about to get these others involved in your case may be enough to get the other party to cooperate. If the other party calls and says "I'll give you the information," give him or her a few days to follow through. Ask when you can expect to receive the FAMILY LAW FINANCIAL AFFIDAVIT and offer to send the other party a blank copy if he or she needs one.

If the other party sends a completed FAMILY LAW FINANCIAL AFFIDAVIT as promised, do not send the subpoena (unless you have reason to believe the information is incomplete or inaccurate). If the other party does not send the information, or you have reason to believe it is incomplete or inaccurate, go ahead with the subpoena. You can send out subpoenas to as many people or organizations as you need, but you will need to use the following procedure for each subpoena.

Notice of Production From Nonparty. The advance notice to the other party is called a NOTICE OF PRODUCTION FROM NONPARTY (see form 36, p.279):

- Complete the top portion of the form according to the instructions on page 21.
- Type the other party's name and address after the words "TO: [all parties]."
- On the line in the main paragraph, type in the name of the person or company, bank, etc., where the subpoena will be sent. If at all possible, use a person's name or title so that the subpoena is directed to a specific person, such as "Jim Jackson, Payroll Director," or "Records Clerk."
- Complete the certificate of service section, including the other party's (or attorney's) name, address, and telephone information below the signature line.

SUBPOENA FOR PRODUCTION OF DOCUMENTS FROM NONPARTY

Next, you will complete a SUBPOENA FOR PRODUCTION OF DOCUMENTS FROM NONPARTY. (see form 37, p.280.) This form will eventually be sent to the person from whom you want to get information. Look at the FAMILY LAW FINANCIAL AFFIDAVIT (form 2 and form 3), and see what type of information is needed. The other party's income information can be obtained from his or her employer. Stock and bond information can be obtained from his or her stock broker, bank account balances from the bank, auto loan balances from the lender, etc. You can have subpoenas issued to any or all of these places, but do not overdue it. Concentrate on income information.

Follow these instructions to complete the SUBPOENA FOR PRODUCTION OF DOCUMENTS FROM NONPARTY:

- Complete the top portion of the form according to the instructions on page 21.
- Type in the other party's employer's (or broker's, bank's, etc.) name and address after the word "TO:." Again, try to use a person's name or title.

- Complete the first paragraph by filling in the information on the appropriate lines as to where and when the person is to appear with the requested information. This could be your home or place of business, the office of a court reporter (you will need to arrange this with the court reporter and they will charge you a fee), or any other appropriate place where you will have access to a copy machine.
- In the space after the first paragraph (after the words "and place the following:") type in a description of the documents or other items you want produced. Be as specific as possible, such as including the other party's Social Security number, an account number, or any other information that will help the person receiving the subpoena to know what you are requesting.
- Call the court clerk to get the information to complete the Americans with Disabilities section on the second page.
- Leave the rest of the spaces blank.

Next, mail a copy of the NOTICE OF PRODUCTION FROM NONPARTY (form 36), along with a copy of the SUBPOENA FOR PRODUCTION OF DOCUMENTS FROM NONPARTY (form 37) and a blank FAMILY LAW FINANCIAL AFFIDAVIT (form 2 or form 3) to the other party (see p. __ to determine whether to send form 2 or form 3). Make sure that you actually mail it on the date you filled in on the certificate of service section of NOTICE OF PRODUCTION FROM NONPARTY (form 36).

If the other party does not file a FAMILY LAW FINANCIAL AFFIDAVIT (form 2 or form 3) within fifteen days, you will complete the SUBPOENA FOR PRODUCTION OF DOCUMENTS FROM NONPARTY (form 37) and have it issued by the court clerk.

- To finish completing the SUBPOENA FOR PRODUCTION OF DOCUMENTS FROM NONPARTY (form 37), below the paragraph that begins "I Hereby Certify," type in the date and your name, address, and telephone information on the appropriate lines, and sign your name on the line marked "Signature of party signing certificate and pleading."

This section will discuss subpoenas that require a person to appear at the hearing and either give testimony (called a *subpoena* or a *subpoena ad testificatum*), or to give testimony and produce documents or other items (called a *subpoena duces tecum*). Before using the forms that appear in Appendix C, check with the court clerk to see if they have subpoena forms. If the clerk has a form, use it. If not, you can use the forms in Appendix C. The instructions below will help you to complete the clerk's forms, as well as the forms in Appendix C.

SUBPOENAS FOR HEARING

Subpoena. In order to force someone to appear at a hearing and testify, you will need to have the person served by the sheriff with a SUBPOENA. (see form 38, p.282.)

Obtain this form from the court clerk if possible. Even if your witness is a friend who wants to appear to testify for you, it is a good idea to have him or her served with a SUBPOENA. The SUBPOENA will enable your friend to get off of work to come to the hearing, and will enable you to have the hearing continued to a later date if your friend has car trouble, or becomes ill, so that he or she cannot make it to the hearing. To complete the SUBPOENA:

☛ Complete the top portion of the form according to the instructions on page 21.

☛ Type in the name and address of the person to be served with the SUBPOENA after the word "TO:" Use an address where the person can be found by the sheriff during the day. You can also complete the PROCESS SERVICE MEMORANDUM, and deliver it to the sheriff along with the SUBPOENA. (see form 18, p.230.)

☛ In the main paragraph, fill in the information for the place and time of the hearing [see the instructions for the NOTICE OF HEARING (GENERAL) (see form 31, p.250.)

☛ Type in your name, address, and telephone information under the heading "Attorney or Party Requesting Subpoena." This will allow the witness to contact you if he or she has any questions, or the sheriff to contact you if he or she has any trouble serving the subpoena.

☛ Take the SUBPOENA to the court clerk for the clerk to issue, then deliver it to the sheriff to have it served. (How to have them issued and served is discussed below.)

Subpoena Duces Tecum. A SUBPOENA DUCES TECUM is simply a subpoena which also requires the witness to bring something with him or her. (see form 39, p.283.) Usually it will be documents or records, but it might also be objects that are relevant to the issues to be decided by the judge (such as a paddle or belt used to spank your child if you are claiming the child was abused). Check with the court clerk to see if they have a SUBPOENA DUCES TECUM form, and use their form if they have one. Otherwise you can use the one in Appendix C. To complete the SUBPOENA DUCES TECUM:

☛ Complete the top portion of the form according to the instructions on page 21.

☛ Type in the name and address of the person to be served with the subpoena after the word "TO:" Use an address where the person can be found by the sheriff during the day. You can also complete the PROCESS SERVICE MEMORANDUM and deliver it to the sheriff along with the subpoena. (see form 16, p.226.)

☛ In the main paragraph, fill in the information for the place and time of the hearing [see the instructions for the NOTICE OF HEARING (GENERAL)] (see form 31, p.250.)

☛ In the space below the words "AND to bring the following items with you:" type in a description of whatever it is you want the witness to bring. This might be such things as "Your police report relating to...[give the date and names of the persons the report relates to]" or "Medical records relating to...[give the person's name]" or "Payroll records relating to...[give the person's name and Social Security number]."

- Type in your name, address, and telephone information under the heading "Attorney or Party Requesting Subpoena." This will allow the witness to contact you if he or she has any questions, or the sheriff to contact you if he or she has any trouble serving the subpoena.
- Take the **Subpoena Duces Tucem** to the court clerk for the clerk to issue, then deliver it to the sheriff to have it served. (How to have subpoenas issued and served is discussed below.)

Getting a Subpoena Issued and Served

To get any type of subpoena issued, take the subpoena to the court clerk. The clerk will sign and date the subpoena, and return it to you. Next, have the sheriff personally serve the subpoena to the person or place named in the subpoena. The sheriff will need at least one extra copy of the subpoena and a check for the service fee. You should also provide the sheriff with a **Process Service Memorandum** that is filled in with the information to help the sheriff find the person to be served. (see form 16, p.226.) Call the sheriff's office if you have any questions about having a subpoena served. After service, the sheriff will file an affidavit verifying when the subpoena was served.

For the **Subpoena for Production of Documents From Nonparty** (form 37), the employer, bank, etc., should send you the requested information. If the employer contacts you and says you must pay for copies, ask how much they will cost and send a check or money order. If the copy costs are not reasonable, tell the employer that you will have the clerk issue a **Subpoena Duces Tecum** to require them to come to the hearing unless they provide the copies at a reasonable cost. If the employer does not provide the information, you can either have the clerk issue a **Subpoena Duces Tecum** for the employer to come to the hearing, or tell the judge at the hearing that the employer did not honor the subpoena and show the judge the subpoena.

There are more procedures you could go through to force the employer to give the information, but it probably is not worth the hassle, and you would probably need an attorney to help you with it. Instead, let the judge order the employer or the other party to provide the information.

For subpoenas for hearing, the person served must appear and testify. Anyone who is served with a subpoena and fails to appear is subject to *contempt of court* penalties of being fined, sentenced to jail, or both.

Testimony of Minor Children

If you intend to have your minor child testify at the hearing, you need to first get the judge's permission. It is generally a bad idea to have your minor children testify. This can cause children great emotional stress, due to being placed in the middle of an argument between their parents and due to the stress of appearing in court and testifying. Therefore, a minor child should only be brought to testify as a last resort.

However, there may be situations (such as cases involving allegations of child abuse) where it will help to have a child testify, or the child may want to testify (such as where the child wants a change in custody). In rare cases, a child may be the only witness who can testify that a parent who claims to have no income is actually employed.

Motion for Testimony and Attendance of Minor Child(ren)

A minor child may not testify without the prior permission of the judge. If you decide that your minor child should testify, you will need to prepare and file a **Motion for Testimony and Attendance of Minor Child(ren)**. (see form 44, p.295.) This form asks the judge's permission for a minor child to be subpoenaed to appear at a hearing or deposition. The form is self-explanatory, and requires you to state why the court should issue the order. This is where you need to state what the child will testify about, and why the child's testimony is necessary (such as: "The child will testify about incidents of physical abuse by the Respondent on January 3, 2002 and January 17, 2002, when only the child and the Respondent were present.")

You will need to notify the other party of your motion, by mailing or delivering a copy of the motion to the other party (or his or her attorney). You will also need to contact the judge's secretary or judicial assistant to find out if a hearing will be required. If so, you will need to schedule a hearing and send the proper hearing notice to the other party.

Order for Testimony and Attendance of Minor Child(ren)

If the judge grants your request, you will need to prepare an **Order for Testimony and Attendance of Minor Child(ren)**. (see form 45, p.297.)

Rules of Evidence

As stated in the Introduction, this book cannot make you a lawyer. However, you should be aware of a few basic rules of evidence. What follows is a very basic explanation, but it may help you avoid some pitfalls, especially if the other parent has a lawyer.

Relevancy The documents you present to the judge and questions that you ask any witnesses should be related to the facts you need to prove. For example, if you are trying to have your child support lowered because you have been laid off from your job, the fact that the other parent gives you a hard time when you come to pick up the child for visitation does not relate (i.e., it "has no relevancy") to the child support issue. Determine what information you need to give the judge to enable him or her to make a decision, and stick to that information.

Hearsay Generally, a witness cannot testify to what someone else told him or her. Such secondhand statements are called *hearsay*.

Example: Suppose you are trying to change custody due to physical abuse, and the other parent's neighbor actually saw the other parent beat your child with an electric cord. You need the neighbor in court to testify to what she saw. You cannot have your cousin testify that the neighbor told him she saw the beating.

Documents This can also apply to documents which contain statements made by someone who is not in court to testify. (There are numerous exceptions to the hearsay rule, making it complicated and difficult to fully understand. However, one important exception (called an *admission against interest*) is that you ***can*** use any statements the other parent made to the person testifying.

Documents must be introduced at the hearing by someone's testimony. You need someone (it can be you) who can identify the paper, say who prepared it, and how he or she knows who prepared it. For example, to introduce documents you received from the other parent's employer, you can testify as to how you got the documents.

Examining Witnesses This refers to questioning your witnesses (*direct examination*) and the other parent's witnesses (*cross-examination*). One problem most non-lawyers have is that they start testifying instead of asking questions. This is not the time for you to explain anything. You need to ask simple questions, and wait for the witness to answer. You should be particularly careful in cross-examining the other parent's witnesses. If you are not very sure what their answer will be, do not ask the question. Do not feel that you must ask questions of each witness. Often it is best to let the witness go without further damaging your case.

Court Proceedings

This section will discuss some general aspects of presenting your case to the judge, general master, or hearing officer. More information that is specific to the type of case you have will be given in later chapters.

Courtroom Manners

There are certain rules of procedure that are used in a court. These are really the rules of good conduct, or good manners, and are designed to keep things orderly. Many of the rules are written down, although some are unwritten customs that have just developed over many years. They are not difficult, and they do make sense.

Show respect for the judge. This basically means, do not do anything to make the judge angry at you, such as arguing with him. Be polite, and call the judge "Your Honor" when you speak to him, such as "Yes, Your Honor," or "Your Honor, I brought proof of my income." Although many lawyers address judges as "Judge," this is not proper.

Showing respect also means wearing appropriate clothing, such as a coat and tie for men and a dress for women. This especially means no T-shirts, blue jeans, shorts, or "revealing" clothing. Many of the following rules also relate to showing respect for the court.

Whenever the judge talks, you listen. Even if the judge interrupts you, stop talking immediately and listen.

Only one person can speak at a time. Each person is allotted his or her own time to speak in court. The judge can only listen to one person at a time, so do not interrupt the other parent when it is his or her turn. And as difficult as it may be, stop talking if the other parent interrupts you. (Let the judge tell the other parent to keep quiet and let you have your say.)

Speak to the judge; not to the other parent. Many people get in front of a judge and begin arguing with each other. They actually turn away from the judge, face each other, and begin arguing as if they are in the room alone. This generally has several negative results: The judge cannot understand what either one is saying since they both start talking at once, they both look like fools for losing control, and the judge gets angry with both of them. So whenever you speak in a courtroom, look only at the judge. Try to pretend that the other parent is not there. Remember, you are there to convince the judge that you should have your divorce judgment changed. You do not need to convince the other parent.

Speak only when it is your turn. The usual procedure is for you to present your case first. When you are done saying all you came to say, the other parent will have a chance to say whatever he or she came to say. Let the other parent have his or her say. When he or she is finished, you will get another chance to respond to what has been said.

Keep calm. Judges like things to go smoothly in their courtrooms. They do not like shouting, name calling, crying, or other displays of emotion. Generally, judges do not like family law cases because they get too emotionally charged. So give your judge a pleasant surprise by keeping calm and focusing on the issues.

Show respect for the other parent. Even if you do not respect the other parent, act like you do. All you have to do is refer to the other parent as "Mr. Smith" or "Ms. Smith" (using his or her correct name, of course).

Following these suggestions will make the judge respect you for your maturity and professional manner and possibly even make him forget for a moment that you are not a lawyer. It will also increase the likelihood that you will get the change you request.

PRESENTING YOUR CASE

The judge will know that you do not have a lawyer, and he or she may help you through the hearing by asking you what he or she needs to know or even telling you what you need to do to present your case. When you first meet the judge, smile and say "Good morning, your Honor," or "Good afternoon, your Honor." Then just follow his or her lead. If he or she starts guiding you, or asking questions, just let him or her control the hearing. Otherwise, be ready to give your brief opening statement, telling the judge what type of petition you filed, the basic reason you filed the petition, and what change you want in the divorce judgment.

The judge may stop you before you have the chance to complete your opening statement and just ask you to present your proof. This is usually done to save time. If this happens just present your proof (which may simply be the FAMILY LAW FINANCIAL AFFIDAVITS filed by you and the other parent. (see forms 2 and 3, p.175 and p.182.)) The judge will probably swear you in, and tell you to proceed. What you do to proceed will depend upon the change you are seeking. Presenting your case will be discussed more in later chapters of this book.

THE JUDGE'S ORDER

After you and the other party have presented your information to the judge, he or she will make a decision. You will need to prepare an order for the judge to sign. There are different orders for each type of case, and they will be discussed in detail in later chapters. Along with the order, you will need to prepare a FINAL DISPOSITION FORM. (see form 9, p.208.) Like the CIVIL COVER SHEET (form 8), this form is required by the courts for administrative purposes. Part I of the FINAL DISPOSITION FORM should be completed exactly the same as the CIVIL COVER SHEET. Under the heading "II. Means of Final Disposition," check the box marked "Disposed by Judge." This form also needs to be dated and signed by you, but be sure to use the date of the final hearing. Take this form with you to the final hearing and give it to the judge at the hearing, along with the order.

7 Establishing Paternity

This chapter will explain the law regarding paternity, and the procedures and instructions for completing the necessary forms for a paternity case.

Florida Paternity Law

In paternity law, there is one term you will frequently see that is not a term commonly used outside of legal circles. That term is *putative father*, which means a man who is alleged to be the father of a child, or who claims to be the father of a child, but has not yet been proven to be the father.

There are two other terms that should be defined here, because, although they are commonly used, their precise legal definition is not always understood. An *illegitimate child* is a child born to a woman who is not married. A *legitimate child* is a child born to a woman who is married (even if her husband is not the child's father). Therefore, a married woman can have a child by someone other than her husband, and the child is still considered legitimate.

Generally, there are five ways that paternity can be established in Florida:

1. A married couple has a child.
2. A child was born out of wedlock, but the mother and father later marry each other.
3. The father acknowledges paternity.
4. A paternity lawsuit is filed by either the mother, the father, or the child; and a court determines paternity.
5. A court in another state has determined paternity.

This chapter will discuss numbers 3 and 4 listed above. No legal procedure is required for numbers 1 or 2. For number 5, the legal procedure has already been completed. (If you and the other parent get married, you can send a copy of your marriage certificate to the Office of Vital Statistics and get an amended birth certificate listing the father. See the discussion of "Acknowledging Paternity" below for information about contacting the Office of Vital Statistics.)

Acknowledging Paternity

The following information relates to the situation where the parents of a child are not married to each other, and where the mother is not married to anyone else. As the law presumes that a child born during a marriage is the child of the husband and wife, someone other than the husband is not allowed to acknowledge paternity.

Paternity may be acknowledged at the time of birth or at a later date. If the child is born in a hospital, and both parents agree to have the father listed on the birth certificate, the hospital will have the necessary form for the parents to sign. If either the mother or the father does not agree, the father cannot be listed on the birth certificate. If either does not agree, the only option the other has is to file a paternity lawsuit.

If the father is not listed on the original birth certificate, he may be added at a later date. However, both the mother and the father must agree to this. If both agree, they can sign a document called an ACKNOWLEDGEMENT OF PATERNITY (this may also be called a *Statement of Paternity*). The signatures of both parties must be notarized. In order to be valid, the ACKNOWLEDGEMENT OF PATERNITY document must contain the social security numbers of both parents. (see form 47, p.302.)

If the father signs an ACKNOWLEDGEMENT OF PATERNITY, he may *rescind* (or cancel) it within sixty days without a reason. After the sixty day period, it may only be rescinded if he can prove it was signed as a result of fraud, duress, or a mistake of fact. The father must be notified of this right before he signs the document.

After the ACKNOWLEDGEMENT OF PATERNITY is signed, it is sent to the Office of Vital Statistics, which is a division of the Florida Department of Health. The Office of Vital Statistics will then issue an amended birth certificate listing the father's name.

More information about amending birth certificates and the ACKNOWLEDGEMENT OF PATERNITY can be obtained from the Office of Vital Statistics by contacting them at one of the following places:

P.O. Box 210
Jacksonville, FL 32231-0042
904-359-6900, Ext. 1024
904-359-6931
www.doh.state.fl.us
VitalStats@doh.state.fl.us

Paternity Lawsuits

Paternity lawsuits are governed by Chapter 742 of the Florida Statutes. A paternity case can be filed by the mother, the putative father, or the child. The most common reason a mother files a paternity suit is to obtain child support. Putative fathers most often file to obtain custody or visitation rights. Paternity suits by the child are rare, but most often occur so that the child may inherit from the putative father.

A special problem may arise if the mother is married to someone other than the father at the time of conception or birth. If a child is conceived or born while the mother was married, the child is presumed to be the child of the mother's husband. This presumption may only be rebutted for a clear and compelling reason, based primarily on the child's best interest.

Therefore, a putative father may not bring a paternity action if the child is born during an intact marriage and the spouses recognize the child as theirs (Fla. Stat. Sec. 742.011). Even if the husband and wife are involved in a divorce, a putative father cannot intervene in the divorce case if the spouses agree to treat the child as a child of their marriage. On the other hand, if a married woman files a paternity suit, the putative father may not base a defense on the presumption that the child is the husband's.

A paternity suit is begun by the filing of a **Petition to Determine Paternity and for Related Relief**. (see form 48, p.304.) Certain other documents will also need to be filed, which will be discussed in detail later in this chapter. The outcome of a paternity suit will most often depend upon the results of scientific testing, which will also be discussed below.

Scientific Paternity Test

There are several types of scientific tests available to assist in determining the paternity of a child. Traditionally, these tests were only done pursuant to a court order in a paternity case. However, in recent years, various companies have begun offering some of these tests to the general public. If you have asked the other party to sign an **Acknowledgement of Paternity**, and he or she is refusing because of doubts about who is the father, you may want to suggest a test to find out. If you have been asked to sign an **Acknowledgement of Paternity**, and are in doubt about who is the father, you may want to suggest a test to find out. In either situation, the test may avoid the time and expense of a paternity suit.

There are four types of testing commonly used in paternity cases:

ABO Test. This is the most basic blood type testing. Blood samples are taken from the mother, the putative father, and the child. These samples are tested to determine each person's blood type, A, B, AB, or O. The putative father may be excluded by such a test.

Example: If the mother has Type A blood and the putative father has Type B, a child of theirs would have to have either Type A or Type B. If the child turns out to have Type O, the child must have inherited it from a man with Type O. Therefore, the putative father could not be this child's father.

However, statistics show that a man who is wrongfully accused of being the father will only be excluded in ten to thirteen percent of cases. This is because of the probability that the real father would have the same blood type as the falsely accused man, and because the child could inherit the mother's blood type.

Red Cell Series. This is an ABO test which adds a test for the Rh factor. This further narrows the matter, but it still allows a man wrongfully accused to be excluded in only half of the cases.

HLA (Human Leukocite Antigen) Test. This test also requires blood samples from the mother, the putative father, and the child. This tests more unique factors in blood. With the HLA test, a man wrongfully accused will be excluded in about ninety percent of the cases.

DNA. One nice feature about DNA testing is that it can be done with samples from only the putative father and the child. Therefore, it can be done if the mother's whereabouts are unknown. It is commonly done by taking saliva samples, so no needles are involved. It is also about 99.9% accurate.

Before the days of HLA and DNA tests, blood tests were used to try to rule out a wrongly accused man, or to support other evidence of paternity. They were not conclusive proof of paternity. At best, the test indicated that the man may be the father. When HLA testing came about, much more significance was attached to the test results. HLA results usually indicated whether the man was the father with better than ninety percent certainty.

Courts tended to rely on the HLA test, so that a positive HLA test would prove paternity unless the putative father came up with very convincing evidence to the contrary (such as proof that he was out of the state when conception occurred, or was sterile). Now, with the high degree of accuracy in DNA testing, the test results leave very little room for doubt either way.

ACKNOWLEDGEMENT OF PATERNITY

If you and the other parent agree on paternity, you can both sign an ACKNOWLEDGEMENT OF PATERNITY. (see form 47, p.302.) Two important requirements for this form to be valid are: (1) both parents must sign it and (2) the social security numbers of both parents must be on the form. The first part of this form is for the father to complete and sign, and the second part is for the mother to complete and sign. Both of you must sign before a notary public. To complete the ACKNOWLEDGEMENT OF PATERNITY, follow the instructions below:

- Fill in the information required for the Statement of Father and the Statement of Mother. This form is self-explanatory, with information about what belongs on each line being indicated under each line.
- In the second paragraph of the Statement of Father section, you will also need to mark an X in the space before either "male" or "female," to indicate the sex of the child.
- You will notice there are spaces to fill in the "full legal name" of the father, mother, and child. You should fill in the same name that is on the person's birth certificate. The only exception is where the person has had his or her name legally changed, in which case it should be the name authorized in the court order granting the name change.
- In the section below the mother's signature, on the line after "COUNTY OF," fill in the name of the county in which you will have the form notarized.
- In the paragraph beginning "Sworn to or affirmed," leave the first line blank (the notary will fill in the date), type the father's name on the second line, and type the mother's name on the third line.
- Both of you need to take the form to a notary public, and sign it on the respective signature lines before the notary. The notary will complete the bottom portion of the form.

Once it is signed by both parties and notarized, the **Acknowledgement of Paternity** form can be sent to the Office of Vital Statistics at the address listed on page 52. If you have any questions, you may also contact the Office of Vital Statistics at the address, phone numbers, or email address listed.

Petition to Establish Paternity and for Related Relief

The basic form to begin a lawsuit to establish paternity is the **Petition to Determine Paternity and for Related Relief**. (see form 48, p.304.) This form may also be used to obtain court orders relating to custody, visitation, and child support, even if paternity has already been legally established. Follow these instructions to complete the form:

- Complete the top portion of the form according to the instructions on page 21.
- On the line in the first (unnumbered) sentence, type in your name.

☛ Under the heading "Section I":

- In paragraph 1, check the space for either "mother" or "father," whichever applies to you. Then fill in each child's name, place of birth, birth date, and sex on the lines indicated.
- In paragraph 2, fill in your current address.
- In paragraph 3, fill in the other party's address.
- In paragraph 9, check either line "a" or line "b," but not both. Check line "a" if paternity has been legally established. If paternity has not been legally established, check line "b," and complete that subparagraph. You will need to list when and where you and the other party had sexual relations. After the phrase "As a result of that sexual intercourse," check the space for either "Petitioner" or "Respondent," whichever applies to the mother (i.e., if you are the mother you would check "Petitioner," if you are the father you would check "Respondent.") In the next sentence, check either "Petitioner" or "Respondent," whichever applies to the father. In the next sentence, check the appropriate space to indicate whether the mother was married at the time of conception or at the time of birth. If the mother was married, fill in the name and address of her husband.
- The heading "Section II. Child Custody, Parental Responsibility, and Visitation" is where you state what you want the judge to order in relation to custody and visitation. The section will deal with parental responsibility, which relates to who makes major decisions about the child's welfare; primary residence, meaning with whom the child will live a majority of the time, and visitation (also called time sharing), which concerns the time the parent not having primary residence will have with the child. (For more information about these matters, which will help you complete this section of the form, see Chapter 8 and Chapter 9.)

☛ To complete Section II:

- In paragraph 1, check the space for either "Mother" or "Father," or "Other," to indicate who currently has the child. If you check "Other," on the line after the word "{explain}" fill in the name of the person who has the child, and their relationship to the child (e.g., "Mary Smith, maternal aunt" or "William and Janet Jones, paternal grandparents").
- Paragraph 2 is to tell the judge if you want shared parental responsibility or sole parental responsibility. In paragraph 2, check either line "a" or line "b," but

not both. Check line "a" if you are requesting that parental responsibility be shared by you and the other parent. Check line "b" if you want sole parental responsibility. If you check line "b," check the space for "Father" or "Mother," whichever applies to you; and on the lines after the word "because," fill in an explanation of why you believe shared parental responsibility would be detrimental to the child.

- Paragraph 3 is to tell the court who you want designated as the child's primary residential parent. Check the space for "Father" if you want the father to be the primary residential parent. Check the space for "Mother" if you want the mother to be the primary residential parent.

  NOTE: *It is suggested that you do not check either "undesignated" or "rotating." These choices are not favored in the law, are only approved in unusual situations, and the judge must have a very good reason for such an order. If you check "undesignated," you are saying that nobody will be designated the primary residential parent.*

  If you check "rotating," it isn't entirely clear what this means. Legal research will reveal some sources that say this means the same as "split custody," which typically refers to a situation where there is more than one child and both parents are designated the primary residential parent of at least one child. Other sources say "rotating" refers to the situation where the child's primary residence alternates between the two parents. The law prefers to keep siblings together and prefers a stable residential environment, therefore the law does not favor either the split custody or the alternating custody situation.

  Regardless of which space you check, on the lines after the word "because," type in an explanation of why you think what you are requesting is in the child's best interests.

- Paragraph 4 is to tell the court what visitation time you want for the parent who is not the primary residential parent. See Chapter 9 for more information about visitation, which will help you complete this section. For items "a" through "f," you may check more than one item. Check all of the items that apply. Check "a" if you don't want the other party to have any visitation. In order to succeed on this request, you will need to prove that the other parent poses an extreme danger to the child. Check "b" if you want limited visitation, which means that you want some kind of limitations or conditions placed on the visitation.

  If you check "b," you should also check "f" and fill in the schedule and limitations you want imposed. Check "c" if you want supervised visitation. This means that some third-party will be present at all times during the visitation, because of some type of concern for the child's safety if left alone with the other parent. Check "d" if you want the exchange of the child for visitation to be supervised or if you want a third-party exchange. Check "e" if you want the judge to determine the visitation arrangement. Check "f" if you want to propose a specific visitation schedule. If you check "f" you will need to type in the details of the schedule you are suggesting, and an explanation of why the schedule is in the best interests of the child.

- In paragraph 5, check either "a" or "b"—but not both. Check "a" if you want the child to keep the name that was entered on his or her birth certificate. Check "b" if you want the child's name changed. If you check "b," type in the child's current name in the first column and the new name you want the child to have in the second column.

☛ The heading "Section III. Child Support" is where you state what you want the judge to order in relation to child support. (For more information about child support, which will help you complete this section of the form, see Chapter 10.) To complete Section III, for paragraphs 1 through 7, check all that apply to your situation.

- Check paragraph 1 if you want child support determined according to the Florida child support guidelines. You will also need to check one of subparagraphs "a," "b," or "c," to indicate when child support begins.

- Check paragraph 2 if you want child support to be more or less than what would be called for by the Florida child support guidelines.

- Check paragraph 3 if you want the judge to order medical or dental insurance coverage, and check the appropriate space to indicate if the father or mother should be ordered to provide the insurance.

- Check paragraph 4 if you want the judge to make an order regarding the payment of medical and dental expenses that are not covered by insurance. Check one of subparagraphs "a," "b," "c," or "d," to indicate how these non-covered expenses should be paid.

- Check paragraph 5 if you want the judge to require the purchase of a life insurance policy on the life of the party paying child support, in order to guarantee child support in the event of the obligor's death. Check one of subparagraphs "a," "b," or "c," to indicate who will pay the life insurance policy premiums.

- Check paragraph 6 if you want the judge to require payment of medical expenses already incurred for the child, including the expenses of birth. Check the space for either "Petitioner," "Respondent," or "Both," to indicate who should pay for these expenses.

- Check paragraph 7 if either you or the other party received any public assistance for the child. Check the space for "Petitioner," "Respondent," or "Both," to indicate which of you received assistance.

☛ Under the heading "Petitioner's Request," indicate what you are asking of the judge. Whatever you check here should match what you checked in Sections I, II, and III. In paragraph 2, check all of the items that apply to what you want. In all cases you will check "a." If you are the mother, in most cases you will be asking for custody and child support, in which case you will also check items "b" through "e." If you are the father, and are only seeking the right to see your child, you would also check item "b."

You would probably want the mother to be the one to ask for child support, instead of asking to pay support and other expenses by checking items "c" through "e." Check item "f" if you asked for a name change in Section II, paragraph 5. If there is anything you want the judge to order that is not reflected elsewhere on this form, check item "g," and type in what you want the judge to order.

☛ *Do not sign this form yet,* since it must be signed before a notary or deputy court clerk. Below the line marked "Signature of Petitioner," fill in your name, address, and telephone information.

☛ Take this form to a notary public or the clerk's office, and sign it before the notary or deputy clerk on the line marked "Signature of Petitioner." Your Petition may now be filed with the clerk.

Civil Cover Sheet

At the time you file your **Petition**, you will also need to file a **Civil Cover Sheet** (see form 8, p.207):

☛ In the section marked "I. Case Style," type in your name on line marked "Petitioner," and the other party's name on the line marked "Respondent." The clerk will give you the case number, and division designation (if any), at the time you file your Petition.

☛ In the section marked "II. Type of Case," check the box in the first column for "Other domestic relations."

☛ At the bottom of the form, type in the date, sign your name on the line marked "Signature of Attorney or Party Initiating Action," and type your address and telephone number on the lines as indicated.

Supporting Forms

In addition to the Petition to Establish Paternity and for Related Relief and the Civil Cover Sheet, you will also need to complete and file the following forms:

- Uniform Child Custody Jurisdiction (UCCJA) Affidavit. (see form 4, p.193.) In all cases you will need to complete and file this form. (See Chapter 8 for instructions for completing form 4.)

- Notice of Social Security Number. (see form 6, p.203.) In all cases you will need to complete and file this form. (See Chapter 4 for instructions for completing form 6.)

- Family Law Financial Affidavit. (see form 2, p.175, and form 3, p.182.) If you or the other party ask for child support, you will need to complete either the Family Law Financial Affidavit (Short Form) (form 2), or the Family Law Financial Affidavit (form 3). (See Chapter 10 for instructions about whether to use form 2 or form 3, and how to complete the form you will need to file.)

- Certificate of Compliance with Mandatory Disclosure. (see form 40, p.284.) (See Chapter 10 for instructions for completing form 40.)

- Child Support Guidelines Worksheet. (see form 5, p.197.) If you or the other party ask for child support, you will need to complete and file a Child Support Guidelines Worksheet. (See Chapter 10 for instructions for completing form 5.)

Under certain circumstances, you may also need to complete and file the following forms:

- Motion for Scientific Paternity Testing. (see form 51, p.317.) If you file this motion, you will also need to complete the Order for Scientific Paternity Testing. (see form 52, p.319.) Instructions for completing both forms included in the next section of this chapter.

- Standard Family Law Interrogatories for Original or Enforcement Proceedings. (see form 34, p.255.) (See Chapter 10 for information about when this form is used and instructions for completing form 34.)

- NOTICE OF SERVICE OF STANDARD FAMILY LAW INTERROGATORIES. (see form 33, p.253.) (See Chapter 10 for information about when to use this form and for instructions for completing form 33.)
- MOTION TO DEVIATE FROM CHILD SUPPORT GUIDELINES. (see form 43, p.291.) You will need to prepare this form if you or the other party ask for child support, and you believe the child support amount should be more or less than what is indicated by the Child Support Guidelines. (See Chapter 10 for instructions for completing form 43.)
- AFFIDAVIT OF INDIGENCY. (see form 1, p.173.) You will use this form if you are financially unable to pay the filing fee and other court costs. (See Chapter 4 for instructions for using and completing form 1.)
- MOTION FOR APPOINTMENT OF GUARDIAN AD LITEM. (see form 41, p.286.) and ORDER APPOINTING GUARDIAN AD LITEM (see form 42, p.288). (See Chapter 8 for instructions for completing forms 41 and 42.)

SCIENTIFIC PATERNITY TESTING

The only way to be sure about paternity is with scientific testing. Therefore, in most cases you will want paternity testing to be done. To ask the court to order testing you will need to prepare and file a MOTION FOR SCIENTIFIC PATERNITY TESTING. (see form 51, p.317.) After the judge makes a decision, you will need to prepare and submit to the judge an ORDER ON MOTION FOR SCIENTIFIC PATERNITY TESTING. (see form 52, p.319.)

MOTION FOR SCIENTIFIC PATERNITY TESTING

To ask the court to order scientific paternity testing, you will need to prepare and file a MOTION FOR SCIENTIFIC PATERNITY TESTING (see form 51, p.317):

- ☛ Complete the top portion of the form according to the instructions on page 21.
- ☛ In the first (unnumbered) paragraph, check the space for "Petitioner" or "Respondent," whichever applies to you.
- ☛ In paragraph 2, fill in the name of each child to be tested, and the child's birthdate.
- ☛ In paragraph 3, check the space for either "Petitioner," "Respondent," or "both Petitioner and Respondent," to indicate who should pay for the testing.
- ☛ Below paragraph 3, complete the certificate of service section of the form to indicate how and when you sent a copy of the MOTION FOR SCIENTIFIC PATERNITY TESTING to the other party, check either "Petitioner" or "Respondent," whichever applies to the other party. Below that, fill in the name, address, and fax number information for either the other party or his or her attorney. If the other party has an attorney, you will send a copy to the attorney instead of to the other party.

- Do not sign this form yet, since it must be signed before a notary or deputy court clerk. Below the line marked "Signature of Party," fill in your name, address, and telephone information.
- Take this form to a notary public or the clerk's office, and sign it before the notary or deputy clerk on the line marked "Signature of Party." Your motion may now be filed with the clerk.

ORDER ON MOTION FOR SCIENTIFIC PATERNITY TESTING

To go along with your motion, you will need to prepare an **ORDER ON MOTION FOR SCIENTIFIC PATERNITY TESTING** (see form 52, p.319):

- Complete the top portion of the form according to the instructions on page 21.
- On the line in the first (unnumbered) paragraph, type in the date of the hearing on the motion.
- In paragraph 2, check either "a" or "b," depending upon whether the judge finds that the mother was married to someone other than the father.

After the phrase "It is therefore ORDERED":

- In paragraph 2, check either "a," or "b," or "c," depending upon when the judge orders everyone to appear for testing. If "b," you will need to fill in the time, date, and location where the testing will be done. If "c," you will need to fill in the city.
- In paragraph 3, check the appropriate spaces to reflect the judge's order about who will pay the cost of the testing.
- Once all of the above items are completed according to the judge's order at the hearing, the order will be submitted to the judge for his or her signature; and for the clerk to complete the clerk's certification.

Answering a Petition to Determine Paternity

This section will discuss what to do if you have been served with a **Petition to Determine Paternity**. If you ignore the matter, a default will be entered against you. There are two forms to choose from for responding to the Petition. If you simply wish to admit or deny the allegations in the Petition, use the **Answer to Petition to Determine Paternity and for Related Relief**. (see form 49, p.309.) However, if you want to ask the judge for anything that is not included in the Petition (such as custody, visitation, or child support), use the **Answer to Petition and Counterclaim to Determine Paternity and for Related Relief**. (see form 50, p.311.) Instructions for each of these forms follows.

Answer to Petition to Determine Paternity and for Related Relief

If you simply wish to admit or deny the allegations in the Petition, you need to prepare and file an **Answer to Petition to Determine Paternity and for Related Relief** (see form 49, p.309):

- Complete the top portion of the form as it appears on the Petition and other papers you received.
- In the first (unnumbered) paragraph, type in your full legal name.
- To complete paragraph 1, you will need to refer to the Petition. On the line at the end of paragraph 1, type in the section and paragraph number from the Petition of each allegation you wish to admit.
- To complete paragraph 2, you will need to refer to the Petition. On the line at the end of paragraph 2, type in the section and paragraph number from the Petition of each allegation you deny.
- To complete paragraph 3, you will need to refer to the Petition. On the line at the end of paragraph 2, type in the section and paragraph number from the Petition of each allegation which you are unable to admit or deny because you don't have enough information to know either way.
- In the paragraph beginning "I certify that a copy," check the space to indicate how you provided a copy of this form to the other party, and fill in the date it was provided.
- Below the heading "Petitioner or his/her attorney," fill in the name of other party (or attorney is he or she has an attorney) and the party's (or attorney's) name, address, the telephone information.

- ☛ Do not sign this form yet. Below the line marked "Signature of Respondent," type in your name, address, and telephone information.
- ☛ Take this form to a notary public or the court clerk's office, and sign it before the notary or a deputy court clerk on the line marked "Signature of Respondent." The notary or clerk will fill in the rest of the form. Your Answer may now be filed.

Answer to Petition and Counterclaim to Determine Paternity and for Related Relief

If, in addition to admitting or denying the allegations in the Petition, you also want to ask for things not already requested in the Petition, you need to prepare and file an **Answer to Petition and Counterclaim to Determine Paternity and for Related Relief**. (see form 50, p.311.) This will include situations such as where the Petition asks that the Petitioner be awarded custody, but you want custody; or where the Petition asks for visitation, but not child support; or where the Petition asks for limited visitation, but you want unlimited visitation.

To complete form 50:

- ☛ Complete the top portion of the form as it appears on the Petition and other papers you received.
- ☛ In the first (unnumbered) paragraph, type in your full legal name.
- ☛ To complete paragraph 1, you will need to refer to the Petition. On the line at the end of paragraph 1, type in the section and paragraph number from the Petition of each allegation you wish to admit.
- ☛ To complete paragraph 2, you will need to refer to the Petition. On the line at the end of paragraph 2, type in the section and paragraph number from the Petition of each allegation you deny.
- ☛ To complete paragraph 3, you will need to refer to the Petition. On the line at the end of paragraph 2, type in the section and paragraph number from the Petition of each allegation which you are unable to admit or deny because you don't have enough information to know either way.
- ☛ Under the heading "Section I. Paternity":
    - In paragraph 1, check the space for either "mother" or "father," whichever applies to you. Then fill in each child's name, place of birth, birth date, and sex on the lines indicated.
    - In paragraph 2, fill in the other party's current address.
    - In paragraph 3, fill in your current address.

- In paragraph 9, check either line "a" or line "b," but *not both*. Check line "a" if paternity has been legally established. If paternity has not been legally established, check line "b," and complete that subparagraph. You will need to list when and where you and the other party had sexual relations.

  After the phrase "As a result of that sexual intercourse," check the space for either "Petitioner" or "Respondent," whichever applies to the mother (i.e., if you are the mother you would check "Petitioner," if you are the father you would check "Respondent.") In the next sentence, check either "Petitioner" or "Respondent," whichever applies to the father. In the next sentence, check the appropriate space to indicate whether the mother was married at the time of conception or at the time of birth. If the mother was married, fill in the name and address of her husband.

☛ In the heading "Section II. Child Custody, Parental Responsibility, and Visitation" state what you want the judge to order in relation to custody and visitation. The section will deal with *parental responsibility*, which relates to who makes major decisions about the child's welfare; *primary residence*, meaning with whom the child will live a majority of the time, and visitation (also called *time sharing*), which concerns the time the parent not having primary residence will have with the child. For more information about these matters, which will help you complete this section of the form, see Chapters 8 and 9.

☛ To complete Section II:

- In paragraph 1, check the space for either "Mother" or "Father," or "Other," to indicate who currently has the child. If you check "Other," on the line after the word "{explain}" fill in the name of the person who has the child, and their relationship to the child (e.g., "Mary Smith, maternal aunt" or "William and Janet Jones, paternal grandparents").

- Paragraph 2 is to tell the judge if you want shared parental responsibility or sole parental responsibility. In paragraph 2, check either line "a" or line "b," but not both. Check line "a" if you are requesting that parental responsibility be shared by you and the other parent. Check line "b" if you want sole parental responsibility. If you check line "b," check the space for "Father" or "Mother," whichever applies to you; and on the lines after the word "because," fill in an explanation of why you believe shared parental responsibility would be detrimental to the child.

- Paragraph 3 is to tell the court who you want designated as the child's primary residential parent. Check the space for "Father" if you want the father to be the primary residential parent. Check the space for "Mother" if you want the mother to be the primary residential parent.

Regardless of which space you check, on the lines after the word "because," type in an explanation of why you think what you are requesting is in the child's best interests.

- Paragraph 4 is to tell the court what visitation time you want for the parent who is not the primary residential parent. (See Chapter 9 for more information about visitation, which will help you complete this section.) For items "a" through "f," you may check more than one item. Check all of the items that apply.

  Check "a" if you don't want the other party to have any visitation. In order to succeed on this request, you will need to prove that the other parent poses an extreme danger to the child. Check "b" if you want limited visitation, which means that you want some kind of limitations or conditions placed on the visitation. If you check "b," you should also check "f" and fill in the schedule and limitations you want imposed. Check "c" if you want supervised visitation. This means that some third-party will be present at all times during the visitation, because of some type of concern for the child's safety if left alone with the other parent.

  Check "d" if you want the exchange of the child for visitation to be supervised or if you want a third-party exchange. Check "e" if you want the judge to determine the visitation arrangement. Check "f" if you want to propose a specific visitation schedule. If you check "f" you will need to type in the details of the schedule you are suggesting, and an explanation of why the schedule is in the best interests of the child.

- In paragraph 5, check either "a" or "b," but *not both*. Check "a" if you want the child to keep the name that was entered on his or her birth certificate. Check "b" if you want the child's name changed. If you check "b," type in the child's current name in the first column and the name you want the child to have in the second column.

☛ The heading "Section III. Child Support" is where you state what you want the judge to order in relation to child support. (For more information about child support, which will help you complete this section of the form, see Chapter 10.) To complete Section III, for paragraphs 1 through 7, check all that apply to your situation.

- Check paragraph 1 if you want child support determined according to the Florida child support guidelines. You will also need to check one of subparagraphs "a," "b," or "c," to indicate when child support begins.

- Check paragraph 2 if you want child support to be more or less than what would be called for by the Florida child support guidelines.

- Check paragraph 3 if you want the judge to order medical or dental insurance coverage, and check the appropriate space to indicate if the father or mother should be ordered to provide the insurance.
- Check paragraph 4 if you want the judge to make an order regarding the payment of medical and dental expenses that are not covered by insurance. Check one of subparagraphs "a," "b," "c," or "d," to indicate how these non-covered expenses should be paid.
- Check paragraph 5 if you want the judge to require the purchase of a life insurance policy on the life of the party paying child support, in order to guarantee child support in the event of the obligor's death. Check one of subparagraphs "a," "b," or "c," to indicate who will pay the life insurance policy premiums.
- Check paragraph 6 if you want the judge to require payment of medical expenses already incurred for the child, including the expenses of birth. Check the space for either "Petitioner," "Respondent," or "Both," to indicate who should pay for these expenses.
- Check paragraph 7 if either you or the other party received any public assistance for the child. Check the space for "Petitioner," "Respondent," or "Both," to indicate which of you received assistance.

☛ Under the heading "Respondent's Request," indicate what you are asking of the judge. Whatever you check here should match what you checked in Sections I, II, and III. In paragraph 2, check all of the items that apply to what you want. In all cases you will check "a." If you are the mother, in most cases you will be asking for custody and child support, in which case you will also check items "b" through "e." If you are the father, and are only seeking the right to see your child, you would also check item "b."

You would probably want the mother to be the one to ask for child support, instead of asking yourself to pay support and other expenses by checking items "c" through "e." Check item "f" if you asked for a name change in Section II, paragraph 5. If there is anything you want the judge to order that is not reflected elsewhere on this form, check item "g," and type in what you want the judge to order.

☛ In the paragraph beginning "I certify that a copy," check the space to indicate how you provided a copy of this form to the other party, and fill in the date it was provided.

☛ Below the heading "Petitioner or his/her attorney," fill in the name of other party (or attorney is he or she has an attorney) and the party's (or attorney's) name, address, the telephone information.

☛ Do not sign this form yet, since it must be signed before a notary public or deputy court clerk. Below the line marked "Signature of Respondent," type in your name, address, and telephone information.

☛ Take this form to a notary public or the court clerk's office, and sign it before the notary or a deputy court clerk on the line marked "Signature of Respondent." The notary or clerk will fill in the rest of the form. Your Answer may now be filed.

OTHER FORMS

In addition to the ANSWER (either form 49 or form 50), you will also need to complete and file the following forms:

- UNIFORM CHILD CUSTODY JURISDICTION (UCCJA) AFFIDAVIT. (see form 4, p.193.) In all cases you will need to complete and file this form. (See Chapter 8 for instructions for completing form 4.)
- NOTICE OF SOCIAL SECURITY NUMBER. (see form 6, p.203.) In all cases you will need to complete and file this form. (See Chapter 4 for instructions for completing form 6.)
- FAMILY LAW FINANCIAL AFFIDAVIT. (see form 2, p.175, and form 3, p.182.) If you or the other party ask for child support, you will need to complete either the FAMILY LAW FINANCIAL AFFIDAVIT (SHORT FORM) (form 2), or the FAMILY LAW FINANCIAL AFFIDAVIT (form 3). See Chapter 10 for instructions about whether to use form 2 or form 3, and how to complete the form you will need to file.
- CERTIFICATE OF COMPLIANCE WITH MANDATORY DISCLOSURE. (see form 40, p.284.) (See Chapter 10 for instructions for completing form 40.)
- CHILD SUPPORT GUIDELINES WORKSHEET. (see form 5, p.197.) If you or the other party ask for child support, you will need to complete and file a CHILD SUPPORT GUIDELINES WORKSHEET. (See Chapter 10 for instructions for completing form 5.)

Under certain circumstances, you may also need to complete and file the following forms:

- MOTION FOR SCIENTIFIC PATERNITY TESTING. (see form 51, p.317.) See the section "Scientific Paternity Testing" earlier in this chapter for instructions for completing form 51. If you file this motion, you will also need to complete the ORDER ON MOTION FOR SCIENTIFIC PATERNITY TESTING. (see form 52, p.319.)
- STANDARD FAMILY LAW INTERROGATORIES FOR ORIGINAL OR ENFORCEMENT PROCEEDINGS. (see form 34, p.255.) (See Chapter 10 for information about when this form is used and instructions for completing form 34.)

- Notice of Service of Standard Family Law Interrogatories. (see form 33, p.253.) (See Chapter 10 for information about when to use this form and for instructions for completing form 33.)
- Motion to Deviate from Child Support Guidelines. (see form 43, p.291.) You will need to prepare this form if you or the other party ask for child support, and you believe the child support amount should be more or less than what is indicated by the Child Support Guidelines. (See Chapter 10 for instructions for completing form 43.)
- Affidavit of Indigency. (see form 1, p.173.) You will use this form if you are financially unable to pay the filing fee and other court costs. (See Chapter 4 for instructions for using and completing form 1.)
- Motion for Appointment of Guardian ad Litem (see form 41, p.286.); and Order Appointing Guardian ad Litem (see form 42, p.288.) (See Chapter 6 for instructions for completing these forms.)

Procedures

This section will briefly discuss the basic procedures of filing with the court clerk, notifying the other party that you have filed a Petition, setting a court date, and notifying the other party of that court date. Generally, this will consist of referring you to other chapters of this book where each of these matters is discussed in greater detail.

Filing with the Court Clerks

Once all of your necessary papers are prepared, you will need to file them with the court clerk. See Chapter 4 for information about filing your court papers.

Notifying the Other Party

You will need to notify the other party by either personal service or by service by publication (if appropriate). (See Chapter 5 for an explanation of how proper notice must be given. Chapter 5 will also explain the procedure to follow for obtaining a default if the other party does not respond to your Petition as required by law.)

Setting a Hearing Date

If the other party responds to your Petition, you will need to schedule a court hearing, and notify the other party of the hearing date. See Chapter 6 for detailed information about scheduling a hearing and sending the required hearing notice.

Preparing and Presenting Your Case

This section will help you to prepare for your court hearing, and explain how to present your case to the judge.

TESTIMONY OF WITNESSES

Other than yourself, the other party, and the expert witness who presents the results of any scientific testing conducted, there may or may not be any other witnesses testifying at the trial. It will all depend upon the situation. If you are the mother and the petitioner, you may have witnesses who can testify to such things as how the putative father behaved as if the child was his, or made statements that the child was his.

If **FAMILY LAW FINANCIAL AFFIDAVITS** have been filed, and all other required financial disclosure has been made, those documents may provide all of the evidence about your financial situation the judge will need to make a decision. The testimony of a third party is required if one of the parties did not file the required papers, or is accused by the other of not providing accurate or complete information. In this situation, you may need to call a third party, such as the other party's employer, bank representative, stock broker, etc., to testify and provide documents regarding the other party's income and assets. (For more about your testimony, see the section below entitled "Presenting Your Proof.")

DOCUMENTS AS EVIDENCE

In most paternity cases, the only documents introduced at the hearing will be the results of the scientific tests. If there are medical expenses, such those incurred for the child's birth, you may need to introduce copies of the medical bills. The only documents concerning your financial situation the court will need to see are the papers already filed with the court. Therefore, it will not be necessary for you to introduce any financial documents into evidence at the hearing.

The only time you may need to introduce other documents is if the other party did not file the required papers, or did not providing accurate or complete information. In this situation, you may need to either introduce documents you have obtained, or call a third party, such as the other party's employer, bank representative, stock broker, etc., to provide documents regarding the other party's income and assets.

OPENING STATEMENT

An opening statement is your chance to briefly tell the judge why you are in court, what you plan to prove, and what you want done. The following is an example of an opening statement:

Example: "Your Honor, we are here on a petition for paternity. I am requesting that the respondent be declared the father of my child, that I be declared the primary residential parent, and that the respondent be ordered to pay child support as required by the child support guidelines. DNA tests have been performed and the results have been filed with the court indicating that the respondent is the father. All required financial information has also been filed. Thank you."

After your opening statement, the other party (or his or her attorney) will have an opportunity to give an opening statement. This is the other party's chance to summarize for the judge why he or she disagrees with what you are asking for.

PRESENTING YOUR PROOF

After the opening statements, it will be your turn to present your proof. Exactly what happens at this point will depend upon what papers have been filed and how the particular judge likes to conduct the hearing. The judge may take over and say that he or she has reviewed the scientific test results and the financial information filed with the court, and ask you and the other party if the information is accurate, and whether either of you have any new information to provide.

If the judge likes a more formal procedure, which is more common in paternity cases than in divorce cases, you will need to present your case in a more formal manner. Tell the judge that you wish to testify. You will then be sworn in as a witness. Have your copy of the **PETITION** ready to use as a checklist for testifying. You will want to state the following:

- your name;
- that you, or the other party, or both of you, live in Florida; and,
- that **FAMILY LAW FINANCIAL AFFIDAVITS** have been filed which accurately reflect the financial status of you and your spouse.

When you are finished, your spouse (or his or her attorney) will be allowed to ask you questions. After these questions have been answered, you will be allowed to call any other witnesses you may have to support your case.

FINAL JUDGMENT

FINAL JUDGMENT OF PATERNITY

After the trial has concluded, and the judge has made his or her rulings, there are two final forms you will need to prepare.

The **FINAL JUDGMENT OF PATERNITY** (see form 53, p.321) will be completed according to the decisions the judge made at the end of the trial. To complete form 53:

- ☛ Complete the top portion of the form according to the instructions on page 21.
- ☛ In paragraph 2, check the space for "By operation of law" if paternity was established prior to filing the paternity case. Check the space for "The Court finds that" if paternity was determined by the court. On the line marked "{full legal name}" type in the full legal name of the father. Where indicated, fill in the name and birth date of each child who is the subject of the paternity order.

☛ The heading "Section I. Custody of and Visitation with Dependent or Minor Child(ren)" sets forth the judges decisions regarding custody and visitation. The section will deal with *parental responsibility*, which relates to who makes major decisions about the child's welfare; *primary residence*, meaning with whom the child will live a majority of the time, and visitation (also called *time sharing*), which concerns the time the parent not having primary residence will have with the child.

☛ To complete Section II:

- In paragraph 2, check only one subparagraph. Check "a" if no decision is being made regarding parental responsibility. Check "b" if shared parental responsibility is ordered, and check the appropriate spaces to reflect what the judge ordered. Check "c" if sole parental responsibility was ordered, and check the appropriate spaces to reflect what the judge ordered.

  If you check "c," after the phrase "Shared parental responsibility would be detrimental to the child(ren) at this time because," type in the reason the judge determined shared parental responsibility would be harmful to the child. If either party raised the issue of parental responsibility, the judge must order shared parental responsibility unless he or she finds that it would be detrimental to the child.

- In paragraph 3, check only one subparagraph to indicate what the judge ordered in relation to visitation by the parent who was not designated as having primary residential responsibility, or who was not awarded sole custody. Check "a" if the judge ordered reasonable visitation without a specific schedule. Check "b" if the judge ordered a specific schedule, and fill in the details or the schedule. Check "c" if the judge denied visitation altogether. If you check "c," you will need to fill in an explanation of the conditions the judge found are detrimental to the child.

- Paragraph 4 will only be completed if the judge orders supervised visitation. If supervised visitation is ordered, check subparagraph "a," "b," or both. Check "a" if the judge designates a particular person to supervise the visitation, and fill in the name of the person. Check "b" if the judge orders visitation to take place at a supervised visitation center, then fill in the address of the center, and check the appropriate space to indicate who is to pay the fee charged by the center.

- Paragraph 5 sets forth any orders regarding how you and the other party are to communicate regarding visitation. Check this paragraph only if it applies, and check the appropriate spaces and fill in any other information needed to state what the judge ordered.

- Paragraph 6 sets forth any order regarding the exchange of the child for visitation. For subparagraphs "a" through "d," check all that apply. If you check "a," type in a description of the location where the exchange is to occur. If you check "c," fill in the name of the person who will handle the exchange. If you check "d," type in whatever other conditions were ordered by the judge for the exchange of the child.

- You will only check the line for paragraph 7 if the judge issued some type of order prohibiting the permanent removal of the child from Florida or some other geographical area. Check the space for "Mother," "Father," or "Both," to indicate who is enjoined. If the injunction prohibits removal from Florida, check the space for "State of Florida." If the injunction prohibits removal from some other geographical area, check the space before "{specify}," and type in a description of that area (e.g., "County of Palm Beach.").

- Check paragraph 8 if there are any other orders relating to parental responsibility or visitation that are not covered elsewhere in Section I. If so, type in these other orders on the line provided (use additional sheets of paper and attach them if necessary).

☛ The heading "Section II. Child Support" is where you state the judge's orders relating to child support. To complete Section II:

- Complete paragraph 1 by checking the appropriate spaces and filling in the correct amounts and percentages.

- In paragraph 2, fill in the child support amount on the first line. Check the space beginning with the words "in accordance with" if the judge ordered the support amount to be paid according to the paying parent's payroll cycle or monthly. If the judge ordered a payment schedule that does not coincide with the payroll cycle and is not monthly, check the space before the word "other," and fill in an explanation of the how often the support amount is to be paid (e.g., "weekly," or "every two weeks").

  Avoid using "bi-monthly" or "semi-monthly," as this often confused people as to whether it means twice per month or every other month (the same confusion occurs if "bi-weekly" or "semi-weekly" is used). You will also need to fill in the date the payments are to begin, and the appropriate information to indicate when child support will end. If the child support is more than five percent higher or lower than called for by the child support guidelines, the judge's reason for this deviation must be stated also.

- In paragraph 3, there are four options for reflecting the judge's order regarding arrearages and retroactive child support. You can check "a," "b," "c," or "b" and "c." If you check "a," you will not check either "b" or "c." If you check "b," check the appropriate space to indicate if medical expenses were incurred by the mother, father, or both, and fill in the amount of these expenses. Fill in the spaces to indicate the percentage of the expenses to be paid by each of you, and check the appropriate space to indicate whether it will be added to the arrearage in subparagraph "c," or paid in some other manner.

If you check "other," fill in and explanation of the payment arrangement the judge ordered. If you check "c," check the appropriate space to indicate whether the mother or father owes a child support arrearage, and fill in the amounts and dates as required. Fill in the total arrearage, and the rate at which it will be paid (in the same manner as you did for the child support in the previous paragraph).

- In paragraph 4, relating to medical or dental insurance coverage, check "a," "b," or both, according to the judge's order. If you check "a," check the appropriate spaces to indicate if the father or mother should be ordered to provide each type of insurance, or whether insurance in not currently available. If you check "b," check the appropriate space to indicate whether expenses not covered by insurance will be shared equally, prorated according to each parent's percentage of their total income, or paid by some other arrangement. If you check "Other," fill in an explanation of how uncovered expenses will be paid.
- Complete paragraph 5 according to what the judge ordered regarding securing child support with life insurance.
- Complete paragraph 6 according to what the judge ordered regarding which parent may claim the tax exemption for the child.
- Use paragraph 7 to type in any orders regarding child support that are not covered elsewhere in Section II.

☛ The heading "Section III. Method of Payment" is where you indicate the judge's orders relating to how child support or alimony is to be paid. To complete Section III:

- In paragraph 1, check either "a" or "b," but not both. If you check "a," fill in the name of the county.
- In paragraph 2, you will check "a" or "b," but not both. In most cases, income withholding will be ordered and you will check "a." If you check "b," fill in the amount of delinquency that will trigger income withholding, fill in the reason the judge decided income withholding is not currently in the child's best interest, and check the appropriate space to indicate whether there is an agreement with the depository or a written agreement signed by you and the other parent for another payment arrangement.

- In paragraph 3, check the appropriate space to indicate whether all, a certain percentage, or none of a bonus will be paid toward an arrearage. If there is no arrearage, or no bonus or other type of one-time payment expected, check the space before the word "No."
- Use paragraph 4 to type in any orders regarding the method of payment of child support or alimony that are not covered elsewhere in Section III.

☛ "Section IV. Child(ren)'s Name(s)" is to indicate whether the judge ordered any child's name changed. If no name changes were ordered, check subparagraph "a." If any name change was ordered, check "b," then fill in the present name and the new name of each child subject to this paternity case.

☛ "Section V. Attorney Fees, Costs, and Suit Money" will reflect any order the judge made regarding a request by either party for the other party to pay attorney fees, costs, scientific tests, and suit money. If neither party made a request, paragraphs 1 and 2 will be left blank. In most cases, there will at least be an order relating to payment of the costs of scientific tests, so paragraph 3 will need to be completed. Compete Section IV as follows:

- Check paragraph 1 if the judge denied a request for attorneys fees, costs, and suit money. You will need to check the appropriate space to indicate whether it was the petitioner's or respondent's request, and fill in the reason the request was denied.
- Check paragraph 2 if the judge granted a request for attorney fees, costs, or suit money. You will need to check the appropriate space to indicate whether the petitioner or respondent is ordered to pay, fill in the amounts for the attorney fees and costs awarded, and fill in the hourly rate and number of hours the attorney fee award is based upon. There is also a space to fill in any other orders relating to the payment of these fees and costs.
- In paragraph 3, check the appropriate space to indicate whether the cost of scientific testing is assessed against the petitioner, the respondent , or in some other manner. If you check "Other," fill in the details of the judge's order regarding payment of the scientific testing expenses (e.g., "equally against the Petitioner and Respondent," or "40% against the Petitioner and 60% against the Respondent," or "Petitioner has already paid such costs, and does not seek contribution from the Respondent").

☛ "Section VI. Other Provisions" is for any other orders the judge made that are not covered elsewhere on this form.

☛ Once form 53 (FINAL JUDGMENT OF PATERNITY) is completed, it is given to the judge for signing. You may either prepare this form immediately after the hearing and then submit it to the judge's secretary or judicial assistant, or prepare it and submit it to the judge within a day or two.

Final Disposition Forms

Along with the **Final Judgment of Paternity**, you will need to prepare and submit a **Final Disposition Form**. (see form 9, p.208.) This form is used by the court for administrative purposes.

- Fill in "Part I. Case Style," exactly the same as the Civil Cover Sheet.
- Under the heading "II. Means of Final Disposition," check the box marked "Disposed by Judge."
- On the line marked "Date," fill in the date of the final hearing.Sign your name on the line marked "Signature of Attorney or Party Initiating Action," and fill in your address and telephone number on the lines so designated.
- Submit the completed **Final Disposition Form** to the judge along with the **Final Judgment of Paternity**.

Custody 8

This chapter will explain how a court goes about making an initial determination about custody. This information basically applies in both divorce cases and paternity cases. Changes in an existing custody order, including in divorce cases, are discussed later in the text.

A parent who wants a court order granting him or her custody will usually also want the other parent to pay child support. Also, unless the other parent poses a danger to the child, the other parent will be entitled to some form of visitation. If you are not married, and only wish to obtain a custody order, you can still use the paternity procedure and forms outlined in the previous chapter, or the petition for support unconnected with dissolution of marriage outlined in Chapter 10.

How Custody is Determined

Florida law provides that "the mother and father jointly are natural guardians of their own children." (Fla. Stat. Sec. 744.301) This statement in the law works fine for a married couple living with their child as a family unit. Problems arise when the parents are not married, or when they are married but separate or divorce. When a dispute arises between parents in these circumstances, other provisions in the law come into play.

For unmarried parents, custody may be resolved through a paternity lawsuit, which is governed by Chapter 742 of the Florida Statutes. Paternity suits are covered primarily in Chapter 7 of this book, although the general information in this chapter about how custody is determined will apply to paternity cases. For married parents, custody can be raised in either a dissolution of marriage (divorce) case or in a petition for support unconnected with dissolution of marriage.

In covering what is traditionally called *custody*, Florida law distinguishes between *primary residence* (where the child lives a majority of the time) and *parental responsibility* (who makes major decisions regarding the child, such as medical care, educational needs, etc.). Many judges and lawyers still refer to this generally as *custody*, and we will too, unless the distinction is significant.

Factors to Consider

In making a decision about custody, the judge will consider the following factors:

- which parent is more likely to allow the other to visit with the child;
- the love, affection, and other emotional ties existing between the child and each parent;
- the ability and willingness of each parent to provide the child with food, clothing, medical care, and other material needs;
- the length of time the child has lived with either parent in a stable environment;
- the permanence, as a family unit, of the proposed custodial home;
- the moral fitness of each parent;
- the mental and physical health of each parent;
- the home, school, and community record of the child;
- the preference of the child, providing the child is of sufficient intelligence and understanding; and,
- any other factory the judge decides is relevant.

The general rule is that the judge should make a determination of what is in the child's best interests. All of the factors listed above are attempts to describe what things are in the best interests of the child. Some of these factors will be more relevant to divorce situations, and others will be more relevant to unmarried parents.

The Special Needs Child

If your child has special needs, the ability of you and the other party to meet those needs may also be considered. Special needs involve the gifted child who has special educational needs, as well as the child with physical or emotional problems and handicaps. This will probably involve expert testimony to verify the child's condition and needs, and show which parent is best able to meet those needs. This does not mean the financial ability to meet the needs, because that can be taken care of by child support. But if the child needs daily in-home physical therapy, the judge may grant custody to the parent who works fewer hours and therefore has more time for the therapy.

Custody Forms

Regardless of whether you are filing a petition for paternity, a petition for dissolution of marriage, a petition for support unconnected with dissolution of marriage, or a petition to change custody, there are certain forms that will need to be filed along with your petition. There are other forms that may be filed, depending upon the circumstances in your case. These forms are discussed in the following sections.

UNIFORM CHILD CUSTODY JURISDICTION ACT (UCCJA) AFFIDAVIT

In all cases involving children you must complete and file a UNIFORM CHILD CUSTODY JURISDICTION ACT (UCCJA) AFFIDAVIT. (see form 4, p.193.) To complete form 4:

- ☛ Complete the top portion of the form according to the instructions on page 21.
- ☛ On the line in the first (unnumbered) paragraph, fill in your name.
- ☛ On the line in paragraph 1, fill in the number of children that are the subject of this case.
- ☛ In paragraph 1, below the heading "The Following Information Is True About Child #1," fill in all blanks with the required information. If the child is not yet five years old, go back to the child's birth.
- ☛ On the second page of the form are spaces for two additional children, if needed. If more than three children are involved in your case, make as many additional copies of the second page as you need to include all of the children.
- ☛ Read paragraphs 2 through 5, and check the appropriate lines and fill in any required information that relates to your situation.
- ☛ In the certificate of service section below paragraph 6, fill in the appropriate spaces to indicate how you provided a copy of this form to the other party (or his or her attorney).
- ☛ Take this form to a notary public, and sign it before the notary. This form should be filed with the court clerk along with your petition.

GUARDIAN AD LITEM

If charges of child abuse or neglect are raised, the judge is required to appoint a *guardian ad litem*. You may also ask the judge to appoint a guardian ad litem in any case. The guardian ad litem will either be an attorney or a person certified by the State Guardian Ad Litem Program. The guardian ad litem has the authority to conduct an investigation to determine what type of custody arrangement is in the child's best interest.

Unless you and the other party are financially unable to pay for the services of the guardian ad litem, either or both of you will be assessed the costs. If the other party poses a danger to your child, but you cannot get the necessary proof, you may want to ask for the appointment of a guardian ad litem. This will require you to prepare the two forms explained in the next section.

Motion for Appointment of Guardian ad Litem

The first form connected with the appointment of a guardian ad litem is the **Motion for Appointment of Guardian ad Litem** (see form 41, p.286):

- ☛ Complete the top portion of the form according to the instructions at the beginning of Chapter 4.
- ☛ In the first (unnumbered) paragraph, check either "Petitioner" or "Respondent," whichever applies to you.
- ☛ In paragraph 1, for each child who is involved in your case, type in the child's name, date of birth, age, sex, and where he or she is currently living, under the appropriate headings.
- ☛ In paragraph 2, check one of the spaces to indicate whether allegations of abuse or neglect were made by either you or the other party in any of the papers either of you have filed with the court.
- ☛ In paragraph 3, check the matters that need to be determined by the judge. The phrase "sole/shared parental responsibility" refers to who should have the responsibility for making major decisions regarding the child. The phrase "primary/secondary residential parent" refers to the question of where the child should live as his or her main residence.
- ☛ In paragraph 4, type in an explanation of why you think a guardian ad litem should be appointed.
- ☛ In the paragraph at the top of the second page of the form, fill in the appropriate spaces to indicate how you provided a copy of this form to the other party (or his or her attorney).
- ☛ Fill in the date, sign your name, and fill in your name, address, and telephone information on the lines indicated.

It is a good idea to check with the guardian ad litem program in the county where your child lives to find out what type of costs to expect. This can become expensive! If you can't afford to pay the fees, you will need to complete and file an **Affidavit of Indigency**. (see form 1, p.173.)

Order Appointing Guardian ad Litem

The other form you will need to complete is the **Order Appointing Guardian Ad Litem**. (see form 42, p.288.) To prepare form 42, all you need to do is complete the top portion of the form according to the instructions at the beginning of Chapter 4.

At the hearing, the judge will either complete the other portions of the form, or tell you what information to insert according to what he or she decides.

You will file the motion with the court clerk, and deliver a copy of the motion and the proposed order to the judge's secretary or judicial assistant. Ask the secretary or judicial assistant if you need to set a hearing, or if the judge will consider the motion without a hearing. If a hearing is required, get a hearing date from the secretary or judicial assistant. (See Chapter 6 for more information about setting a hearing date). If a hearing is necessary, you will need to mail a copy of your motion, and a **NOTICE OF HEARING** (form 25 or form 31) to the other party (or his or her attorney).

PREPARING AND PRESENTING YOUR CASE

The witnesses you choose to have testify will depend upon what you are trying to prove at the hearing. Witnesses may include relatives, friends, neighbors, police officers, CFS investigators, doctors and psychologists, and your child's school teachers and counselors. You will need to decide who you think would be a witness to help your position, and who the other party might use to hurt your position.

SELECTING AND INTERVIEWING WITNESSES

First, make a list of each fact you want to prove at the hearing. Again, this will depend upon the reasons you are asking for a change in custody. Beside each fact, write down the name of the witness or witnesses you believe will be able to testify to that fact. Next, make a list of each potential witness, their address and telephone number, what fact they will prove for you, and what you expect each would say in court. You can use the **WITNESS TESTIMONY WORKSHEET** to help you. (see worksheet 2, p.167.) See the "Questioning Witnesses" section of this chapter, page 83.

Your next step is to talk to each potential witness to be sure of what they will say at the hearing. Never assume what a witness will say at the hearing. Many cases have been lost by a witness giving surprise testimony at a hearing. With regard to questioning witnesses at hearings, one of the first lessons law students are taught is: "Never ask a question unless you know what the answer will be." For each witness you interview, you want to ask the specific questions you might ask at the hearing and also allow the witness to describe what he or she saw, heard, and "knows." This will allow you to find out new information and will possibly lead you to other witnesses.

There is a big danger of a witness telling you one thing before the hearing, then changing his or her testimony at the hearing. The best way to reduce this danger is to take the witness' *deposition*. This is where you have the sheriff serve a notice on the witness to appear at a specific place and time to answer questions before a court reporter. Unfortunately, this can be very expensive. You will have to pay for the court reporter to show up and record the testimony and pay for the reporter to type up a record or *transcript* of the deposition. You can expect to pay about $45 for the court reporter, plus at least $100 per hour of testimony transcribed. The advantage to having a transcript is that you can use it to contradict the witness if he or she says something different at the hearing. Most lawyers only take depositions of the witnesses for the opposing parent. They do extensive questioning of their own witnesses and tell them that they will be expected to give the same testimony at the hearing.

One alternative is to ask the witness to give you a written, signed statement of what they saw, heard, and know. It may also help to have someone with you when you interview the witness, so that person can testify to the original statements if the witness changes his or her story at the hearing. The important message here is to be as sure as possible what your witnesses will say before you put them on the witness stand.

Private Investigators. If you are basing your change of custody on abuse or the lifestyle of the other party, you may want to hire a private investigator to help you prove it (if you can afford the fee). You do not necessarily want to rely on CFS investigators, who are frequently inexperienced undertrained, underpaid, and overworked.

Expert Witnesses. Sometimes, especially in custody and alimony cases, it is necessary to have an expert witness testify. An expert witness is someone you are having testify because of his or her special education, training or experience, such as a doctor or psychologist. An expert witness will testify to something that requires special training for an evaluation and a professional opinion.

At the hearing, it is first necessary to have the judge determine that the witness is qualified as an expert. This is usually done by asking the witness to tell his or her profession and to describe his or her training and job experience. Once this is done, you say to the judge, "I would like this witness qualified as an expert."

Notifying Witnesses

The best way to notify witnesses of your hearing date is by having the sheriff serve them with a SUBPOENA. (see form 38, p.282) It's a good idea to call your witnesses to let them know of the hearing date, and that they will be receiving a SUBPOENA. It is not absolutely necessary to serve a SUBPOENA on witnesses who are willing to come and help you. But if they have car trouble or are ill on the hearing date, the judge will probably not continue the hearing so they can testify at a later date unless they were served with a SUBPOENA.

For doctors, psychologists, school teachers, police officers, CFS investigators, etc., it is absolutely necessary that you serve them with subpoenas. This should be done at least five days before the hearing, but no earlier than about two weeks before. Police officers must be served at least five days before or they do not need to appear. If you just need the person to testify, use a regular SUBPOENA (see form 38, p.282). If you need the person to bring records or other evidence (such as a police report, medical records, etc.), you need to use the **SUBPOENA DUCES TECUM** (see form 39, p.283). See Chapter 6 for information on how to prepare and serve subpoenas.

QUESTIONING WITNESSES

In questioning witnesses at the hearing, you want to show three basic things: who the witness is, what the witness knows, and how the witness knows it. The **WITNESS TESTIMONY WORKSHEET** (worksheet 1) will help you prepare for questioning your witnesses at the hearing. Make a copy of the **WITNESS TESTIMONY WORKSHEET** for each witness you will be calling (including yourself) and fill it in as follows:

1. Type in a short reminder of what you expect this witness to prove by his or her testimony, in the box marked "Purpose of Witness."
2. For questions in Part I, type in the answers you expect from the witness.
3. If your witness is a relative, friend, neighbor, or other non-expert witness, skip Part II. If your witness is a CFS investigator, police officer, or other person whose occupation is significant to your case (but who will be testifying to facts from first-hand knowledge and will not be asked to give opinions based upon their expertise), type in the answers you expect from the witness. for questions 1 through 4 in Part II. If the witness is an expert (that is, will be giving opinions based upon their expertise), complete all of Part II.
4. Part III is for you to type in the questions you want to ask the witness to prove your position, and the expected answer to each question. Refer back to what you put in the "Purpose of Witness" section when deciding on your questions.

Keep in mind that most judges try to finish hearings as soon as possible. Therefore, you don't want your witnesses to get off the track of what they need to say to prove your case. To prepare your witnesses, you should go over the questions you will ask with the witness a day or two before the hearing. This will reassure you that the witness will give the testimony you want and will understand your questions. Use the Witness Testimony Worksheet to prepare your questions and review them with the witness.

You will also want to decide the order in which the witnesses will testify. Generally, you will want to have them testify in an order that will make sense, so the judge can understand the facts you are trying to present. However, to accommodate the doctor, police officer, etc., you may want to have them testify first so you don't keep them from their business longer than necessary.

DOCUMENTS AS EVIDENCE

Have copies of all documents you may want to present to the judge and arrange them in the order you will present them. Generally, a document must be introduced by the person who prepared it. For example, if you are going to present a doctor's medical records about an injury for which your child was treated, you will need to have the doctor talk about the records during his testimony. So keep in mind the order in which your witnesses will testify when you are arranging your documents.

9 VISITATION

This chapter explains how judges commonly make decisions regarding visitation. This information basically applies in both divorce and paternity cases. If you are not married, and only wish to obtain a visitation order, you can still use the paternity procedure and forms outlined in Chapter 7. If you are married, the issue of visitation should be raised in your divorce case. In a divorce case, there are procedures and forms for obtaining temporary visitation.

HOW VISITATION IS DETERMINED

Visitation is the time a child spends with the parent who is not designated the primary residential parent. It can be any length of time, from a few hours per week to an entire summer. Visitation is presumed to be in a child's best interest, and it will be up to the parent with custody to prove otherwise if he or she wants visitation limited or denied. Unlike the areas of custody and support, there are no Florida Statutes that set forth any criteria or guidelines for visitation. The Florida Legislature has left this subject up to the judges.

The most common visitation schedule is alternate weekends and one weekday each week. In addition to the weekly visitation, it is common for the court to set a visitation schedule of sharing holidays, school vacations, birthdays, and other important events. It is common to alternate these special days (e.g., you have the child for Thanksgiving this year, the other parent has the child for Thanksgiving next year). The following is a list of holidays you may want to consider in proposing a visitation schedule. Some of these are listed because they are days that the schools in Florida are commonly closed, and others are to remind you of other days that may be important to you or your child.

- Your child's birthday
- Your birthday
- Your spouse's birthday
- Labor Day
- Rosh Hashanah
- Yom Kippur
- Columbus Day
- Halloween
- Thanksgiving Day
- Hanukkah
- Christmas Eve
- Christmas Day
- School Christmas vacation
- New Year's Eve
- New Year's Day
- Martin Luther King, Jr. Day
- President's Day
- Valentine's Day
- St. Patrick's Day
- Easter
- School spring vacation
- Passover
- Mother's Day
- Father's Day
- Fourth of July
- Other relatives' birthdays
- Other non-school days
- Summer vacation
- Any other holiday or day that is important to you, the other parent, or your child.

Visitation Forms

Regardless of whether you are filing a petition for paternity, a petition for dissolution of marriage, a petition for support unconnected with dissolution of marriage, or a petition to change visitation, there are certain forms that will need to be filed along with your petition. There are other forms that may be filed, depending upon the circumstances in your case. These forms include:

- **Uniform Child Custody Jurisdiction Act (UCCJA) Affidavit** (see form 4, p.193.) This form must be filed in all visitation cases. (See Chapter 8 for instructions for completing form 4.)
- **Motion for Appointment of Guardian ad Litem** (see form 41, p.286.) This form may be filed if allegations of abuse or neglect are involved in your visitation dispute. If you file this form, you will also need to prepare an **Order Appointing Guardian ad Litem**. (see form 42, p.288.) (See Chapter 8 for instructions for completing form 41 and form 42.)

Preparing and Presenting Your Case

In most cases, it will not be necessary to have any witnesses testify. (The only exception is if you want to severely limit or terminate visitation because the other party poses a threat to the child. In such cases, review all of Chapter 8, which discusses the factors for custody, some of which may also be used in a visitation case.) Generally, your statements to the judge that the current visitation arrangement is not working will be enough.

Again, in most cases, this will simply involve thinking about what you want to tell the judge. Basically, you want to point out the visitation provision in your judgment or any more recent visitation order, briefly explain some of the problems you have had with the other party regarding visitation, and tell the judge what kind of visitation order you would like to end these problems. The following is an example of such an opening statement:

> "Your Honor, we are here on a petition to modify visitation. The judgment currently provides for 'reasonable and liberal visitation.' This arrangement has not been working. My ex-husband never brings the children home at the agreed upon time, frequently arrives an hour late to pick them up or forgets to pick them up at all, and last Christmas Eve he was to have them home by 8:00 P.M., but kept them until 3:00 P.M. on Christmas Day. I would like an order specifying alternate weekend visitation from 7:00 P.M. Friday until 5:00 P.M. Sunday. If he doesn't arrive to pick up the children or call to advise me of a delay by 7:20 P.M., visitation may be cancelled for that weekend. I would also like the order to provide for visitation on alternate holidays from 9:00 A.M. to 8:00 P.M., and that the holidays be designated as New Year's Day, Easter Day, Memorial Day, Fourth of July, Labor Day, Thanksgiving Day, Christmas Eve, and Christmas Day."

You are telling the judge three things:

1. what the current visitation order is;
2. why you want it changed; and,
3. what outcome you desire.

The judge will then hear the other party's story. You may get a chance to respond, and then the judge will make a decision. Have paper and pen ready, so you can write down what the judge orders and can prepare the visitation order.

CHILD SUPPORT 10

This chapter will explain how child support is determined in all types of cases. It will also provide details of the forms and procedures for asking a court for what is called *support unconnected with dissolution of marriage with dependent or minor children*. In order to use this particular procedure, there are two requirements: (1) you must be married to the other parent of the child, and (2) neither you nor your spouse has filed for dissolution of marriage (divorce).

If you are not married to the other parent, you will need to use the paternity procedure described in Chapter 7. If you are married to the other parent, but one of you has filed for divorce, you will need to seek temporary or permanent child support as part of the divorce case.

HOW CHILD SUPPORT IS DETERMINED

Two factors are used to determine the amount of child support: (1) the needs of the child, and (2) the financial ability of each parent to meet those needs. Florida has established a formula to be used in calculating the needs of the child and each parent's ability to meet those needs. The following steps are used in determining the proper amount of child support:

- You and the other parent each provide proof of your gross incomes.
- Taxes and certain other deductions are allowed to determine each of your *net* incomes.
- Your net incomes are added together to arrive at your *combined* income.
- The combined income and the number of children you have are used to establish the children's needs. This is done by reading a chart (which is found in Appendix A of this book, and is explained in detail later).

- The net income of the parent without custody is divided by the combined income. This will give you the non-custodial parent's share (or percentage) of the combined income.
- That percentage is multiplied by the needs of the children to arrive at the amount of support to be paid by the parent without custody.

Most people can use this procedure. However, if your and the other parent's combined income is less than $650 per month these guidelines cannot be used. If your combined income is over $10,000 per month, you will need to add a certain percentage of the amount over $10,000; the amount of that additional percentage depending upon the number of children.

Also, the judge may depart from the guidelines by up to five percent, after considering the needs of the child and each parent's age, station in life, standard of living, and financial status. A written reason must be given in the **FINAL JUDGMENT** if the judge departs by more than five percent. These guidelines will be discussed more in this chapter, and their text can be found in Appendix A of this book. (Fla. Stat. Sec. 61.30).

The judge can also adjust the amount of child support in consideration of the following factors:

- extraordinary medical, psychological, educational, or dental expenses;
- independent income of the child, but not including supplemental security income for a child;
- the payment of support for a parent (that is, the parent of one of the parties) which regularly has been paid and for which there is a demonstrated need;
- seasonal variations in one or both parent's incomes or expenses;
- the age of the child, taking into account the greater needs of older children;
- special needs, such as costs associated with the disability of a child, that have traditionally been met by the family even though fulfilling those needs will cause the support to exceed the guidelines;
- the total available assets of the parents and the child;
- the impact of the Internal Revenue Service dependency exemption and waiver of that exemption (the judge may order the custodial parent to execute a waiver of the exemption if the non-custodial parent is current in child support payments);
- if the child support guidelines would require the non-custodial parent to pay more than fifty-one percent of his or her gross income for a single support order; or,
- any other adjustment needed to achieve an equitable result, such as to allow for a reasonable and necessary expense or debt which the parties jointly incurred during marriage.

Also, when the non-custodial parent has visitation for "a substantial amount of time," support must be adjusted based upon:

- the amount of time each child will spend with each parent;
- the needs of each child;
- the direct and indirect financial expenses for each child. Direct expenses include such things as food, clothing, and school activities. Indirect expenses include such things as mortgage or rent payments, utilities, and automobile expenses;
- the comparative income of each parent, considering all relevant factors provided in Section 61.30(2)(a) of the Florida Statutes;
- the station in life of each parent and each child;
- the standard of living experienced by the entire family during the marriage; or,
- the financial status and ability of each parent.

Most cases will be determined by the parents' incomes, using the child support tables in the Florida Statutes. The only exception is if you and the other parent can show that one or more of the factors listed above apply to your case. Some of the factors listed above will be of less significance or of no significance at all, such as in a case where you and the other parent are not married and have never lived together with the child as a family unit.

Child Support Guidelines Worksheet

The **Child Support Guidelines Worksheet** is used to calculate the proper amount of child support. (see form 5, p.197.) You will note that there is a column for the "Father" and a column for the "Mother." Be sure to fill in the information under the proper column. This form has fairly detailed instructions for each item, which should be sufficient for you to complete the form. However, if you have any difficulty, the following comments and examples may further assist you.

- Complete the top portion of the form according to the instructions at the beginning of Chapter 4, page 21.
- In the first, unnumbered paragraph, type in your name.
- In item "1. Present Net Monthly Income," fill in the net income figures from line 27 of your **Family Law Financial Affidavit** (form 2 or 3) and from line 27 of your spouse's **Family Law Financial Affidavit**. (If you are just evaluating your situation, you will not have your spouse's **Family Law Financial Affidavit**, so you will have to use your best estimate of your spouse's net income.)
- In item "2. Combined Present Net Monthly Income," add the figures from item 1a and item 1b, and fill in the total on line 2. The combined income is your net income added to your spouse's net income.

Example: The father's net income is $1,800 per month. The mother's net income is $1,200 per month. This would give a combined income of $3,000 (1,800 + 1,200).

☛ For item "3. Basic Monthly Obligation," fill in the number of children subject to the support order on the line beginning "There is (are) {number} ____ minor child(ren)..." Next, turn to the child support guidelines chart in Appendix A, beginning on page 155 of this book, which comes from Section 61.30(6) of the Florida Statutes. Read down the first column to your combined income, then read across to the column for the number of children for which support is owed. Write in the needs indicated by the support chart on line 3.

Example: With a combined income of $3,000 per month, find the figure "3,000" in the left column of the child support guidelines chart, then read across for the number of children. For one child the needs are $644 per month; for two children the needs are $1,001; for three children the needs are $1,252, etc. For our example, let's assume you have two children, so their monthly needs are $1,001.

☛ In item "4. Percentage of Financial Responsibility," you will determine each parent's percentage share of the combined income. To get your share, divide your net income from item 1 by the combined income from line 2.

Example: To get the father's percentage, divide $1,800 by $3,000, which will give you ".6" or six percent. To get the mother's percentage, divide $1,200 by $3,000, which will give you ".4" or four percent. The father's percentage goes on line 4a and the mother's on line 4b. (You will note that this item of the form calls for a percentage, which requires dropping the decimal point. Using our example, ".4" would be shown in item 4b as "40%," not as ".4%."

☛ In item "5. Share of Basic Monthly Obligation," multiply the needs (or basic obligation) by the father's percentage share ($1,001 x .6 = $600.60). This gives the amount of the children's needs the father would be expected to contribute. Next, multiply the needs by the mother's percentage share ($1,001 x .4 = $400.40). This is the amount the mother would be expected to contribute. Write in the contribution of you and your spouse on lines 5a and 5b.

NOTE: *How you complete the remainder of the form will depend upon your visitation arrangement. If the noncustodial parent will have overnight visitation less than 146 days in the year, you will complete items 6 through 9, and item 17 (skipping items 10 through*

16). If the noncustodial parent will have overnight visitation at least 146 days in the year, you will skip items 6 through 9, and complete items 10 through 17.

- Remember, you will only compete items 6 through 9 if the noncustodial parent will have overnight visitation less than 146 days in the year. For item "6. Total Monthly Child Care Costs," if you or your spouse are paying for child care, fill in the monthly child care costs on line 6.
- In item "7. Percentage of Child Care Costs," multiply the figure on line 6 by .75, and fill in the answer on line 7. Next, multiply the figure on line 7 by the percentage in line 4a, and fill in the answer on line 7a. This is the father's share of the child care costs. Next, multiply the figure on line 7 by the percentage in line 4b, and fill in the answer on line 7b. This is the mother's share of the child care costs.
- For item "8. Total Monthly Child(ren)'s Health Insurance Costs," if you or your spouse are paying for health insurance for your children, fill in the monthly cost of the insurance on line 8. This is only the insurance cost related to the children. Next, multiply the figure on line 8 by the percentage in line 4a, and fill in the answer on line 8a. This is the father's share of the children's health insurance costs. Next, multiply the figure on line 8 by the percentage in line 4b, and fill in the answer on line 8b. This is the mother's share of the children's health insurance costs.
- In item "9. Total Monthly Obligation," add the figures on lines 5a, 7a, and 8a, and fill in the answer on line 9a. This gives the father's total share of the child support obligation. Next, add the figures on lines 5b, 7b, and 8b, and fill in the answer on line 9b. This is the mother's total share of the child support obligation. If you have completed items 6 through 9, ignore items 10 through 16, and skip down to the instructions for item 17.
- Remember, you will only complete items 10 through 16 if the noncustodial parent will have overnight visitation at least 146 days of the year. In item "10. Shared Parenting Adjustment," take the figures from lines 5a and 5b and fill them in where indicated. Take the amount from line 5a , multiply it by 1.5, and fill in the answer on line 10a. Then take the amount from line 5b, multiply it by 1.5, and fill in the answer on line 10b.
- In item "11. Percentage of Overnight Stays," fill in the number of nights the children will spend with the father each year on the line in the sentence that reads: "The child(ren) spend(s) ____ Overnight stays with the father each year." Take this number, multiply it by 100, then divide the answer by 365 and fill in that answer on line 11a.

For example, if the children will spend 150 nights with the father, you would multiply 150 by 100, which would give you 15,000. Then you would divide 15,000 by 365, which would give you 41.09, which can be rounded off to 41.

Next, fill in the number of nights the children will spend with the mother each year on the line in the sentence that reads: "The child(ren) spend(s) ____ Overnight stays with the mother each year." Take this number, multiply it by 100, then divide by 365 and fill in the answer on line 11b.

- In item "12. Adjusted Financial Responsibility," multiply the amount on line 10a by the percentage on line 11a, and fill in the answer on line 12a. You will need to insert a decimal point to do this. (For example, if the figure on line 11a is "41%," you would multiply line 10a by .41.) Next, multiply the amount on line 10b by the percentage on line 11b, and fill in the answer on line 12b.
- In item "13. Total Monthly Child Care Costs," if you or your spouse are paying for child care, fill in the monthly child care costs on line 13. Next, multiply the figure on line 13 by the percentage on line 4a, and fill in the answer on line 13a. This is the father's share of the child care costs. Next, multiply the figure on line 13 by the percentage on line 4b, and fill in the answer on line 13b. This is the mother's share of the child care costs.
- For item "14. Total Monthly Child(ren)'s Health Insurance Costs," if you or your spouse are paying for health insurance for your children, fill in the monthly cost of the insurance on line 14. This is only the insurance cost related to the children. Next, multiply the figure on line 14 by the percentage in line 4a, and fill in the answer on line 14a. This is the father's share of the children's health insurance costs. Next, multiply the figure on line 14 by the percentage in line 4b, and fill in the answer on line 14b. This is the mother's share of the children's health insurance costs.
- In item "15. Total Monthly Obligation," add the amounts from lines 12a, 13a, and 14a, and fill in the answer on line 15a. This is the father's total child support obligation. Next, add the amounts from lines 12b, 13b, and 14b, and fill in the answer on line 15b. This is the mother's total child support obligation.
- In item "16. Monetary Transfer," if the amount on line 15a is larger than the amount on line 15b, subtract line 15b from line 15a. If line 15a is smaller than line 15b, subtract line 15a from line 15b. Fill in the answer on line 16. If line 15a is larger than line 15b, then the amount on line 16 is the monthly child support the father will pay to the mother. If line 15a is smaller than line 15b, then the amount on line 16 is the monthly child support the mother will pay to the father.

- In item "17. Adjustments to Guidelines Amount," in most cases you will check line "b. Deviation from the guidelines amount is NOT requested." However, if your child has special needs (such as because of a physical or mental handicap, because the child is in a special private school for gifted children, etc.), or there are any other reasons you think the child support guidelines are not giving a proper result, you can check line a, and file MOTION TO DEVIATE FROM CHILD SUPPORT GUIDELINES. (see form 43, p.291.)
- Fill in the certificate of service section to indicate how and when you sent or delivered a copy of the form to your spouse (or his or her attorney); and fill in your spouse's (or spouse's attorney's) name, address, and telephone information.
- Sign your name before a notary public or court clerk on the line marked "Signature of Party," and fill in the date, your name, address, and telephone information on the lines indicated.

MOTION TO DEVIATE FROM CHILD SUPPORT GUIDELINES

If there are unusual circumstances in your case that would make the regular child support guidelines insufficient, you can ask the judge to deviate from the guidelines. You do this by checking line "a" in item 10 of the CHILD SUPPORT GUIDELINES WORKSHEET (see form 5, p.197), and filing a MOTION TO DEVIATE FROM CHILD SUPPORT GUIDELINES. (see form 43, p.291.) If you read form 12, it will tell you what types of situations would justify deviating from the guidelines.

The following situation might also lead to one party filing this motion: If one party voluntarily reduces his or her income or quits a job, the judge can determine that it was done to avoid child support and refuse to recognize the reduction or loss of income. The judge will then order support as if that party were still receiving the income. This is called *imputed income*. An exception is made where the parent is required to take such an action to stay home and care for a young, ill, or handicapped child. If this question arises, the judge will decide whether the parent needs to stay home. If you are the one in this situation, be ready to explain your reasons.

To complete the MOTION TO DEVIATE FROM CHILD SUPPORT GUIDELINES (form 43):

- Complete the top portion of the form according to the instructions on page 21.
- In the line immediately above "Section I," check "Petitioner."
- In "Section I," if you are requesting more child support than is called for by the guidelines, check the line for "a." Check any of items 1 through 14 under "a" that apply.
  - If you are requesting less child support than is called for by the guidelines, check the line for "b." Check any of items 1 through 15 under "b" that apply. Under either of these choices are a few blank lines where you need to explain any of the items you select. If necessary, you can add additional sheets for your explanation.

- Complete "Section II. Income and Assets of Child(ren) Common to Both Parties," and "Section III. Expenses for Child(ren) Common to Both Parties." Just follow the instructions on the form itself.

  NOTE: *In order for the judge to consider your request to deviate from the guidelines, you will need to file a* **FAMILY LAW FINANCIAL AFFIDAVIT** *(form 2 or 3), and the* **CHILD SUPPORT GUIDELINES WORKSHEET** *(form 5).*

- Fill in the certificate of service section (beginning with "I have filed, ...") to indicate how and when you sent or delivered a copy of the form to the other parent (or his or her attorney); and fill in the other parent's (or attorney's) name, address, and telephone information.

- Sign your name before a notary public or court clerk on the line marked "Signature," and fill in the date, your name, address, and telephone information on the lines indicated.

- File this form with the court clerk.

PETITION FOR SUPPORT UNCONNECTED WITH DISSOLUTION OF MARRIAGE WITH DEPENDENT OR MINOR CHILD(REN)

The basic form you will file to ask the court for child support is the **PETITION FOR SUPPORT UNCONNECTED WITH DISSOLUTION OF MARRIAGE WITH DEPENDENT OR MINOR CHILD(REN)**. (see form 10, p.209.) As stated at the beginning of this chapter, you may only use this form if (1) you are married to the other parent, and (2) no dissolution of marriage (divorce) case has been filed by you or your spouse. To complete form 10:

- Complete the top portion of the form according to the instructions on page 21.

- In the first (unnumbered) paragraph, type in your name, and check one of the spaces for either "Husband" or "Wife," whichever applies to you.

- In paragraph 1, check the space for "Husband," "Wife," or "Both," to indicate which of you live in Florida.

- In paragraph 2, on the line beginning with the word "Petitioner," check the appropriate space to indicate whether you are in the military service. On the line beginning with the word "Respondent," check the appropriate space to indicate whether your spouse is in the military service.

- ☛ In paragraph 3, on the appropriate lines as indicated on the form, fill in the date of your marriage; the city, state, and country where you were married; and the date you and your spouse separated. Note the box to check if the date of separation is approximate.
- ☛ In paragraph 4, for subparagraphs "a" through "d," check all that apply. If you check "a," fill in the date the baby is due. If you check "b," fill in each minor child's name, place of birth, birth date, and sex of all children of you and your spouse on the lines as indicated. If you check "c," fill in each minor child's name, place of birth, birth date, and sex of all children of any children born or conceived during your marriage that are not children of both you and your spouse. If you check "d," fill in the name, place of birth, birth date, and sex of each child of you and your spouse who is age eighteen or older and dependent upon you due to a mental or physical incapacity.
- ☛ Under the heading "Section I. Spousal Support (Alimony)," check either paragraph 1 or 2, but not both. If you check paragraph 2, you will need to fill in the amount of alimony you want; whether it should be paid every week, every other week, or every month; the date it should begin; and how long it should continue (specify the date or event when it will end); write in an explanation of why you should get alimony, and any special requests; and check the last space if you want life insurance to guarantee payment in the event of your spouse's death.
- ☛ Under the heading "Section II. Child Support," for paragraphs 1 through 5, check all that apply to what you would like the judge to order. For each paragraph that you check, fill in the information required by that paragraph.
- ☛ The heading "Section III. Other Relief," is a place you can type in anything you want the judge to order that was not covered elsewhere on this form.
- ☛ Under the heading "Section IV. Petitioner's Request," you will check each item that reflects what you want the judge to order. Item "a" is to request alimony; item "b" requests child support; and item "c" requests anything that you typed in Section III, as well as anything else you didn't think of that may come up at a court hearing.
- ☛ Do not sign this form yet, as it must be signed before a notary public or a deputy court clerk. Fill in your name, address, and telephone information on the lines below the line marked "Signature of Petitioner."
- ☛ Take this form to a notary public or to the court clerk's office, and sign in before the notary or deputy clerk on the line marked "Signature of Petitioner." Your Petition may now be filed.

FAMILY LAW FINANCIAL AFFIDAVIT

Rule 12.105(c) of the Florida Family Law Rules requires both parties to complete and file a **FAMILY LAW FINANCIAL AFFIDAVIT**. (see form 2, p.175, or form 3, p.182.) The **FAMILY LAW FINANCIAL AFFIDAVIT (SHORT FORM)** is used if you have an annual income or annual expenses of less than $50,000. (see form 2, p.175.) If annual income or annual expenses are $50,000 of more, the other **FAMILY LAW FINANCIAL AFFIDAVIT** is used. (see form 3, p.182.) The form to be used is determined by each of you separately.

Example: If your income is less than $50,000 and the other parent's income is more than $50,000, you will file Form 2 and your spouse will file Form 3. Form 3 if more detailed than Form 2, but both require the same type of information about the following four areas: your income, expenses, assets, and debts.

FAMILY LAW FINANCIAL AFFIDAVIT (SHORT FORM)

Since the child support guidelines use monthly income figures, the **FAMILY LAW FINANCIAL AFFIDAVIT** is also figured on a monthly basis. If you are paid weekly, or every two weeks, you will need to convert your income to a monthly figure. The same conversion will be required for any of your expenses that are not paid monthly. To convert weekly amounts to monthly amounts, take the weekly figure and multiply it by 4.3 (there are roughly 4.3 weeks to a month). To convert from every two weeks, divide the amount of your check by 2, then multiply that by 4.3.

Fill in all of the blank spaces on the **FAMILY LAW FINANCIAL AFFIDAVIT** form, then take it to a notary public or to the clerk's office before you sign it. You will sign before the notary or a deputy clerk, and file it along with your **PETITION**. Most of the blanks on the **FAMILY LAW FINANCIAL AFFIDAVIT** clearly indicate what information is to be filled in there; however, the following information may answer some questions.

Regarding the **FAMILY LAW FINANCIAL AFFIDAVIT (SHORT FORM)** (form 2, p.175.):

- Complete the top portion of the form according to the instructions in Chapter 4.
- Type your name in the blank in the first paragraph.
- Fill in the information about your employment and income. If you are unemployed, you will need to check the box and attach a sheet explaining what efforts you are making to seek employment.
- For each item listed in "Section I. Present Monthly Gross Income," fill in the monthly amount (before taxes) that you receive. Total the amounts you listed and fill in the total on line 17. Next, complete section marked "Present Monthly Deductions." Total the deductions and fill in the total on line 26. Next, subtract the amount on line 26 from the amount on line 17, and fill in the answer on line 27.

- For "Section II. Average Monthly Expenses," simply refer to each item listed and estimate as best you can the amount you spend on that item in a month. If a particular item is an annual expense, such as auto insurance, convert it to a monthly amount.
- To complete the sections marked "Section III: Assets and Liabilities":
  - In the subsection marked "A. Assets," fill in the value for each item listed. Ignore the boxes before each item, and the columns marked "Nonmarital," because these only relate to original divorce cases–not to modification cases.
  - In the subsection marked "B. Liabilities," fill in the amount owed for each type of debt listed. Again, ignore the boxes before the items, and the columns marked "Nonmarital."
  - For the subsection marked "C. Contingent Assets and Liabilities," read the instructions for that subsection on the form, and fill in any information that applies.
- In "Section IV: Child Support Guidelines Worksheet," check the line for "A Child Support Guidelines Worksheet IS NOT being filed in this case."
- At the top of the fifth page, fill in the appropriate information to indicate how and when you sent or delivered a copy of the form to your ex-spouse (or his or her attorney); and fill in your ex-spouse's (or attorney's) name, address, and telephone information.
- Do not sign this form yet. Fill in your name, address, and telephone information on the lines below the signature line.
- Take this form to a notary public, and sign before the notary on the line marked "Signature of Party."

Family Law Financial Affidavit (Long Form)

To complete the **Family Law Financial Affidavit** (see form 3, p.182):

- Complete the top portion of the form according to the instructions in Chapter 4.
- Type in your name in the blank in the first paragraph.

- In "Section I. Income," fill in the information about yourself, and your employment and income. If you are unemployed, you will need to check the box and attach a sheet explaining what efforts you are making to seek employment. Under the subsection marked "Last Year's Gross Income," fill in the gross income amount from your W-2 or 1099 forms. For each item listed under "Present Monthly Gross Income," fill in the monthly amount (before taxes) that you receive. Total the amounts you listed and fill in the total on line 17. Next, complete section marked "Present Monthly Deductions." Total the deductions and fill in the total on line 26. Next, subtract the amount on line 26 from the amount on line 17, and fill in the answer on line 27.
- For the section marked "Section II. Average Monthly Expenses," simply refer to each item listed and estimate as best you can the amount you spend on that item in a month. If a particular item is an annual expense, such as auto insurance, convert it to a monthly amount. Add up amounts and fill in subtotals and totals where indicated. Complete the subsection marked "Summary."
- To complete the sections marked "Section III: Assets and Liabilities:"
    - In the subsection marked "A. Assets," fill in the value for each item listed. Ignore the boxes before each item and the columns marked "Nonmarital" because these only relate to original divorce cases–not to modification cases.
    - In the subsection marked "B. Liabilities/Debts," fill in the amount owed for each type of debt listed. Again, ignore the boxes before the items, and the columns marked "Nonmarital."
    - For the subsection marked "C. Net Worth," fill in the total assets figure and the total liabilities figure; subtract liabilities from assets; and fill in the answer on the line marked "Total Net Worth."
    - For the subsection marked "D. Contingent Assets and Liabilities," read the instructions for that subsection on the form and fill in any information that applies.
    - Ignore the subsection marked "E."
- Under the heading "Attachments," check the line for "A Child Support Guidelines Worksheet IS NOT being filed in this case."
- Fill in the certificate of service section to indicate how and when you sent or delivered a copy of the form to your ex-spouse (or his or her attorney); and fill in your ex-spouse's (or attorney's) name, address, and telephone information.
- Do not sign this form yet. Fill in your name, address, and telephone information on the lines below the signature line.
- Take this form to a notary public, and sign before the notary on the line marked "Signature of Party."

FINANCIAL DISCLOSURE AND INTERROGATORIES

In any case involving a request for child support, there are several financial disclosure requirements. First, be sure to read Rule 12.285 of the Family Law Rules of Procedure (found in Appendix A of this book)—particularly subsection (d). This rule describes the financial disclosure requirements you must satisfy.

If you or your spouse have an annual income or annual expenses of $50,000 of more, you (or your spouse) must file answers to the STANDARD FAMILY LAW INTERROGATORIES FOR ORIGINAL OR ENFORCEMENT PROCEEDINGS. (see form 34, p.255.) Of course, if you earn $50,000 or more per year, you may have enough at stake to justify hiring a lawyer to represent you.

NOTE: *If you are requesting a change to an existing child support order, you will instead use the* STANDARD FAMILY LAW INTERROGATORIES FOR MODIFICATION PROCEEDINGS. *(see form 35, p.268.)*

The following information will discuss the forms you will need to file in connection with these disclosure requirements.

STANDARD FAMILY LAW INTERROGATORIES FOR ORIGINAL OR ENFORCEMENT PROCEEDINGS

To complete the STANDARD FAMILY LAW INTERROGATORIES FOR ORIGINAL OR ENFORCEMENT PROCEEDINGS (see form 34, p.255):

- Complete the top portion of the form according to the instructions on page 21.
- Type in the answer to each question. If you need more space, type in "see attached sheet," and attach additional sheets of paper with your answers. Be sure to indicate the number of the question you are answering on the additional sheets.
- On the first page add the words "Answers to" just above the title "Standard Family Law Interrogatories."
- Send a copy of your answers to your spouse.

To prove to the court that you have answered the interrogatories, check the appropriate box on the CERTIFICATE OF COMPLIANCE WITH MANDATORY DISCLOSURE (form 40). (See the instructions for form 40 on page 102.) If your spouse has annual income or expenses of $50,000 or more, he or she will need to provide you with the answers even if you do not request them.

CERTIFICATE OF COMPLIANCE WITH MANDATORY DISCLOSURE

The CERTIFICATE OF COMPLIANCE WITH MANDATORY DISCLOSURE must be filed in all cases. (see form 40, p.284.) It is used to satisfy the judge that you have provided your spouse with the required documents and a FAMILY LAW FINANCIAL AFFIDAVIT. (A copy of this form should also be given to your spouse, so that he or she can complete it to certify that he or she has provided the required information to you.)

To complete the **CERTIFICATE OF COMPLIANCE WITH MANDATORY DISCLOSURE** (see form 40, p.284):

- ☛ Complete the top portion of the form according to the instructions on page 21.
- ☛ In the first (unnumbered) paragraph, type in your name.
- ☛ Skip the section marked "1. For Temporary Financial Relief Only."
- ☛ In paragraph marked "2. For Initial, Supplemental, and Permanent Financial Relief," type in the date the documents were mailed or personally delivered to the other parent. For items "a" through "q," check all that apply.
- ☛ Fill in the certificate of service section after item "q," to indicate how and where you provided a copy of this form to the other parent or his or her attorney.
- ☛ Fill in the date, sign your name on the line marked "Signature of Party," and fill in your name, address, and telephone numbers on the lines indicated.
- ☛ Mail a copy of this form to your spouse in the manner indicated in the certificate of service section.
- ☛ File the original of this form with the court clerk.

NOTICE OF SERVICE OF STANDARD FAMILY LAW INTERROGATORIES

If the other parent has annual income and expenses of less than $50,000, you may still require him or her to submit answers to the standard interrogatories. To do so, send the other parent a copy of form 34, and file a **NOTICE OF SERVICE OF STANDARD FAMILY LAW INTERROGATORIES** with the clerk. (see form 33, p.253) To complete form 33:

- ☛ Fill in the top portion of the form according to the instructions on page 21.
- ☛ On the lines in the main paragraph, type your name, the date the **STANDARD FAMILY LAW INTERROGATORIES** (form 31) were served on the other parent, and the other parent's name (or his or her attorney's name).
- ☛ Check the space for "Original or Enforcement Proceedings."
- ☛ Below the sentence beginning "I am requesting," check the line for each type of questions you want the other parent to answer. This will require you to read the Standard Family Law Interrogatories to see what questions are asked. If there are questions you would like answered that are not in form 31, you may type out your additional questions and attach them to form 30. If you do this, you will need to fill in the number of new questions you are asking on the line where indicated.

- ☛ Complete the certificate of service section to indicate how you will provide the other parent with a copy of form 30. Fill in the other parent's or attorney's information.
- ☛ Sign your name on the line marked "Signature of Party," and type in your name, address, and telephone number information below the signature line.
- ☛ Send or deliver a copy of the form to the other parent in the manner you indicated in the certificate of service section.
- ☛ File the original with the court clerk.

The other parent has thirty days from the date he or she receives the interrogatories to send you answers and file a copy of his or her answers with the clerk.

Other Forms

In addition to the forms discussed above, there are several other forms that you will, or may, need to file along with your PETITION. These are:

- CIVIL COVER SHEET. (see form 8, p.207.) This form must be completed and filed along with the PETITION in all cases. (See Chapter 4 for instructions for completing form 8.)
- UNIFORM CHILD CUSTODY JURISDICTION ACT (UCCJA) AFFIDAVIT. (see form 4, p.193.) This form must be filed in all cases. (See Chapter 8 for instructions for completing form 4.)
- NOTICE OF SOCIAL SECURITY NUMBER(S) (see form 6, p.203.) This form must be filed in all cases.
- AFFIDAVIT OF INDIGENCY (see form 1, p.173.) You will file this form if you are financially unable to pay the filing fee and other court costs. (See Chapter 4 for instructions for completing form 1.)

Procedures

This section will briefly discuss the basic procedures of filing with the court clerk, notifying your spouse that you have filed a PETITION, setting a court date, and notifying your spouse of that court date. Generally, this will consist of referring you to other chapters of this book where each of these matters is discussed in greater detail.

Filing with the Court Clerk

Once all of your necessary papers are prepared, you will need to file them with the court clerk. See Chapter 4 for information about filing your court papers.

Notifying the Other Parent

You will need to notify your spouse by either personal service or by service by publication (if appropriate). See Chapter 5 for an explanation of how proper notice must be given. That chapter will also explain the procedure to follow for obtaining a default if your spouse does not respond to your **Petition** as required by law.

Setting a Hearing Date

If your spouse responds to your **Petition**, you will need to schedule a court hearing, and notify your spouse of the hearing date. See Chapter 6 for detailed information about scheduling a hearing and sending the required hearing notice.

Preparing and Presenting Your Case

This section will help you to prepare for your court hearing, and explain how to present your case to the judge.

In most cases asking for child support, the only testimony offered is that of the parties. If **Family Law Financial Affidavits** have been filed, all other required financial disclosure has been made, and a **Child Support Guidelines Worksheet** filed, those documents will provide all of the evidence the judge will need to make a decision. For more about your testimony, see the section below entitled "Presenting Your Proof."

Testimony of Witnesses

The only time the testimony of a third party is required is if one of the parties did not file the required papers, or is accused by the other of not providing accurate or complete information. In this situation, you may need to call a third party, such as the other party's employer, bank representative, stock broker, etc., to testify and provide documents regarding the other party's income and assets. If you decide this is necessary, see Chapter 6 for information about obtaining documents, having subpoenas issued, and having third-party witnesses testify.

Documents as Evidence

In most cases asking for child support, the only documents the court will need to see are the papers already filed with the court. Therefore, it will not be necessary for you to introduce any documents into evidence at the hearing.

The only time you may need to introduce other documents is if your spouse did not file the required papers, or did not providing accurate or complete information. In this situation, you may need to either introduce documents you have obtained, or call a third party, such as the other party's employer, bank representative, stock broker, etc., to provide documents regarding the other party's income and assets. If you decide this is necessary, see Chapter 6 for information about obtaining documents, having subpoenas issued, and having witnesses testify and present documents as evidence.

Opening Statement

An opening statement is your chance to briefly tell the judge why you are in court, what you plan to prove, and what you want done. The following is an example of an opening statement:

Example: "Your Honor, we are here on a petition for support unconnected with dissolution of marriage. I am requesting an order for child support in the amount of $376 per month. This is based on the information contained in the Family Law Financial Affidavits and the Child Support Guidelines Worksheet which have been filed with the court. Thank you."

After your opening statement, your spouse (or his or her attorney) will have an opportunity to give an opening statement. This is your spouse's chance to summarize for the judge why he or she disagrees with what you are asking for.

Presenting Your Proof

After the opening statements, it will be your turn to present your proof. Exactly what happens at this point will depend upon what papers have been filed and how the particular judge likes to conduct the hearing. The judge may take over and say that he or she has reviewed the financial information filed with the court, and ask you and your spouse if the information is accurate, and whether either of you have any new information to provide. If satisfied that the financial information is correct, the judge may just state that he or she is ordering child support based upon the child support guidelines.

If the judge likes a more formal procedure, you will need to tell the judge that you wish to give testimony. You will then be sworn in as a witness. Have your copy of the PETITION ready to use as a checklist for testifying. You will want to state the following:

- your name;
- that you, or your spouse, or both of you, live in Florida;
- the date and place of your marriage;
- the date, or approximate date, when you and your spouse separated;
- the names and ages of your children for whom you are requesting support;
- that FAMILY LAW FINANCIAL AFFIDAVITS have been filed, which accurately reflect the financial status of you and your spouse;
- that a CHILD SUPPORT GUIDELINES WORKSHEET has been filed, and the amount of child support that is calculated pursuant to the guidelines. (If you are requesting child support in an amount that is different from the guidelines, be prepared to explain why the guidelines should not be followed.); and,
- any other things you are requesting as stated in your PETITION, including any request for alimony, medical/dental insurance, a request for payment of medical/dental expenses not covered by insurance, and a request for life insurance to secure support.

Final Judgment

After you present your case, your spouse will be entitled to present his or her case. Once the judge has heard from both sides, he or she will make a decision. The judge's decision will then need to be put into a written order. This section will explain the two forms you will need to complete in order to finish your case.

Final Judgment for Support Unconnected with Dissolution of Marriage with Dependent or Minor Child(ren)

Following what the judge decides, you will need to complete the **Final Judgment for Support Unconnected with Dissolution of Marriage with Dependent or Minor Child(ren)**. (see form 10, p.209.) To complete form 10:

- Complete the top portion of the form according to the instructions on page 21.
- In paragraph 2, fill in the name and birth date of each child who is subject to the support order.
- Under the heading "Section I. Alimony":
    - In paragraph 1, check the first space if the judge denies your request for alimony. Check the second space if the judge grants your request for alimony, and, for subparagraphs "a" through "d," check all subparagraphs that reflect what the judge ordered. For each subparagraph you check, fill in all of the information required by that subparagraph.
    - In paragraph 2, check the space for either "Awarding" or "Denying," depending upon whether the judge granted your request for alimony. If the judge stated any reasons in addition to those listed in subparagraphs "a" through "f," write those reasons on the lines provided. Note there is a box to check if extra pages are needed.
    - In paragraph 3, check either "a" or "b," but not both. If you check "b," fill in all of the required information in that subparagraph.
    - In paragraph 4, for subparagraphs "a" and "b," check all that apply; and fill in the required information for any subparagraph checked.
    - Paragraph 5 is for any other matters relating to alimony ordered by the judge that are not covered elsewhere in Section I.

☛ Under the heading "Section II. Child Support":

- In paragraph 1, check the space for either "Mother" or "Father," to indicate who will pay child support. Check the next space for either "Mother" or "Father," to indicate which of you filed the Child Support Guidelines Worksheet. Fill in your and your spouse's incomes, the child support guidelines percentages, the monthly child care costs, and the monthly health/dental insurance costs on the appropriate lines.
- In paragraph 2, fill in the amount of child support, check the appropriate space to indicate when it is to be paid, and fill in the date payments are to begin. Check one of the spaces to indicate when child support will end. If the judge decided that the child support guidelines should not be followed and deviates from the guidelines by five percent or more (either up or down), fill in the reasons for deviating from the guidelines on the lines at the end of paragraph 2. You may have to ask the judge how he or she wants this subsection completed.
- In paragraph 3, check "a" if no retroactive child support was awarded. Check "b" if retroactive child support was awarded. If you check "b," fill in all of the blanks, which are self-explanatory.
- Paragraph 4 needs to be completed if the judge makes an order regarding health and dental insurance. Check "a," "b," or both. For any subparagraph you check, fill in all of the blanks, which are self-explanatory.
- If the judge ordered life insurance to secure payment of support, fill in the required information in paragraph 5, which is self-explanatory.
- If the judge made an order regarding the tax exemption for the child, complete paragraph 6.
- Paragraph 7 is for any other matters relating to child support ordered by the judge that are not covered elsewhere in Section II.

☛ Under the heading "Section III. Method of Payment":

- In paragraph 1, check "a" if the judge ordered payment through the Central Governmental Depository, and fill in the name of the county. Check "b" if the judge did not order payment through the Central Governmental Depository.
- In paragraph 2, check "a" if the judge ordered income withholding to begin immediately. Check "b" if the judge ordered income withholding deferred. If you check "b," fill in the amount of delinquency that will trigger income withholding, and type in the judge's explanation of why income withholding is not in the best interests of the children. Usually the judge will order payments through the Central Governmental Depository by way of an income

deduction order, in which case the parent who will pay support will be referred to the appropriate place (usually the court clerk, Central Governmental Depository, or support enforcement office) to get the necessary paperwork done to implement the income deduction. This is done by one of these agencies sending an Income Deduction Notice to the employer of the person who is paying support.

- Paragraph 3 is for an order that all, some, or none of the obligor's bonus or other one-time payment be applied to child support.
- Paragraph 4 is for any other orders relating to the method of payment that are not covered elsewhere in Section III.

☛ "Section IV. Attorney Fees, Costs, and Suit Money" will need to be completed if either party requested the other party to pay any of these expenses. If such a request was made, check paragraph 1 or 2, and fill in the blanks. Of course, if you are asking for attorney fees you have hired an attorney, and he or she will be preparing this form. If attorney fees and court costs have been requested by either party, the judge must state why the request is granted or denied, so you will have to ask the judge how he or she what this section completed.

☛ "Section V. Other Provisions" is where you would state any other orders the judge makes that are not stated elsewhere on this form.

Once you have filled in all of the required information, this form will be submitted to the judge for his or her signature.

Final Disposition Form

Similar to the **Civil Cover Sheet** (form 8), the **Final Disposition Form** is another form required by the courts for their administrative purposes. (see form 9, p.208.) (See Chapter 7 for instructions for completing form 9.)

Changing Custody 11

This chapter will discuss changing an existing custody order. This information will apply to changing a custody order in both divorce cases and paternity cases.

How a Change in Custody is Determined

In covering what is traditionally called *custody*, Florida law distinguishes between *primary residence* (where the child lives a majority of the time) and *parental responsibility* (who makes major decisions regarding the child, such as medical care, educational needs, etc.). Many judges and lawyers still refer to this generally as custody, and we will as well, unless the distinction is significant.

If your situation has reached the point where you are reading this chapter, you probably want your child to live with you, and you want the sole parental responsibility for making major decisions about your child's welfare. Your first step is to read your divorce judgment or other custody order to see how it describes your current custody/parental responsibility situation. Most divorce judgments designate the primary residence with one parent, but provide for joint parental responsibility. Florida law favors joint parental responsibility.

Factors to Consider

The following factors are those that a judge is required to consider in awarding custody initially, as opposed to changing custody. Some of these factors may also apply in a change of custody situation, and the relative importance of each factor may be different in considering a change of custody. The factors are:

- which parent is more likely to allow the other to visit with the child? (If the other party is denying you visitation, or is causing serious problems with visitation or your relationship with your child, this may justify a change in custody.

However, it may also be viewed by the judge as only requiring a more specific visitation order, or only require that the judge instruct the other party to follow the current visitation order. If you are using this as the reason to request a change in custody, be ready to assure the judge that you will do a better job of fostering a good relationship between the child and the other parent.);

- the love, affection, and other emotional ties existing between the child and each parent;
- the ability and willingness of each parent to provide the child with food, clothing, medical care, and other material needs;
- the length of time the child has lived with either parent in a stable environment(This may be the most significant factor in a fight to change custody, because the courts are reluctant to remove a child from a stable environment unless there is a very good reason.);
- the permanence, as a family unit, of the proposed custodial home;
- the moral fitness of each parent;
- the mental and physical health of each parent;
- the home, school, and community record of the child;
- the preference of the child, providing the child is of sufficient intelligence and understanding (Especially if your child is older, you may want to give a lot of consideration to where the child wants to live.); and,
- any other factor the judge decides is relevant.

While some of these factors will come into play in your attempt to change custody, these are not necessarily the same factors the judge will consider. To justify a change in custody, you will need to show that the child's needs and the parents' circumstances have changed since the current custody order was entered. Or, you must show that the current custody arrangement has failed (such as where the other party is not following the current custody or visitation order). If the child is in a stable environment, it will be difficult to get the judge to upset things by changing custody.

Generally, you will need to prove that the child is in some kind of danger by staying in the other party's custody. Other factors that have been considered in change of custody cases include the sex of the child; the relocation of one of the parents; and the morals, race, religion, and social views of the parents which have an effect on the child's welfare. These things may be considered, but they do not necessarily decide the question. The primary concern is the *best interest* of the child, with a strong presumption in favor of maintaining a stable home environment.

You will need to look at your current custody order to see if there are any statements about why custody was awarded to the other party. If custody was based upon your agreement, there will probably be no such statement. In filing a petition to change custody, the following factors should be considered:

Financial Inability. It is almost impossible to justify a change of custody on the grounds that the other parent lacks the ability to provide for your child. This is because the other parent's difficulty can be fixed by you paying child support! However, while financial inability will not get you a change of custody, financial unwillingness may. This is where you can prove that the other party is not using the child support and other available financial resources to care for the child. In other words, the other party has the money, but is not using it to provide for the child. This may also constitute neglect, which is covered below. You will need to show an actual negative effect on the child. Mere speculation will not be enough.

Health of the Parents. This relates to both physical and mental health. To obtain a change of custody you will need to prove that the other party has a mental or physical condition which renders him or her unable to adequately take care of the child. This will require testimony of expert witnesses, especially doctors or psychologists who have examined or treated the other party. It may also require you to show that your child is actually not receiving proper care. If you believe the other party suffers from a mental problem, you can file a motion for a psychological evaluation.

Lifestyle and Beliefs of the Parents. Generally, a custodial parent is allowed to have his or her own beliefs, morals and lifestyle as long as it doesn't affect his or her ability to be a parent and raise the child. Here again, you will probably need expert witness testimony to prove a negative effect on the child. One of the big issues today is drug abuse. If you believe the other party is a drug abuser, you can file a motion to have the other party tested for drugs.

Warning: Drug abuse is a charge that is frequently made in custody disputes, often without any real proof. Don't make such a charge lightly.

Abuse and Neglect. If you suspect that the other party is physically abusing your child, you are required by law to call the *Department of Children and Families Services* (CFS) (their toll-free number is 800-962-2873). CFS will investigate, and if they find abuse you may be able to use their investigators as witnesses to justify a change in custody. In most cases, if CFS cannot prove abuse (and they often cannot), you will not be able to either. Also, be aware that it is a criminal offense to make a false abuse report to CFS, so don't do it simply to harass the other party.

If CFS does find abuse or neglect, it may remove the child from the other party's home, temporarily place the child with you or another relative, and file a petition in juvenile court to get a court order permanently removing the child from the other party's home. However, if CFS believes that the child would not be any better off in your custody, the child may end up with other relatives, or in a foster home, for a long period of time while you or the other party take parenting courses and see psychologists.

A CFS investigation may result in an administrative hearing that is similar to a trial and may involve your child being called to testify. This can be traumatic. It could also trigger a criminal investigation by the police, criminal abuse or neglect charges against the other party, and your child being interviewed by police officers, State Attorney Office investigators and lawyers, and being called to testify at depositions and in a criminal trial. These things can take months to complete with no guarantee that anything will be sufficiently proven. This should not discourage you from pursuing the matter if you really believe the other party is abusing or neglecting your child, but you should be aware of the situation in which you may be getting yourself and your child involved.

Physical Abuse. In order to make a physical abuse charge hold up, you will generally need to show some kind of an injury and how the injury occurred. This may require you to decide if you want to drag your child into court to testify about what happened. It may also require bringing doctors to court to testify.

Sexual Abuse. This is usually even more difficult to prove than physical abuse, especially if it involves a young child and no physical evidence of abuse (as determined by a doctor). You will also need to consider whether you want to have your child testify–this will probably be unavoidable if you want to pursue the matter. As with physical abuse, you also need to be aware that children sometimes make up stories of abuse in an attempt to manipulate their parents. CFS social workers and psychologists may tell you that young children do not make up sexual abuse stories, but they are wrong. Even a physician's conclusion that there has been sexual abuse cannot be relied upon, as many other medical problems can create symptoms similar to those caused by - sexual abuse.

Emotional Abuse. Emotional abuse is impossible to prove unless you can get a psychologist or psychiatrist to testify that something the other party did caused serious psychological damage to your child. This must clearly be different than the problems caused by the divorce itself.

Neglect. Neglect can mean failing to provide adequate housing, food, clothing, medical care, or education.

THE "SPECIAL NEEDS" CHILD

If your child has "special needs," the ability of you and the other party to meet these needs may also be considered. Special needs involve the gifted child who has special educational needs, as well as the child with physical or mental problems and handicaps. This will probably involve expert testimony to verify the child's condition and needs, and show which parent is best able to meet those needs. For example, if your handicapped child needs frequent at-home physical therapy, the judge may not change custody if you work full time and the other party stays at home with the children.

RELATIONSHIP TO SUPPORT AND VISITATION

A change in child custody will also result in a change in child support and visitation. If you get custody of your child, the other party may be required to pay child support. If you do not want child support, the judge will probably go along with no support as long as you can satisfy the judge that you have the financial ability to take care of your child.

If you will have custody, you need to consider the other party's visitation rights. If you and the other party got along fine with whatever visitation arrangement is in your divorce judgment, you may be able to simply reverse the situation now that you have custody. But if your petition to change custody has led to bitter disputes with the other party, it is a good idea to get a detailed visitation order to minimize problems in the future.

SUPPLEMENTAL PETITION TO MODIFY CUSTODY OR VISITATION AND OTHER RELIEF

The basic form used to ask for a change in custody is the **SUPPLEMENTAL PETITION TO MODIFY CUSTODY OR VISITATION AND OTHER RELIEF**. (see form 13, p.217.) You will see that there are also provisions in this form to ask for child support because a change in child support usually goes with a change in custody. To complete form 13:

- Complete the top portion of the form according to the instructions in Chapter 4.
- On the line in the first, unnumbered paragraph, fill in your name.
- In paragraph 1, check the space for "dissolution of marriage," and fill in the date of the final judgment. You will need to attach a copy of the divorce judgment, and any subsequent custody orders.
- In paragraph 2, fill in the number of the paragraph (or paragraphs) in the most recent order relating to custody. This will either be the paragraphs in your divorce or paternity judgment, or in the last modification order if custody has been modified since the divorce judgment. Check the appropriate space to indicate whether you are seeking to modify the "final judgment" or the "most recent modification" of the judgment.
- In the space below paragraph 3, you will need to type in a brief explanation of what circumstances have changed since the last custody order that would justify a change in custody. This is basically a statement of the reason you want to change custody.

- In paragraph 4, check the space for "custody," and in the space after paragraph 4, type in what you want the new custody order to do. For example, if the current order gives the other parent sole custody and you want sole custody: "To transfer sole custody of the two minor children from the Respondent to the Petitioner." Or, if the current order provides for joint custody and you want sole custody: "To award the Petitioner sole custody of the minor child."
- In paragraph 5, type in an explanation of why a change in custody is in the best interest of the children. This may be obvious from what you have already stated in paragraph 3, but you will still need to fill in paragraph 5.
- Read paragraphs 6 through 9, and be sure to file the additional forms required by these paragraphs.
- Paragraph 10 is to be used for any matters not covered elsewhere in the form.
- Take this form to a notary public and sign it before the notary.

Financial Disclosure Documents

Because a change in custody almost always results in a change in child support, you will need to complete and file several financial disclosure forms.

Family Law Financial Affidavit

You and the other party will each need to file either a **Family Law Financial Affidavit (Short Form)** (form 2) or **Family Law Financial Affidavit** (form 3). Filing one of these forms is required. To determine which **Family Law Financial Affidavit** you need (form 2 or form 3), and for instructions for completing it, see the instructions for these forms in Chapter 10. Also, be sure to read the chapters relating to child support and visitation, as a change in custody will also require a change in child support and visitation.

Interrogatories are written questions that one party submits to the other. The party receiving the interrogatories must provide written answers that are certified under oath. This means they are the same as testifying in court, and the person answering can be charged with *perjury* or *contempt of court* for not answering truthfully.

STANDARD FAMILY LAW INTERROGATORIES FOR MODIFICATION PROCEEDINGS

The Family Law Rules of Procedure require that any party with an annual income or annual expenses of $50,000 or more must provide answers to the STANDARD FAMILY LAW INTERROGATORIES FOR MODIFICATION PROCEEDINGS. (see form 35, p.268.) Therefore, if you have an annual income of more than $50,000 or annual expenses of more than $50,000, you will need to file answers to the STANDARD FAMILY LAW INTERROGATORIES FOR MODIFICATION PROCEEDINGS (form 35). To complete form 35:

- Complete the top portion of the form according to the instructions on page 21.
- On the first page of the form, add the words "Answers to" just above the title "Standard Family Law Interrogatories for Modification Proceedings."
- Type in the answers to each question. If you need more space, type in "see attached sheet," and attach additional sheets of paper to the form. On any such additional sheet, be sure to indicate the number of the question you are answering.
- Send a copy of the completed form to the other party (or his or her attorney).

CERTIFICATE OF COMPLIANCE WITH MANDATORY DISCLOSURE

To show the court that you have provided the other party with a FAMILY LAW FINANCIAL AFFIDAVIT (form 2 or form 3), and all required financial information, you will need to file a CERTIFICATE OF COMPLIANCE WITH MANDATORY DISCLOSURE. (see form 40, p.284.) (See Chapter 10 for instructions on completing form 40.)

NOTICE OF SERVICE OF STANDARD FAMILY LAW INTERROGATORIES

If the other party has an annual income and annual expenses of less than $50,000, he or she is not required to *automatically* file answers to the STANDARD FAMILY LAW INTERROGATORIES FOR MODIFICATION PROCEEDINGS. However, you may still require him or her to provide these answers. To do so, send the other party a copy of form 35, and prepare and file a NOTICE OF SERVICE OF STANDARD FAMILY LAW INTERROGATORIES (see form 33, p.253):

- Complete the top portion of the form according to the instructions on page 21.
- On the lines in the main paragraph, type your name, the date the STANDARD FAMILY LAW INTERROGATORIES FOR MODIFICATION PROCEEDINGS (form 35) was sent to the other party, and the other party's name (or his or her attorney's name).
- Check the space for "Modification Proceedings."
- Below the sentence beginning "I am requesting," check the line for each type of questions you want the other party to answer. This will require you to read the STANDARD FAMILY LAW INTERROGATORIES FOR MODIFICATION PROCEEDINGS (form 35) to see what questions are asked. If there are questions you like answered that are not in form 35, you may type out your additional questions and attach them to form 35. If you do this, you will need to fill in the number of the new questions you are asking on the line where indicated.

- Complete the certificate of service section to indicate how you will provide the other party with a copy of form 33. Fill in the other party's, or attorney's, information.
- Sign your name on the line marked "Signature of Party," and type in your name, address, and telephone number information below the signature line.
- Send or deliver a copy of the form to the other party (or attorney) in the manner you indicated in the certificate of service section.
- File the original with the court clerk.

The other party has thirty days from the date he or she receives the interrogatories to send you answers, and to file a copy of his or her answers with the clerk.

UCCJA, Guardian Ad Litem, and Your Case

In all cases involving custody or visitation, you must complete the **Uniform Child Custody Jurisdiction Act (UCCJA) Affidavit**. Furthermore, if there are charges of abuse or neglect, a court must appoint a *guardian ad litem*. Finally, you must prepare and present a case, possibly with witnesses and documents. (see Chapter 8 for information on all these things.)

Judgment Forms

Once the judge announces his or her decision, there are two more forms you will need to complete.

Supplemental Final Judgment of Modification of Parental Responsibility/ Visitation

At the hearing, you will need to present the judge with a **Supplemental Final Judgment of Modification of Parental Responsibility/Visitation** (form 54). To complete this form:

- Complete the top portion of the form according to the instructions in Chapter 4.
- Under the heading "Section I. Findings:"
  - In paragraph 2, type in the date of the most recent custody order. This may be in your divorce or paternity judgment, or a subsequent order modifying the judgment.

- In paragraph 3, type in a brief description of what circumstances the judge determines have changed.
- In paragraph 4, type in a brief statement of why the judge decided the change of custody is in the best interest of the children.

☛ Under the heading "Section II. Custody of and Visitation With Dependent or Minor Child(ren):"

- In paragraph 2, fill in the names and birthdates of your children.
- In paragraph 3 through 9, check the appropriate spaces and fill in the necessary information to reflect what the judge ordered regarding custody and visitation.

☛ Under the headings for "Section III. Child Support," "Section IV. Method of Payment," and "Section V. Attorney Fees, Costs, and Suit Money," check the appropriate spaces and fill in the necessary information to reflect what the judge ordered regarding these matters. Leave any items blank that do not apply. "Section VI. Other," is to add anything else the judge orders that is not covered elsewhere in the form.

☛ Once you have completed all items according to what the judge ordered, you will give the form to the judge for his or her signature. If you have time to get the form completed right at the hearing, you may be able to hand it to the judge for signature at that time. Otherwise, you will need to prepare the form after you leave the hearing room, and take or send it to the judge within a couple of days. You can ask the judge which way he or she prefers for you to handle submission of the order for signature.

FINAL DISPOSITION FORM

Like the CIVIL COVER SHEET (form 8), the FINAL DISPOSITION FORM (form 9) is another form required by the courts for their administrative purposes. Part I of the form should be completed exactly the same as the CIVIL COVER SHEET, but be sure to fill in the case number, judge, and division. Under the heading "II. Means of Final Disposition," check the box marked "Disposed by Judge." (If you have a trial on a contested case, check the box marked "Disposed by Non-Jury Trial.") This form also needs to be dated and signed by you, but be sure to use the date of the final hearing. Also, fill in your address and phone number below the signature line. Take this form with you to the final hearing. You will need to give it to the judge at the hearing so that it can be included in your file when it is sent to the court clerk.

12 Changing Visitation

Of all the provisions in a divorce judgment, visitation is the easiest to get modified. All you generally need to show is that the current arrangement is not working. This may be due to a change in circumstances (such as one party moving farther away), or because the current order is too general and a more rigid schedule is needed. In such cases you want to be specific, so there is no room for the other party to be uncertain about what is required. If the current order is already specific, but the other party is not following it, you need to file a motion to enforce the order rather than to modify the order.

If you have custody and you are seeking to completely terminate visitation between your child and the other party, you will need to show that the other party poses a serious danger to the child. (This will be very similar to asking for a change in custody, so be sure to read Chapter 8 of this book.)

If your judgment or current court order denies you all visitation and you are asking the judge to start giving you visitation, you will need to show a significant change in the circumstances which made the judge deny visitation in the first place. Legally, there is no relationship between child support and visitation. Therefore, if the other party fails to pay child support, you cannot legally refuse visitation. Also, if the other party refuses to allow you visitation, you cannot legally refuse to pay child support.

SUPPLEMENTAL PETITION TO MODIFY CUSTODY OR VISITATION AND OTHER RELIEF

The SUPPLEMENTAL PETITION TO MODIFY CUSTODY OR VISITATION AND OTHER RELIEF (form 13 is the basic form used to ask the court for a change in visitation. (You will note that this is the same form used to ask for a change in custody.) To complete form 13:

- Complete the top portion of the form according to the instructions in Chapter 4.
- On the line in the first, unnumbered paragraph, fill in your name.
- In paragraph 1, check the space for either "dissolution of marriage" or "paternity," whichever applies to your situation; and fill in the date of the final judgment. You will need to attach a copy of the judgment and any subsequent visitation orders.
- In paragraph 2, fill in the number of the paragraph (or paragraphs) in the most recent order relating to visitation. This will either be the paragraphs in your judgment, or in the last modification order if visitation has been modified since the judgment. Check the appropriate space to indicate whether you are seeking to modify the "final judgment" or the "most recent modification" of the judgment.
- In the space below paragraph 3, you will need to type in a brief explanation of what circumstances have changed since the last visitation order that would justify a change in the visitation order. This is basically a statement of the reason you want to change your visitation arrangement.
- In paragraph 4, check the space for "visitation," and in the space after paragraph 4, type in what you want the new visitation order to say.
- In paragraph 5, type in an explanation of why a change in visitation is in the best interest of the children. This may be obvious from what you have already stated in paragraph 3, but you will still need to fill in paragraph 5.
- Read paragraphs 6 through 9. In most cases, a change in visitation will not affect child support, in which event you should cross out paragraphs 6 and 7. If the visitation change you are seeking is so great that you believe it should result in a change in child support (such as if the child will be living with you three days each week), you will need to complete and file the forms men-

tioned in paragraphs 6 and 7. You will need to compete and file a **UNIFORM CHILD CUSTODY JURISDICTION ACT** (UCCJA) **AFFIDAVIT** (form 4) as indicated in paragraph 8. If you have not done so previously, you will also need to complete and file a **NOTICE OF SOCIAL SECURITY NUMBER** (form 6).

- Paragraph 10 is to be used for any matters not covered elsewhere in the form and will not be used in most cases.
- Take this form to a notary public and sign it before the notary.

OTHER FORMS

UNIFORM CHILD CUSTODY JURISDICTION ACT (UCCJA) AFFIDAVIT

You should complete and file a **UNIFORM CHILD CUSTODY JURISDICTION ACT** (UCCJA) **AFFIDAVIT** (form 4) (See Chapter 6 for information about completing form 4). Although this form may not be legally necessary unless you or the other party live outside of Florida, the judge may interpret paragraph 8 of the **PETITION** (form 13) as requiring form 4 in all visitation cases. Also, having this form in the court's file may make the judge feel more comfortable about going ahead with a hearing and issuing a new visitation order.

CHILD SUPPORT GUIDELINES WORKSHEET

As indicated above, if you believe the visitation change you are requesting should result in a change in child support, will need to file a **CHILD SUPPORT GUIDELINES WORKSHEET** (form 5). (See the instructions for form 5 in Chapter 10.)

FAMILY LAW FINANCIAL AFFIDAVIT

If you are also asking for a change in child support, or if the other party has requested a change in child support in response to your request to change visitation, you will need to prepare and file a **FAMILY LAW FINANCIAL AFFIDAVIT** (form 2 or form 3). (See the instructions for forms 2 and 3 in Chapter 10.)

NOTICE OF SOCIAL SECURITY NUMBER

Finally, as indicted above, if you have not done so previously, you will also need to complete and file a **NOTICE OF SOCIAL SECURITY NUMBER** (form 6).

FILING WITH THE COURT CLERK

See Chapter 4 for information about filing your papers with the court clerk. See Chapter 5 for information about notifying the other parent, and Chapter 6 for information about setting a court date. If you are seeking to terminate the other parent's visitation altogether, you may also need to file some of the forms discussed in the section in Chapter 7 regarding "Guardian Ad Litem."

Preparing and Presenting Your Case

In most cases, it will not be necessary to have any witnesses testify. (The only exception is if you want to severely limit or terminate visitation because the other party poses a threat to the child. In such cases, review all of Chapter 8, which discusses the factors for custody, some of which may also be used in a visitation case. Generally, your statements to the judge that the current visitation arrangement is not working will be enough.

Again, in most cases, this will simply involve thinking about what you want to tell the judge. Basically, you want to point out the visitation provision in your judgment or any more recent visitation order, briefly explain some of the problems you have had with the other party regarding visitation, and tell the judge what kind of visitation order you would like to end these problems. The following is an example of such an opening statement:

> "Your Honor, we are here on a petition to modify visitation. The judgment currently provides for 'reasonable and liberal visitation.' This arrangement has not been working. My ex-husband never brings the children home at the agreed upon time, frequently arrives an hour late to pick them up or forgets to pick them up at all, and last Christmas Eve he was to have them home by 8:00 P.M., but kept them until 3:00 P.M. on Christmas Day. I would like an order specifying alternate weekend visitation from 7:00 P.M. Friday until 5:00 P.M. Sunday. If he doesn't arrive to pick up the children or call to advise me of a delay by 7:20 P.M., visitation may be cancelled for that weekend. I would also like the order to provide for visitation on alternate holidays from 9:00 A.M. to 8:00 P.M., and that the holidays be designated as New Year's Day, Easter Day, Memorial Day, Fourth of July, Labor Day, Thanksgiving Day, Christmas Eve, and Christmas Day."

You are telling the judge three things:

1. what the current visitation order is;
2. why you want it changed; and,
3. what outcome you desire.

The judge will then hear the other party's story. You may get a chance to respond, and then the judge will make a decision. Have paper and pen ready, so you can write down what the judge orders and can prepare the visitation order.

JUDGMENT FORMS

SUPPLEMENTAL FINAL JUDGMENT OF MODIFICATION OF PARENTAL RESPONSIBILITY/VISITATION

At the hearing, you will need to present the judge with a SUPPLEMENTAL FINAL JUDGMENT OF MODIFICATION OF PARENTAL RESPONSIBILITY/VISITATION (form 54) which is the same form used for changes in custody. (Refer to the instructions for form 54 in Chapter 11.) The main difference in using form 54 here is that you will not need to fill in information about custody and child support (unless either of these matters were raised by you or the other party).

NOTE: *See page 76 for information about the* ***FINAL DISPOSITION FORM.***

13 Changing Child Support

This chapter will explain the forms and procedures for seeking an increase or decrease in child support. This includes requests to change child support ordered in a judgment of dissolution of marriage, a judgment of paternity, or a judgment of support unconnected with dissolution of marriage.

How a Change in Child Support is Determined

Two factors are used to determine the amount of support:

1. the needs of the child and
2. the financial ability of each parent to meet those needs.

Florida has established a formula to be used in calculating both the needs of the child and each parent's ability to meet those needs. The following steps are used in determining the proper amount of support:

1. You and the other parent each provide proof of your *gross* incomes.
2. Taxes and other deductions are allowed to determine each of your *net* incomes.
3. Your net incomes are added together to arrive at your *combined income.*
4. The combined income and the number of children you have are used to establish the children's needs. (This is done by reading a chart.)
5. The net income of the parent without custody is divided by the combined income. This gives that parent's percentage of the combined income.
6. That percentage is multiplied by the needs of the children to arrive at the amount of support to be paid by the parent without custody.

This procedure can be used by most people. However, if you and the other party's combined income is less than $650 per month these guidelines can't be used. If your combined income is over $10,000 per month, you will need to add a percentage of the amount over $10,000, depending upon the number of children. Also, the judge may depart from the guidelines by up to five percent (a written reason must be given in the judgment if the judge departs by more than fiver percent). These guidelines will be discussed more below, and their text can be found in Appendix A, Section 61.30, Florida Statutes. An increase or decrease in child support will only be allowed if this calculation results in a significantly different amount than what is currently ordered.

The judge may depart slightly from the guidelines after considering the needs of the child and each parent's age, station in life, standard of living, and financial status. The judge can also adjust the amount of child support in consideration of the following factors:

- the impact of IRS dependency exemption or waiver of the exemption (the judge may also order the custodial parent to sign a waiver of the exemption);
- whether the guidelines would require the payment of more than fifty-five percent of the payor's gross income; and
- the amount of time the noncustodial parent has visitation.

Evaluating Your Situation

In order to modify child support, you will need to show that one or more of the following have occurred:

1. your income has gone down significantly;
2. the other parent's income has gone up significantly;.
3. your child's special needs have changed; or,
4. the current guidelines would justify a change of fifteen percent or $50, whichever is greater.

As the child's needs are generally determined by the parents' incomes, most cases will be determined by the parents' incomes, using the child support tables in the Florida Statutes. The only exception is where your child has some special needs, such as for medical treatment for a disability, that exceed the needs presumed by your incomes. These special needs will be discussed more later in this chapter.

Because needs or ability to pay must have changed, it is important for you to get any information you can regarding your and the other parent's financial situations at the time the original judgment was entered. The best source would be the FINANCIAL AFFIDAVITS you both filed. If you do not have copies, go to the court clerk's office and get copies of the FINANCIAL AFFIDAVITS from your divorce or paternity file. Compare your current incomes with the incomes in the original FINANCIAL AFFIDAVITS to see how things have changed. A change of a few dollars won't justify a change in child support. The change must be substantial.

The CHILD SUPPORT GUIDELINES WORKSHEET is used to calculate the proper amount of child support. (see form 5, p.197.) It is important to get the most accurate income information possible about yourself and the other parent. Completing form 5 will give you a good idea of how much of a child support change is called for, if any, so that you can decide whether you should file a petition.

Because you will need to file form 5 with the court, make a copy of it to use now. Here you are only trying to get a rough idea of the amount of child support to expect, so you can compare it to the current child support amount and decide if it is worth your time and effort to ask for an increase or decrease. Later, after you have more accurate income information, you will complete the final copy to file along with your petition. As you prepare your form to file, you will refer back to this section for instructions on completing it.

CHILD SUPPORT GUIDELINES WORKSHEET

To complete the CHILD SUPPORT GUIDELINES WORKSHEET (form 5):

- Complete the top portion of the form according to the instructions on page 21.
- In the first, unnumbered paragraph, type in your name.
- In item "1. Present Net Monthly Income," fill in the net income from line 27 of your FAMILY LAW FINANCIAL AFFIDAVIT (form 2 or 3), and the other parent's net income from line 3 of his or her FAMILY LAW FINANCIAL AFFIDAVIT. If you are just evaluating your situation to decide if you should file, you will not have the other parent's FAMILY LAW FINANCIAL AFFIDAVIT, so you will just have to use your best estimate of the other parent's net income.
- In item "2. Combined Present Net Monthly Income," add the two figures from item 1 and fill in the total. The *combined income* is your net income added to your ex-spouse's net income. For example: Your net income is $1,200 per month. Your the other parent's net income is $1,800 per month. This would give you a combined income of $3,000 (1,200 + 1,800). Add your monthly net income and your the other parent's monthly net monthly income. This is your combined income, which should be written in on line 2.
- For item "3. Basic Monthly Obligation," fill in the number of children subject to the support order on the line beginning "There is (are) {number} _____ minor child(ren)..." Next, turn to the child support guidelines chart in Appendix A, beginning on page 155 of this book, which comes from Section 61.30(6),

Florida Statutes. Read down the first column to your combined income, then read across to the column for the number of children for which support is owed. This figure will give you the needs of your children. Write in the needs indicated by the support table on line 3.

Again using our example of a combined income of $3,000 per month, find the figure "3,000" in the left column of the child support guidelines chart, then read across for the number of children. For one child the needs are $644 per month; for two children the needs are $1,001; for three children the needs are $1,252, etc. For our example, let's assume you have two children, so their monthly needs are $1,001.

- In item "4. Percent of Financial Responsibility," you will determine each parent's percentage share of the combined income. To get your share, divide your net income from item 1 by the combined income from line 2. Using our example: $1,200 divided by $3,000 = .4. Next, divide the other parent's net income from line 1 by the combined income from line 2 ($1,800 divided by $3,000 = .6). Write your percentages, and the other parent's on lines 4a and 4b. (You will note that this item of the form calls for a percentage, which requires dropping the decimal point.)

- For item "5. Share of Basic Monthly Obligation," multiply the needs (or *basic obligation*) by your percentage share ($1,001 x .4 = $400.40). This gives you the amount of your children's needs you would be expected to contribute according to the current guidelines. Now multiply the needs by the other parent's percentage share ($1,001 x .6 = $600.60). This is the amount the other parent would be expected to contribute according to the current guidelines. Write in the contributions of you and the other parent on lines 5a and 5b. Whichever parent does not have custody will be ordered to pay support according to this calculation. In our example, if you have custody the other parent will be ordered to pay $600.60 per month. If the other parent has custody, you will be ordered to pay $400.40 per month. (If you and the other parent are each going to have custody of one child, the support will be offset, so that the other parent would pay $200.20 per month ($600.60–$400.40).

- For item "6. Total Monthly Child Care Costs," if you or the other parent are paying for child care, fill in the monthly child care costs on line 6.

- In item "7. Percentage of Child Care Costs," multiply the figure on line 6 by .75, and fill in the answer on line 7. Next, multiply the figure on line 7 by the percentage from line 4a, and fill in the answer on line 7a. This gives the father's share of the child care costs. Next, multiply the figure on line 7 by the percentage from line 4b, and fill in the answer on line 7b. This gives the mother's share of the child care costs.

- For item "8. Total Monthly Child(ren)'s Health Insurance Costs," if you or the other parent are paying for health insurance for your children, fill in the monthly cost of the insurance on line 8 (only fill in the insurance cost related to the children). Next, multiply the figure on line 8 by the percentage from line 4a, and fill in the answer on line 8a. This gives the father's share of the health insurance costs. Next, multiply the figure on line 8 by the percentage from line 4b, and fill in the answer on line 8b. This gives the mother's share of the health insurance costs.

- In item "9. Total Monthly Obligation," add the figures on lines 5a, 7a, and 8a; and fill in the answer on line 9a. This gives the father's total share of the child support obligation. Next, add the figures on lines 5b, 7b, and 8b; and fill in the answer on line 9b. This gives the mother's total share of the child support obligation.

- In item "10. Adjustments to Guidelines Amount," in most cases you will check line "b. Deviation from the guidelines amount is NOT requested." However, if your child has special needs (such as because of a physical or mental handicap, because the child is in a special private school for gifted children, etc.), or if there are any other reasons you think the child support guidelines are not giving a proper result; you can check line a, and file a MOTION TO DEVIATE FROM CHILD SUPPORT GUIDELINES (form 43).

- Fill in the certificate of service section to indicate how and when you sent or delivered a copy of the form to the other parent (or his or her attorney); and fill in the other parent's (or attorney's) name, address, and telephone information.

- Fill in the date, sign your name on the line marked "Signature of Party," and fill in your name, address, and telephone information on the lines below the signature line.

> ***Warning*:** Do not stop or reduce child support payments unless you get an order signed by the judge allowing you to do so. If you do this without a court order, you will accumulate a child support arrearage, and will risk contempt of court proceedings.

Supplemental Petition for Modification of Child Support

The basic form used to ask for an increase or decrease in child support is the SUPPLEMENTAL PETITION FOR MODIFICATION OF CHILD SUPPORT (see form 14, p.220):

- ☛ Complete the top portion of the form according to the instructions on page 21.
- ☛ In the first (unnumbered) paragraph, fill in your name.
- ☛ In paragraph 1, if you are seeking a change in an order in a divorce case, check the box for "of dissolution of marriage." If you are seeking a change in a support order in a paternity case, check the box for "of paternity." If you are seeking to change a support order in any other type of case, check the box for "for support unconnected with a dissolution of marriage." On the line in paragraph 1, fill in the date of the final judgment.
- ☛ In paragraph 2, fill in paragraph numbers from your judgment or the last child support order which you are seeking to change. Check the appropriate box to indicate whether you are seeking to change the "final judgment" or the "most recent modification thereof." Fill in the current amount of the child support order, check the box for whether it is paid each week, every other week, or every month; and fill in the date the current order became effective.
- ☛ In paragraph 3, type in an explanation of what circumstances have changed since the current child support order was entered that would justify a change. For example: "The noncustodial parent's income has significantly increased," or "The child's medical needs have drastically increased."
- ☛ In paragraph 4, type in how you want the child support order changed. For example: "Increase child support to $200 per week," or "Decrease child support to $100 per week."
- ☛ In paragraph 5, type in a brief explanation of why your requested child support change would be in the best interests of the child.
- ☛ Complete the certificate of service section to indicate how and when you sent or delivered a copy of the form to the other party (or his or her attorney); and fill in the other party's (or attorney's) name, address, and telephone information.
- ☛ Do not sign this form yet. Type your name, address, and telephone information where indicated below the line marked "Signature of party signing certificate and pleading."

☛ Attach a copy of your judgment, copies of any subsequent orders modifying child support, and the completed CHILD SUPPORT GUIDELINES WORKSHEET (form 5) to the SUPPLEMENTAL PETITION.

☛ Take this form to a notary and sign it before the notary. Your SUPPLEMENTAL PETITION is now ready for filing.

OTHER FORMS

In addition to the SUPPLEMENTAL PETITION, you will or may need to file certain other forms. These include:

- CHILD SUPPORT GUIDELINES WORKSHEET (see form 5, p.197.) (See the subsection in Chapter 10 for instructions for preparing the CHILD SUPPORT GUIDELINES WORKSHEET.)
- MOTION TO DEVIATE FROM CHILD SUPPORT GUIDELINES (see form 43, p.291.) (See Chapter 10 for instructions for preparing the MOTION TO DEVIATE FROM CHILD SUPPORT GUIDELINES.)
- FAMILY LAW FINANCIAL AFFIDAVIT (SHORT FORM) (see form 2, p.175.); or FAMILY LAW FINANCIAL AFFIDAVIT (see form 3, p.182.) (See Chapter 10 for instructions about when to use each form and how to complete whichever of these forms you need.)
- STANDARD FAMILY LAW INTERROGATORIES FOR MODIFICATION PROCEEDINGS (see form 35, p.268.) (See Chapter 12 for information on when this form is needed, and how to complete it.)
- CERTIFICATE OF COMPLIANCE WITH MANDATORY DISCLOSURE (see form 40, p.284.) (See Chapter 10, for information about how to complete form 40.)
- NOTICE OF SERVICE OF STANDARD FAMILY LAW INTERROGATORIES (see form 33, p.253.) (See Chapter 12 for information about when to use form 33 and how to complete it.)

Filing with the Court Clerk

Once all of your necessary papers are prepared, you will need to file them with the court clerk. See Chapter 4 for information about filing your court papers.

See Chapter 5 for information about notifying the other party, and Chapter 6 for information about setting a court date. When you send the other party a **Notice of Hearing** (form 25, form 26, or form 31), you will need to enclose a blank **Family Law Financial Affidavit** (form 2 or form 3) for the other party to complete and file. You will send the **Family Law Financial Affidavit (Short Form)** (see form 2, p.175) if the other party has an annual income or annual expenses of less than $50,000; and send the **Family Law Financial Affidavit** (see form 3, p.182) if the other party has an annual income or annual expenses of $50,000 or more. If you aren't sure of which form to send, you can either make the best guess possible based on what you know or suspect, or send a copy of each form. A copy of your **Notice of Hearing** must also be filed with the clerk.

Preparing and Presenting Your Case

Your proof will mostly be the information in your **Supplemental Petition for Modification of Child Support** (form 14) and **Family Law Financial Affidavit** (form 2 or form 3). If the other parent fails to file a Family Law Financial Affidavit and you obtained information from his or her employer through a **Subpoena for Production of Documents from Nonparty** (form 37), this information will also be part of your proof.

Opening Statement

You will basically want to tell the judge three things: why you are in court (to ask for an increase or decrease in child support), why you are asking for a change, and what the new child support order should be. First you will make a short opening statement, then you will present whatever proof you have.

The following is an example of an opening statement:

> "Your Honor, we are here on a petition to increase child support. The divorce judgment ordered my ex-spouse to pay child support in the amount of $583.20 per month for our two children. Since the entry of the divorce judgment, my ex-husband's net income has increased from $1,800 per month to $2,300 per month, and I have lost my job due to an illness and am without income. These changes are reflected in the Family Law Financial Affidavits filed by my ex-husband and myself. Therefore, considering the minimum support schedule, I am asking for an increase in child support to $768 per month."

Presenting Your Proof

Next, you will present your proof (which may simply be the **Family Law Financial Affidavits** filed by you and the other party). The judge will probably swear you in, and tell you to proceed. For the situation above, you might present the judge with a letter from your former employer indicating the last day you worked, and a letter from your doctor verifying your illness and how it affects your ability to work. You would also want to refer the judge to your **Family Law Financial Affidavit**, which should be in the court file. Simply tell the judge what each document is. Your statement might be like this:

> "I have filed a **Family Law Financial Affidavit** showing my current expenses and lack of income, and a **Child Support Guidelines Worksheet** calculating the proper amount of support under the minimum support schedule. My ex-husband has filed a **Family Law Financial Affidavit** verifying his income. I have with me a copy of the **Family Law Financial Affidavit** I filed just before the judgment was issued, a letter from my last employer verifying my last day of work, and a letter from my doctor regarding my medical condition."

The judge will ask you any questions he or she may have, then give the other party an opportunity to make a statement or to ask you questions. He may give you a chance to respond to what the other party says, and ask you more questions. Just answer the judge's questions honestly and as best you can. Be prepared to guide the judge through the calculations in your **Child Support Guidelines Worksheet** to show him how you arrived at the support amount for which you are asking. After the judge has heard all of the facts, he will announce his decision.

Judgment Forms

After the judge makes a decision, there are two forms you will need to prepare. One is the **Supplemental Final Judgment Modifying Child Support** (see form 55, p.335), which will become your new support order. The other is a **Final Disposition Form** (see form 9, p.208), which is a simple form that provides the court with statistical information for administrative purposes. How to complete each of these forms is explained below.

Supplemental Final Judgment Modifying Child Support

What the judge decides will need to be put into the **Supplemental Final Judgment Modifying Child Support**. (see form 55, p.335.) If you aren't sure how to complete an item, ask the judge how he or she wants you to complete it. Keep in mind that you are filling in this form according to what the judge finds and orders. To complete form 55:

☛ Complete the top portion of the form according to the instructions on page 21.

☛ Under the heading "Section I. Findings":

- In paragraph 2, fill in the names and birthdates of the minor children who are subject to the support order.

- In paragraph 3, type in the date the last support order was entered. This may be the date of your original judgment if this is the first change that has been made.

- In paragraph 4, type in an explanation of what circumstances have changed since the last support order was entered. This will often be the same as what you included in your SUPPLEMENTAL PETITION FOR MODIFICATION OF CHILD SUPPORT (see form 14, p.220.). However, you will also need to listen to what the judge says on this subject at the hearing. The change in circumstances mentioned by the judge is what needs to be in this paragraph.

- In paragraph 5, type in an explanation of why it is in the best interests of the children that child support be changed. Again, listen to what the judge says at the hearing. The reason given by the judge is what needs to be in this paragraph. This will often be the same thing that you included in your SUPPLEMENTAL PETITION FOR MODIFICATION OF CHILD SUPPORT (see form 14, p.220.).

☛ Under the heading "Section II. Child Support":

- In paragraph 1, check the box for either "Mother" or "Father" to indicate who will pay child support. Fill in your income and the other party's income, the child support guidelines percentage for each of you, the monthly child care costs, and the monthly health/dental insurance costs on the appropriate lines. Get this information from the CHILD SUPPORT GUIDELINES WORKSHEET (form 5).

- In paragraph 2, fill in the amount of child support, and check the box for when it is to be paid, as ordered by the judge at the hearing. If the judge decided that the child support guidelines should not be followed and deviates from the guidelines by five percent or more (up or down), fill in the reasons the judge gave for deviating from the guidelines on the lines at the end of paragraph 2. You may have to ask the judge how he or she wants this subsection completed.

- Paragraph 3 needs to be completed if there are arrearages in child support. Check either line "a" or "b," or both. If you check "b," fill in all of the blanks, which are self-explanatory.

- Paragraph 4 needs to be completed if the judge makes an order that includes health or dental insurance. Check either line "a" or "b," or both. If you check "b," fill in all of the blanks, which are self-explanatory.

- Paragraph 5 needs to be completed if the judge orders the party paying support to obtain life insurance to guarantee payment of support. Fill in all of the blanks, which are self-explanatory.

- Paragraph 6 needs to be completed if the judge makes an order regarding which party will be entitled to claim the tax exemption for the children. Fill in the blanks, which are self-explanatory.

- If the judge makes any other orders about child support that are not covered elsewhere in "Section II," enter them in paragraph 7. You may use additional sheets if necessary.

☛ Under the heading "Section III. Method of Payment":

- In paragraph 1, check line "a" if the judge ordered payment through the Central Government Depository (and fill in the name of the county). Check line "b" if the judge did not order payment through the Central Government Depository.

- In paragraph 2, check line "a" if the judge ordered income withholding to begin immediately. Check line "b" if the judge ordered income withholding deferred. If you check line "b," fill in the amount of delinquency that will trigger income withholding, and type in an explanation of why the judge decided income withholding is not in the best interest of the children. Usually, the judge will order payments through the Central Government Depository by way of an income deduction order, in which case you should be referred to the appropriate place (usually either the court clerk, Central Government Depository, or support enforcement office) to get the necessary paperwork done to implement the income deduction. This is done by one of these agencies sending an Income Deduction Notice to the employer of the person who is paying support.

- Paragraph 3 is for an order that all, some, or none of the payor's bonus or other one-time payment be applied to child support.

- Paragraph 4 is for any other orders regarding the method of payment that are not covered elsewhere in "Section III."

- "Section IV. Attorney Fees, Costs, and Suit Money" will need to be completed if either party requested the other to pay any of these expenses. If such a request was made, check paragraph 1 or 2, and fill in the blanks. Of course, if you are asking for attorney fees you have hired an attorney, and he or she will be the one preparing this form. If attorney fees and court costs have been requested by either party, the judge must state why he or she grants or denies such a request, so you may need to ask the judge how he or she wants this section completed.

- Paragraph 1 in "Section V. Other" is for adding anything the judge orders that is not covered elsewhere in this form.

- Once all of the information has been filled in, the order needs to be presented to the judge for him or her to fill in the date and sign the order. You can either present it to the judge at the hearing, or deliver or mail it to the judge's office later. If you decide to deliver or mail it, you will need to mail a copy to the other party (or attorney) at the same time, and also file a **CERTIFICATE OF SERVICE** to verify you have done so. (see form 21, p.236.)

If you are uncertain how to fill in any portion of this form, ask the judge how he or she would like them completed. After all, you are preparing the form to accurately reflect the judge's decision, and eventually the judge will have to approve and sign this form.

NOTE: *See Chapter 7 for information about the* ***FINAL DISPOSITION FORM.***

14 Enforcement Proceedings

This chapter will discuss the enforcement of custody, visitation, and child support orders. The procedures and forms for each type of enforcement problem are very similar. Many use the same forms, with slight variations in how they are filled out.

Law and Procedure

This section will briefly discuss the law and court procedures relating to violations of court orders for custody, visitation, and child support. The specific forms and procedures for each type of violation will be explained in later sections of this chapter.

The Law

The law concerning violations of court orders is fairly simple. If you do not do what the judge ordered, you can be held in contempt of court. Being held in contempt of court means the judge can throw you in jail, and set certain conditions for your release. If the violation relates to custody or visitation, the condition is typically that you promise not to violate the order again. If the violation is a failure to pay child support, the condition is typically that you pay a certain amount of money.

A violation of a judge's order can also be the criminal offense of *interference with custody*, which is a third degree felony under Section 787.03 of the Florida Statutes. (See Appendix A for the full text of this statute.) This law is discussed further in the section of this chapter on "Custody Enforcement."

The Procedure

The procedure is also fairly simple. If the other party violates the judge's order, you file a motion for contempt to let the judge know that there has been a violation of the order. The other party is then required to appear before the judge and either explain why the order was violated, or argue that the order was not violated. If the judge is not satisfied with the other party's explanation, the judge may find him or her in contempt of court and impose a variety of sanctions. If the other party does not appear in court, the judge may issue a warrant for his or her arrest.

You will need to provide the other party with a copy of your motion and a notice of hearing. This can be done by mail or delivery, but the best way is to have the other party personally served by the sheriff. The danger in using mail or delivering the papers yourself is that if the other party does not show up for the hearing, and the judge has some doubt about whether the other party actually received notice, the judge may not issue a warrant. But if the other party was personally served, there will be no doubt that he or she actually received notice.

Custody Enforcement

The violation of a custody order is usually considered to be more serious than violations of either visitation or child support orders. A custody order violation is really a form of kidnapping. You have two options in dealing with a custody order violation:

1. File a **Motion for Civil Contempt/Enforcement** (see form 46, p.299):
2. File a complaint with your local law enforcement agency. As stated above, a violation of a custody order can also be the criminal offense of *interference with custody*, which is defined in Section 787.03 of the Florida Statutes. The law provides for certain defenses, and if the law enforcement agency believes any of these defenses exist, they may refuse to pursue the matter. Therefore, before you call the police or sheriff's office, turn to page 160 in Appendix A of this book and read Section 787.03 carefully. If, after reading it, you believe that none of the defenses apply, call your local law enforcement agency and explain what has occurred. This may be the quickest way to get your child returned.

Motion for Civil Contempt/Enforcement

The typical ways for a custody order to be violated are failing to return the child after visitation, and picking up the child when it is not the other party's scheduled visitation period. If the other party has violated the custody order, you can complete and file a **Motion for Civil Contempt/Enforcement** (see form 46, p.299):

- ☛ Complete the top portion of the form according to the instructions on page 21. This portion of the form should be the same as your original judgment. If you were listed as the "Petitioner" on the judgment, you will still be listed as the "Petitioner" of this form. If you were listed as the "Respondent" on the judgment, you will still be listed as the "Respondent" of this form.

- In the first (unnumbered) paragraph, check the spaces for "Petitioner" and "Respondent," as they apply to you and the other party.
- In paragraph 1, fill in the title of the order which the other party has violated. If there haven't been any modifications since the original final judgment was entered, this will be the title that appears on the final judgment. Depending upon when the judgment was entered, and what type of case you had, the title may vary (e.g., Judgment of Divorce, Final Judgment of Dissolution of Marriage, Judgment of Paternity). If the other party has violated a modified order, fill in the title that appears on the first page of that order (e.g., Order Modifying Judgment of Divorce, Order Modifying Custody). Also fill in the date of the order that was violated, and the identity of the court that entered it (e.g., Circuit Court, Tampa, Florida).

NOTE: *There is also a box to check if the judgment or order is not from the same court where you are filing this motion (in which event you will need to attach a copy of the judgment or order).*

- In paragraph 2, fill in a statement as to what the order required for custody. For example: "The Petitioner was designated as the primary residential parent," or "The Petitioner as granted sole parental responsibility."
- In paragraph 3, fill in a statement of how the order has been violated. For example: "The Respondent failed to return the child from visitation on July 4, 2002, and continues to refuse to return the child."
- In paragraph 4, indicate what you want the judge to do. For a violation a custody order, you should check items "a," "e," "f," and "h." You may also want to check item "l," and ask for some other order. This might be a request to terminate visitation, or limit visitation in some manner.
- Complete the certificate of service section, including the other party's name, address, and telephone number.
- Take this form to a notary public or to the court clerk's office, and sign it before the notary or a deputy clerk.

Notice of Hearing

You will need to follow the standard procedures indicated in Chapters 4 and 5 to file this form with the clerk, obtain a hearing date, and properly notify the other party. At the hearing you will need to produce evidence of the other party's violation of the custody order. Often, this will just be your testimony. If anyone else was present when the child was to be returned to you, or when you attempted to pick up the child, or heard the other party refuse to return the child, they can also testify. If you decide that the child should testify, be sure to read the section on "Testimony of Minor Children" in Chapter 6.

You will need to schedule a hearing date for your motion. See Chapter 6 for more information about how to schedule a hearing. Then, depending upon whether the hearing is scheduled with the judge or a general master, you will then need to prepare either a NOTICE OF HEARING (GENERAL) (see form 31, p.250) or a NOTICE OF HEARING BEFORE GENERAL MASTER (see form 25, p.242). (See Chapter 6 for instructions for preparing these forms.)

VISITATION ENFORCEMENT

This section will discuss the forms and procedures for enforcing visitation orders.

Before beginning with this procedure, consider whether the problems you are having with visitation could be resolved by a more specific visitation order. If so, you may instead want to ask for a change in your visitation order by filing a SUPPLEMENTAL PETITION TO MODIFY CUSTODY OR VISITATION FOR OTHER RELIEF. (see form 13, p.217.) (See Chapter 12 for more information about changing a visitation order.)

Example: Your current visitation order says you get the children on alternate weekends "beginning after school on Friday." The kids get out of school at 2:55 p.m., and are home by 3:30 p.m. You arrive at the other parent's house at 3:30, but the children are never ready to go before 4:30 p.m. This problem may be resolved by changing the order to read "beginning at 4:00 p.m. on Friday."

MOTION FOR CIVIL CONTEMPT/ ENFORCEMENT

If you already have a sufficiently specific visitation order, but the other party is not following it, you will need to file forms to enforce (not change) the current visitation order. To do this, you will complete and file a MOTION FOR CIVIL CONTEMPT/ENFORCEMENT (see form 46, p.299):

- Complete the top portion of the form according to the instructions on page 21. This portion of the form should be the same as your original judgment. If you were listed as the "Petitioner" on the judgment, you will still be listed as the "Petitioner" of this form. If you were listed as the "Respondent" on the judgment, you will still be listed as the "Respondent" of this form.

- In the first (unnumbered) paragraph, check the spaces for "Petitioner" and "Respondent," as they apply to you and the other party.

- In paragraph 1, fill in the title of the order which the other party has violated. If there haven't been any modifications since the original final judgment was entered, this will be the title that appears on the final judgment. Depending upon when the judgment was entered, and what type of case you had, the title may vary (e.g., Judgment of Divorce, Final Judgment of Dissolution of Marriage, Judgment of Paternity). If the other party has violated a modified order, fill in the title that appears on the first page of that order (e.g., Order Modifying Judgment of Divorce, Order Modifying Visitation). Also fill in the date of the order that was violated, and the identity of the court that entered it (e.g., Circuit Court, Tampa, Florida). Note that there is also a box to check if the judgment or order is not from the same court where you are filing this motion (in which event you will need to attach a copy of the judgment or order).

- In paragraph 2, fill in a statement as to what the order required for visitation. For example: "The Respondent was ordered to allow visitation on alternate weekends, from 5:00 p.m. on Friday, until 5:00 p.m. on Sunday."
- In paragraph 3, fill in a statement of how the order has been violated. For example: "The Respondent failed to allow visitation for the past three scheduled visitation periods," or "The Respondent has returned the minor children from visitation at least two hours late for every visitation period since February 12, 2002."

- In paragraph 4, indicate what you want the judge to do. This will depend upon the nature of the visitation problem. The following information will help you decide how to fill out paragraph 4:

  - ***Failure to allow visitation.*** For the failure of the other party to allow visitation, check items "a," "e," "f," and "k." This includes situations where you were denied part of your visitation, such as where the children weren't ready at the time they were scheduled to begin visitation. However, it is not a good idea to go before a judge because of a single incident of your children being late, or because they are late by a few minutes. Most judges would regard these situations as trivial and not worthy of the court's time.

    Under item "k," type in what make-up visitation you want. For example, if the current order gives you visitation on alternate weekends, and the other party denied you visitation for two weekends, indicate the dates you want those two weekends made up (e.g., "the weekends of May 11th and May 18th, 2002").

  - ***Other noncompliance.*** For other types of failure to comply with the visitation order, check items "a," "e," and "f." [Note: Just in case you are curious, neither the author nor several other attorneys consulted could determine the difference between items "a" and "f."] If you check these items, the judge will probably give the other party a lecture about following the requirements of the visitation order "to the letter."

- ***Fines.*** If you want the other party fined for the noncompliance, you can also check items "g" or "h." Item "g" should be used if the other party's noncompliance cost you money. For example, if you had purchased tickets to take your child to an amusement park, museum, sporting event, etc.; and were unable to use them because of the denial of visitation. Item "h" should be used if you want the other party fined as punishment and as an incentive not to violate the visitation order again. Judges will often only grant this request if there has been one or more previous court hearings where the other party was found to have violated the visitation order.

- ***Incarceration.*** If you want the other party held in jail as an incentive to comply with the visitation order in the future, you can check item "i." Judges will usually only grant this request if there have been prior court hearings where the other party has been found to have intentionally not complied with the visitation order, or if the other party indicates to the judge that he or she does not intend to comply. In such cases, the judge will usually order the person held in jail for a certain period of time (such as fifteen days, thirty days, etc.), but provide that early release can be obtained by the person assuring the judge that they intend to comply with the order.

☛ Complete the certificate of service section, including the other party's name, address, and telephone number.

☛ Take this form to a notary public or to the court clerk's office, and sign it before the notary or a deputy clerk.

You will need to follow the standard procedures indicated in Chapters 4 and 5 to file this form with the clerk, obtain a hearing date, and properly notify the other party. At the hearing you will need to produce evidence of the other party's failure to comply with the visitation order. Often, this will just be your testimony. If anyone else was present when you attempted to pick up the child (or when the other party returned the child late, or when whatever else occurred that violated the order), they can also testify. If you decide that the child should testify, be sure to read the section on "Testimony of Children" in Chapter 6.

NOTICE OF HEARING

See Chapter 6 for information on scheduling a date for your motion.

Child Support Enforcement

This section will explain the forms and procedure for enforcing child support orders.

Motion for Civil Contempt/ Enforcement

If the other party has failed to pay the court ordered child support, will need to complete and file a **Motion for Civil Contempt/Enforcement** (see form 46, p.299):

- Complete the top portion of the form according to the instructions on page 21. This portion of the form should be the same as your original judgment. If you were listed as the "Petitioner" on the judgment, you will still be listed as the "Petitioner" of this form. If you were listed as the "Respondent" on the judgment, you will still be listed as the "Respondent" of this form.
- In the first (unnumbered) paragraph, check the spaces for "Petitioner" and "Respondent," as they apply to you and the other party.
- In paragraph 1, fill in the title of the order which the other party has violated. If there haven't been any modifications since the original final judgment was entered, this will be the title that appears on the final judgment. Depending upon when the judgment was entered, and what type of case you had, the title may vary (e.g., Judgment of Divorce, Final Judgment of Dissolution of Marriage, Judgment of Paternity). If the other party has violated a modified order, fill in the title that appears on the first page of that order (e.g., Order Modifying Judgment of Divorce, Order Modifying Child Support). Also fill in the date of the order that was violated, and the identity of the court that entered it (e.g., Circuit Court, Tampa, Florida). Note that there is also a box to check if the judgment or order is not from the same court where you are filing this motion (in which event you will need to attach a copy of the judgment or order).
- In paragraph 2, fill in a statement as to what the order required for child support. For example: "The Respondent was ordered to pay the sum of $200 per month for the support of one minor child."
- In paragraph 3, fill in a statement of how the child support order has been violated. For example: "The Respondent failed to make child support payments for the months of March, April, May, and July, 2002."
- In paragraph 4, indicate what you want the judge to do. For a failure to pay child support situation, check items "a," "e," "f," and "i."

NOTE: *Just in case you are curious, neither the author nor several other attorneys consulted could determine the difference between items "a" and "f."*

You can also check item "l," and type in that you want the other party held in jail until he or she pays a certain amount of the arrearage that is owed.

Example: "That the Respondent be incarcerated until such time as he pays the sum of $500 toward the arrearage owed." If you do not do this, the judge will decide the period of incarceration and the amount needed to get out of jail earlier.

- Complete the certificate of service section, including the other party's name, address, and telephone number.
- Take this form to a notary public or to the court clerk's office, and sign it before the notary or a deputy clerk.

You will need to follow the standard procedures indicated in Chapters 4 and 5 to file this form with the clerk, obtain a hearing date, and properly notify the other party. At the hearing you will need to produce evidence of the other party's failure to pay and ability to pay. This can consist of such things as your testimony and written records of payment, account statements from the Central Governmental Depository, and records you subpoena from the other party's employer, bank, stock broker, etc.

NOTICE OF HEARING

See Chapter 6 for more information on scheduling a date for your motion.

NOTE: *There is also an approved form titled Notice of Hearing on Motion for Civil Contempt/Enforcement, however, it is a poorly drafted form, will not work for hearings before a general master, will not work for anything but child support, and one of the hearing notices listed above will work fine.] Be sure to read the section below on "Notifying the Other Party."*

NOTIFYING THE OTHER PARTY

Regardless of whether you are seeking enforcement of custody, visitation, or child support, you will need to provide the other party with a copy of your motion and a notice of hearing. This can be done by mail or delivery, but the best way is to have the other party personally served by the sheriff. The danger in using mail or delivering the papers yourself is that if the other party does not show up for the hearing, and the judge has some doubt about whether the other party actually received notice, the judge may not issue a warrant. But if the other party was personally served, there will be no doubt that he or she actually received notice.

Glossary

This glossary provides general definitions. Not all of the terms in this glossary are found in this book. Other terms are included because you may encounter them in the course of dealing with the courts, lawyer, various agencies, or in any legal research you may conduct. Any of these terms may be specifically defined by the laws of Florida. If any term is specifically defined by Florida law, that particular definition will be used by the courts.

A

acknowledgment. A statement, written or oral, made before a person authorized by law to administer oaths (such as a notary public).

acknowledgment of paternity. A notarized statement, signed by both parents before a notary public, verifying the paternity of a child.

adult. In Florida, and most states, a person eighteen years of age or older.

affiant. The legal term for a person who signs an affidavit.

affidavit. A person's written statement of facts, signed under oath before a person authorized to administer oaths (such as a notary public or court clerk).

age of majority. The age at which a person legally becomes an adult; which is eighteen in Florida and most states.

agent. A person who is given authority to act on behalf of another person or other legal entity.

alimony. Money that the court orders one spouse to pay the other spouse as support for living costs after a divorce or separation.

appeal. Asking for an order to be reconsidered or reviewed.

appellate court. Those courts that only hear appeals and not a full trial.

B

business day. Any day other than a Saturday, Sunday, or legal holiday.

C

circuit court. A court with jurisdiction over a specific geographical area, such as a district.

Clerk of Court Child Support Collection System or CLERC System. The automated system, integrating all clerks of court and depositories, through which payment data and State Case Registry data is transmitted to the automated child support enforcement system of the Florida Department of Revenue.

creditor. A person or institution to whom money is owed.

cross-examination. Questions that the other party asks of your witness or questions you ask of the other party's witness.

custodial parent. The parent with whom the child maintains his or her primary residence.

custody. The authority to decide for the welfare of a child and to make all decisions regarding his or her care.

D

debtor. A person or institution who owes money.

decedent. A person who has died.

dependent child. A child who has reached the age of majority, but is still dependent upon his or her parents due to physical or mental disability.

deposition. Questions posed under oath and are recorded by a court reporter.

depository. The central governmental depository established by Florida law to perform depository functions and to receive, record, report, disburse, monitor, and otherwise handle alimony and child support payments not otherwise required to be processed by the State Disbursement Unit.

direct examination. Questions you ask of your own witnesses or questions the other party asks of his or her own witnesses.

dissolution of marriage. Another term for divorce; legally dissolving a marriage.

E

execute. To sign a legal document, in the legally required manner (e.g., before witnesses or a notary public), thereby making it effective.

F

Federal Case Registry of Child Support Orders. The automated registry of support order abstracts and other information established and maintained by the United States Department of Health and Human Services.

fee agreement. An arrangement between an attorney and client regarding how an attorney will be paid.

G

general master. An attorney appointed by the court to hear certain types of matters in the place of the judge.

guardian ad litem. A person, usually a lawyer, who is appointed by the court to represent the best interests of a minor.

guardian ad litem. A person appointed by the court to represent the best interests of a child.

H

hearsay. Statements made out of court, usually not allowed as evidence.

I

illegitimate child. A child born to a woman who is not married.

income. As used in chapter 61 of Florida Statutes (relating to child support and alimony), any form of payment to an individual, regardless of source, including, but not limited to: wages, salary, commissions and bonuses, compensation as an independent contractor, worker's compensation, disability benefits, annuity and retirement benefits, pensions, dividends, interest, royalties, trusts, and any other payments, made by any person, private entity, federal or state government, or any unit of local government. United States Department of Veterans Affairs disability benefits and unemployment compensation, as defined in chapter 443 of the Florida Statutes, are excluded from this definition of income except for purposes of establishing an amount of support.

income deduction (also called income withholding). When child support or alimony payments are deducted from the obligee's paycheck by his or her employer.

instrument. A legal term for a document.

IV-D (pronounced "Four D") services. Services provided pursuant to Title IV-D of the Social Security Act, 42 U.S.C. §651 et seq.

L

legitimate child. A child born to a woman who is married (even if her husband is not the child's father).

M

maintenance. A shortened version of the term separate maintenance. See alimony.

mediation. An alternative dispute resolution procedure, in which a third party tries to help the parties resolve a dispute.

minor child. A person under the age of eighteen.

N

natural father. A child's biological father.

noncustodial parent. The parent with whom the child does not maintain his or her primary residence.

notary public. A person who is legally authorized by the state to acknowledge signatures on legal documents.

O

obligee. The person to whom payments are made pursuant to a court order for alimony or child support.

obligor. A person responsible for making payments pursuant to a court order for alimony or child support.

P

parental responsibility. Used in Florida law to describe decision-making responsibility for a minor.

paternity. Fatherhood.

payor. An employer, former employer, or any other person or agency providing or administering income to an obligor.

personal property. All property other than land and things permanently attached to the land (such as buildings).

primary residential parent. See custodial parent.

putative father. A man who is alleged to be the father of a child; or who claims to be the father of a child, but has not yet been proven to be the father.

R

recording. The process of filing a deed, mortgage, court judgment, or other legal document with the court clerk's office (this does not apply to papers filed with the clerk's office in a lawsuit).

relevancy. Testimony or other evidence that relates to the matter to be decided by the judge or jury.

S

secondary residential parent. The parent who is not the primary residential, or custodial, parent.

separate maintenance. See alimony.

shared parental responsibility. A court-ordered relationship in which both parents retain full parental rights and responsibilities with respect to their child and in which both parents confer with each other so that major decisions affecting the welfare of the child will be determined jointly.

sole parental responsibility. A court-ordered relationship in which one parent makes decisions regarding a minor child.

spousal support. Another term for alimony.

State Case Registry. The automated registry maintained by the Title IV-D agency, containing records of each Title IV-D case and of each support order established or modified in the state on or after October 1, 1998.

State Disbursement Unit. The unit established and operated by the Title IV-D agency to provide one central address for collection and disbursement of child support payments made in cases enforced by the department pursuant to Title IV-D of the Social Security Act and in cases not being enforced by the department in which the support order was initially issued in this state on or after January 1, 1994, and in which the obligor's child support obligation is being paid through income deduction order.

subpoena. A legal document, issued by a court, to compel the attendance of a person at a hearing or deposition.

subpoena duces tecum. A legal document, issued by a court, to compel a person to produce a document or other tangible item at a hearing or deposition.

summons. A legal document, usually accompanying a complaint or petition, advising a person that he or she is being sued and must respond within a certain period of time in order to avoid losing by default.

support. Child support and spousal support or alimony.

support order. A judgment, decree, or order, whether temporary or final, issued by a court for the support and maintenance of a child which provides for monetary support, health care, arrearages, or past support; and a judgment, decree, or order, whether temporary or final, issued by a court for the support and maintenance of a child and the spouse or former spouse of the obligor with whom the child is living which provides for monetary support, health care, arrearages, or past support.

T

temporary child support. Child support that is ordered while a case is pending, and before final judgment.

temporary custody.Custody that is awarded while a case is pending, and before a final judgment.

temporary visitation. Visitation that is awarded while a case is pending, and before a final judgment.

tenancy by the entirety. This is essentially the same as joint tenancy, but it can only occur between a husband and wife. Upon the death of one spouse, the property automatically passes to the surviving spouse. In states which do no have a tenancy by the entirety, spouses typically hold property as joint tenants with rights of survivorship.

tenancy in common. A way for two or more people to own property, whereby if one of the owners dies, his or her interest in the property passes to his or her heirs (not to the other co-owners).

title. A document that proves ownership of property.

trial court. The court that hears all of the evidence, witnesses, and arguments for the first time in order to make a decision.

V

visitation. The time a noncustodial parent is granted to spend with his or her minor child.

Appendix A: Selected Florida Statutes and Court Rules

This Appendix contains excerpts from the Florida Statutes relating to custody, visitation, child support, and alimony. It also contains the financial disclosure requirements of the Family Law Rules of Procedure.

Florida Statutes

The following statutes are in numerical order. Where you see asterisks (* * * * *), it means that a portion of that particular section has been omitted.

Chapter 61
Dissolution of Marriage; Support; Custody

61.09 Alimony and child support unconnected with dissolution.— If a person having the ability to contribute to the maintenance of his or her spouse and support of his or her minor child fails to do so, the spouse who is not receiving support or who has custody of the child or with whom the child has primary residence may apply to the court for alimony and for support for the child without seeking dissolution of marriage, and the court shall enter an order as it deems just and proper.

61.10 Adjudication of obligation to support spouse or minor child unconnected with dissolution; child custody, child's primary residence, and visitation. Except when relief is afforded by some other pending civil action or proceeding, a spouse residing in this state apart from his or her spouse and minor child, whether or not such separation is through his or her fault, may obtain an adjudication of obligation to maintain the spouse and minor child, if any. The court shall adjudicate his or her financial obligations to the spouse and child, shall establish the child's primary residence, and shall determine the custody and visitation rights of the parties. Such an action does not preclude either party from maintaining any other proceeding under this chapter for other or additional relief at any time.

61.13 Custody and support of children; visitation rights; power of court in making orders.—

(1)(a) In a proceeding for dissolution of marriage, the court may at any time order either or both parents who owe a duty of support to a child to pay support in accordance with the guidelines in s. 61.30. The court initially entering an order requiring one or both parents to make child support payments shall have continuing jurisdiction after the entry of the initial order to modify the amount and terms and conditions of the child support payments when the modification is found necessary by the court in the best interests of the child, when the child reaches majority, or when there is a substantial change in the circumstances of the parties. The court initially entering a child support order shall also have continuing jurisdiction to require the obligee to report to the court on terms prescribed by the court regarding the disposition of the child support payments.

(b) Each order for child support shall contain a provision for health insurance for the minor child when the insurance is reasonably available. Insurance is reasonably available if either the obligor or obligee has access at a reasonable rate to group insurance. The court may require the obligor either to provide health insurance coverage or to reimburse the obligee for the cost of health insurance coverage for the minor child when coverage is provided by the obligee. In either event, the court shall apportion the cost of coverage, and any noncovered medical, dental, and prescription medication expenses of the child, to both parties by adding the cost to the basic obligation determined pursuant to s. 61.30(6). The court may order that payment of uncovered medical, dental, and prescription medication expenses of the minor child be made directly to the payee on a percentage basis.

1. A copy of the court order for insurance coverage shall be served on the obligor's payor or union by the obligee or the IV-D agency when the following conditions are met:

a. The obligor fails to provide written proof to the obligee or the IV-D agency within 30 days of receiving effective notice of the court order, that the insurance has been obtained or that application for insurability has been made;

b. The obligee or IV-D agency serves written notice of its intent to enforce medical support on the obligor by mail at the obligor's last known address; and

c. The obligor fails within 15 days after the mailing of the notice to provide written proof to the obligee or the IV-D agency that the insurance coverage existed as of the date of mailing.

* * * * *

(c) To the extent necessary to protect an award of child support, the court may order the obligor to purchase or maintain a life insurance policy or a bond, or to otherwise secure the child support award with any other assets which may be suitable for that purpose.

(d)1. Unless the provisions of subparagraph 3. apply, all child support orders entered on or after January 1, 1985, shall direct that the payments of child support be made as provided in s. 61.181 through the depository in the county where the court is located. All child support orders shall provide the full name, date of birth, and social security number of each minor child who is the subject of the child support order.

2. Unless the provisions of subparagraph 3. apply, all child support orders entered before January 1, 1985, shall be modified by the court to direct that payments of child support shall be made through the depository in the county where the court is located upon the subsequent appearance of either or both parents to modify or enforce the order, or in any related proceeding.

3. If both parties request and the court finds that it is in the best interest of the child, support payments need not be directed through the depository. The order of support shall provide, or shall be deemed to provide, that either party may subsequently apply to the depository to require direction of the payments through the depository. The court shall provide a copy of the order to the depository.

4. If the parties elect not to require that support payments be made through the depository, any party may subsequently file an affidavit with the depository alleging a default in payment of child support and stating that the party wishes to require that payments be made through the depository. The party shall provide copies of the affidavit to the court and to each other party. Fifteen days after receipt of the affidavit, the depository shall notify both parties that future payments shall be paid through the depository.

* * * * *

(e) In a judicial circuit with a work experience and job training pilot project, if the obligor is unemployed or has no income and does not have an account at a financial institution, then the court shall order the obligor to seek employment, if the obligor is able to engage in employment, and to immediately notify the court upon obtaining employment, upon obtaining any income, or upon obtaining any ownership of any asset with a value of $500 or more. If the obligor is still unemployed 30 days after any order for support, the court may order the obligor to enroll in the work experience, job placement, and job training pilot program for noncustodial parents as established in s. 409.2565, if the obligor is eligible for entrance into the pilot program.

(2)(a)The court shall have jurisdiction to determine custody, notwithstanding that the child is not physically present in this state at the time of filing any proceeding under this chapter, if it appears to the court that the child was removed from this state for the primary purpose of removing the child from the jurisdiction of the court in an attempt to avoid a determination or modification of custody.

(b)1. The court shall determine all matters relating to custody of each minor child of the parties in accordance with the best interests of the child and in accordance with the Uniform Child Custody Jurisdiction Act. It is the public policy of this state to assure that each minor child has frequent and continuing contact with both parents after the parents separate or the marriage of the parties is dissolved and to encourage parents to share the rights and responsibilities, and joys, of childrearing. After considering all relevant facts, the father of the child shall be given the same consideration as the mother in determining the primary residence of a child irrespective of the age or sex of the child.

2. The court shall order that the parental responsibility for a minor child be shared by both parents unless the court finds that shared parental responsibility would be detrimental to them child. Evidence that a parent has been convicted of a felony of the third degree or higher involving domestic violence, as defined in s. 741.28 and chapter 775, or meets the criteria of s. 39.806(1)(d), creates a rebuttable presumption of detriment to the child. If the presumption is not rebutted, shared parental responsibility, including visitation, residence of the child, and decisions made regarding the child, may not be granted to the convicted parent. However, the convicted parent is not

relieved of any obligation to provide financial support. If the court determines that shared parental responsibility would be detrimental to the child, it may order sole parental responsibility and make such arrangements for visitation as will best protect the child or abused spouse from further harm. Whether or not there is a conviction of any offense of domestic violence or child abuse or the existence of an injunction for protection against domestic violence, the court shall consider evidence of domestic violence or child abuse as evidence of detriment to the child.

a. In ordering shared parental responsibility, the court may consider the expressed desires of the parents and may grant to one party the ultimate responsibility over specific aspects of the child's welfare or may divide those responsibilities between the parties based on the best interests of the child. Areas of responsibility may include primary residence, education, medical and dental care, and any other responsibilities that the court finds unique to a particular family.

b. The court shall order "sole parental responsibility, with or without visitation rights, to the other parent when it is in the best interests of" the minor child.

c. The court may award the grandparents visitation rights with a minor child if it is in the child's best interest. Grandparents have legal standing to seek judicial enforcement of such an award. This section does not require that grandparents be made parties or given notice of dissolution pleadings or proceedings, nor do grandparents have legal standing as "contestants" as defined in s. 61.1306. A court may not order that a child be kept within the state or jurisdiction of the court solely for the purpose of permitting visitation by the grandparents.

3. Access to records and information pertaining to a minor child, including, but not limited to, medical, dental, and school records, may not be denied to a parent because the parent is not the child's primary residential parent. Full rights under this subparagraph apply to either parent unless a court order specifically revokes these rights, including any restrictions on these rights as provided in a domestic violence injunction. A parent having rights under this subparagraph has the same rights upon request as to form, substance, and manner of access as are available to the other parent of a child, including, without limitation, the right to in-person communication with medical, dental, and education providers.

* * * * *

(d) No presumption shall arise in favor of or against a request to relocate when a primary residential parent seeks to move the child and the move will materially affect the current schedule of contact and access with the secondary residential parent. In making a determination as to whether the primary residential parent may relocate with a child, the court must consider the following factors:

1. Whether the move would be likely to improve the general quality of life for both the residential parent and the child.

2. The extent to which visitation rights have been allowed and exercised.

3. Whether the primary residential parent, once out of the jurisdiction, will be likely to comply with any substitute visitation arrangements.

4. Whether the substitute visitation will be adequate to foster a continuing meaningful relationship between the child and the secondary residential parent.

5. Whether the cost of transportation is financially affordable by one or both parties.

6. Whether the move is in the best interests of the child.

(3)For purposes of shared parental responsibility and primary residence, the best interests of the child shall include an evaluation of all factors affecting the welfare and interests of the child, including, but not limited to:

(a) The parent who is more likely to allow the child frequent and continuing contact with the nonresidential parent.

(b) The love, affection, and other emotional ties existing between the parents and the child.

(c) The capacity and disposition of the parents to provide the child with food, clothing, medical care or other remedial care recognized and permitted under the laws of this state in lieu of medical care, and other material needs.

(d) The length of time the child has lived in a stable, satisfactory environment and the desirability of maintaining continuity.

(e) The permanence, as a family unit, of the existing or proposed custodial home.

(f) The moral fitness of the parents.

(g) The mental and physical health of the parents.

(h) The home, school, and community record of the child.

(i) The reasonable preference of the child, if the court deems the child to be of sufficient intelligence, understanding, and experience to express a preference.

(j) The willingness and ability of each parent to facilitate and encourage a close and continuing parent-child relationship between the child and the other parent.

(k) Evidence that any party has knowingly provided false

information to the court regarding a domestic violence proceeding pursuant to s. 741.30.

(l) Evidence of domestic violence or child abuse.

(m) Any other fact considered by the court to be relevant.

(4)(a) When a noncustodial parent who is ordered to pay child support or alimony and who is awarded visitation rights fails to pay child support or alimony, the custodial parent shall not refuse to honor the noncustodial parent's visitation rights.

(b) When a custodial parent refuses to honor a noncustodial parent's visitation rights, the noncustodial parent shall not fail to pay any ordered child support or alimony.

(c) When a custodial parent refuses to honor a noncustodial parent's or grandparent's visitation rights without proper cause, the court shall, after calculating the amount of visitation improperly denied, award the noncustodial parent or grandparent a sufficient amount of extra visitation to compensate the noncustodial parent or grandparent, which visitation shall be ordered as expeditiously as possible in a manner consistent with the best interests of the child and scheduled in a manner that is convenient for the person deprived of visitation. In ordering any makeup visitation, the court shall schedule such visitation in a manner that is consistent with the best interests of the child or children and that is convenient for the noncustodial parent or grandparent. In addition, the court:

1. May order the custodial parent to pay reasonable court costs and attorney's fees incurred by the noncustodial parent or grandparent to enforce their visitation rights or make up improperly denied visitation;

2. May order the custodial parent to attend the parenting course approved by the judicial circuit;

3. May order the custodial parent to do community service if the order will not interfere with the welfare of the child;

4. May order the custodial parent to have the financial burden of promoting frequent and continuing contact when the custodial parent and child reside further than 60 miles from the noncustodial parent;

5. May award custody, rotating custody, or primary residence to the noncustodial parent, upon the request of the noncustodial parent, if the award is in the best interests of the child; or

6. May impose any other reasonable sanction as a result of noncompliance.

(d) A person who violates this subsection may be punished by contempt of court or other remedies as the court deems appropriate.

(5) The court may make specific orders for the care and custody of the minor child as from the circumstances of the parties and the nature of the case is equitable and provide for child support in accordance with the guidelines in s. 61.30. An award of shared parental responsibility of a minor child does not preclude the court from entering an order for child support of the child.

(6) In any proceeding under this section, the court may not deny shared parental responsibility, custody, or visitation rights to a parent or grandparent solely because that parent or grandparent is or is believed to be infected with human immunodeficiency virus; but the court may condition such rights upon the parent's or grandparent's agreement to observe measures approved by the Centers for Disease Control and Prevention of the United States Public Health Service or by the Department of Health for preventing the spread of human immunodeficiency virus to the child.

(7) In any case where the child is actually residing with a grandparent in a stable relationship, whether the court has awarded custody to the grandparent or not, the court may recognize the grandparents as having the same standing as parents for evaluating what custody arrangements are in the best interest of the child.

(8) If the court orders that parental responsibility, including visitation, be shared by both parents, the court may not deny the noncustodial parent overnight contact and access to or visitation with the child solely because of the age or sex of the child.

61.14 Enforcement and modification of support, maintenance, or alimony agreements or orders.—

(1)(a) When the parties enter into an agreement for payments for, or instead of, support, maintenance, or alimony, whether in connection with a proceeding for dissolution or separate maintenance or with any voluntary property settlement, or when a party is required by court order to make any payments, and the circumstances or the financial ability of either party changes or the child who is a beneficiary of an agreement or court order as described herein reaches majority after the execution of the agreement or the rendition of the order, either party may apply to the circuit court of the circuit in which the parties, or either of them, resided at the date of the execution of the agreement or reside at the date of the application, or in which the agreement was executed or in which the order was rendered, for an order decreasing or increasing the amount of support, maintenance, or alimony, and the court has jurisdiction to make orders as equity requires, with due regard to the changed circumstances or the financial ability of the parties or the child, decreasing, increasing, or confirming the amount of separate support, maintenance, or alimony provided for in the agreement or order. A finding that medical insurance is reasonably available or the child support guidelines in s. 61.30 may constitute changed circumstances. Except as otherwise provided in s. 61.30(11)(c), the court may modify an order of support, maintenance, or alimony by increasing or decreasing the support, maintenance, or alimony retroactively to the date of the filing of the action or supplemental action for modification as equity requires, giving due regard to the changed circumstances or the financial ability of the parties or the child.

(b) In Title IV-D cases reviewed pursuant to the 3-year review and adjustment cycle, no substantial change of circumstance need be proven to warrant a modification.

* * * * *

(4) If a party applies for a reduction of alimony or child support and the circumstances justify the reduction, the court may make the reduction of alimony or child support regardless of whether or not the party applying for it has fully paid the accrued obligations to the other party at the time of the application or at the time of the order of modification.

(5)(a) When a court of competent jurisdiction enters an order for the payment of alimony or child support or both, the court shall make a finding of the obligor's imputed or actual present ability to comply with the order. If the obligor subsequently fails to pay alimony or support and a contempt hearing is held, the original order of the court creates a presumption that the obligor has the present ability to pay the alimony or support and to purge himself or herself from the contempt. At the contempt hearing, the obligor shall have the burden of proof to show that he or she lacks the ability to purge himself or herself from the contempt. This presumption is adopted as a presumption under s. 90.302(2) to implement the public policy of this state that children shall be maintained from the resources of their parents and as provided for in s. 409.2551, and that spouses be maintained as provided for in s. 61.08. The court shall state in its order the reasons for granting or denying the contempt.

(b) In a judicial circuit with a work experience and job training pilot project, if at the time of the contempt hearing the obligor is unemployed or has no income, then the court shall order the obligor to seek employment, if the obligor is able to engage in employment, and to immediately notify the court upon obtaining employment, upon obtaining any income, or upon obtaining any ownership of any asset with a value of $500 or more. If the obligor is still unemployed 30 days after any order for support, the court may order the obligor to enroll in a work experience, job placement, and job training program for noncustodial parents as established in s. 409.2565, if the obligor is eligible for entrance into the pilot program.

* * * * *

61.30 Child support guidelines; retroactive child support.—

(1)(a) The child support guideline amount as determined by this section presumptively establishes the amount the trier of fact shall order as child support in an initial proceeding for such support or in a proceeding for modification of an existing order for such support, whether the proceeding arises under this or another chapter. The trier of fact may order payment of child support which varies, plus or minus 5 percent, from the guideline amount, after considering all relevant factors, including the needs of the child or children, age, station in life, standard of living, and the financial status and ability of each parent. The trier of fact may order payment of child support in an amount which varies more than 5 percent from such guideline amount only upon a written finding explaining why ordering payment of such guideline amount would be unjust or inappropriate. Notwithstanding the variance limitations of this section, the trier of fact shall order payment of child support which varies from the guideline amount as provided in paragraph (11)(b) whenever any of the children are required by court order or mediation agreement to spend a substantial amount of time with the primary and secondary residential parents. This requirement applies to any living arrangement, whether temporary or permanent.

(b) The guidelines may provide the basis for proving a substantial change in circumstances upon which a modification of an existing order may be granted. However, the difference between the existing monthly obligation and the amount provided for under the guidelines shall be at least 15 percent or $50, whichever amount is greater, before the court may find that the guidelines provide a substantial change in circumstances.

(c) In Title IV-D cases reviewed pursuant to the 3-year review and adjustment cycle, no change of circumstance need be proven to warrant a modification.

(2) Income shall be determined on a monthly basis for the obligor and for the obligee as follows:

(a) Gross income shall include, but is not limited to, the following items:

1. Salary or wages.

2. Bonuses, commissions, allowances, overtime, tips, and other similar payments.

3. Business income from sources such as self-employment, partnership, close corporations, and independent contracts. "Business income" means gross receipts minus ordinary and necessary expenses required to produce income.

4. Disability benefits.

5. All workers' compensation benefits and settlements.

6. Unemployment compensation.

7. Pension, retirement, or annuity payments.

8. Social security benefits.

9. Spousal support received from a previous marriage or court ordered in the marriage before the court.

10. Interest and dividends.

11. Rental income, which is gross receipts minus ordinary and necessary expenses required to produce the income.

12. Income from royalties, trusts, or estates.

13. Reimbursed expenses or in kind payments to the extent that they reduce living expenses.

14. Gains derived from dealings in property, unless the gain is nonrecurring.

(b) Income on a monthly basis shall be imputed to an unemployed or underemployed parent when such employment or underemployment is found to be voluntary on that parent's part, absent physical or mental incapacity or other circumstances over which the parent has no control. In the event of such voluntary unemployment or underemployment, the employment potential and probable earnings level of the parent shall be determined based upon his or her recent work history, occupational qualifications, and prevailing earnings level in the community; however, the court may refuse to impute income to a primary residential parent if the court finds it necessary for the parent to stay home with the child.

(c) Public assistance as defined in s. 409.2554 shall be excluded from gross income.

(3) Allowable deductions from gross income shall include:

(a) Federal, state, and local income tax deductions, adjusted for actual filing status and allowable dependents and income tax liabilities.

(b) Federal insurance contributions or self-employment tax.

(c) Mandatory union dues.

(d) Mandatory retirement payments.

(e) Health insurance payments, excluding payments for coverage of the minor child.

(f) Court-ordered support for other children which is actually paid.

(g) Spousal support paid pursuant to a court order from a previous marriage or the marriage before the court.

(4) Net income for the obligor and net income for the obligee shall be computed by subtracting allowable deductions from gross income.

(5) Net income for the obligor and net income for the obligee shall be added together for a combined net income.

(6) The following schedules shall be applied to the combined net income to determine the minimum child support need:

(See Child Support Schedule on pages ___-___)

For combined monthly available income less than the amount set out on the above schedules, the parent should be ordered to pay a child support amount, determined on a case-by-case basis, to establish the principle of payment and lay the basis for increased orders should the parent's income increase in the future. For combined monthly available income greater than the amount set out in the above schedules, the obligation shall be the minimum amount of support provided by the guidelines plus the following percentages multiplied by the amount of income over $10,000:

Child or Children

One	Two	Three
Four	Five	Six
5.0%	7.5%	9.5%
11.0%	12.0%	12.5%

(7) Child care costs incurred on behalf of the children due to employment, job search, or education calculated to result in employment or to enhance income of current employment of either parent shall be reduced by 25 percent and then shall be added to the basic obligation. After the adjusted child care costs are added to the basic obligation, any moneys prepaid by the noncustodial parent for child care costs for the child or children of this action shall be deducted from that noncustodial parent's child support obligation for that child or those children. Child care costs shall not exceed the level required to provide quality care from a licensed source for the children.

(8) Health insurance costs resulting from coverage ordered pursuant to s. 61.13(1)(b), and any noncovered medical, dental, and prescription medication expenses of the child, shall be added to the basic obligation unless these expenses have been ordered to be separately paid on a percentage basis. After the health insurance costs are added to the basic obligation, any moneys prepaid by the noncustodial parent for health-related costs for the child or children of this action shall be deducted from that noncustodial parent's child support obligation for that child or those children.

(9) Each parent's percentage share of the child support need shall be determined by dividing each parent's net income by the combined net income.

(10) Each parent's actual dollar share of the child support need shall be determined by multiplying the minimum child support need by each parent's percentage share.

(11)(a) The court may adjust the minimum child support award, or either or both parents' share of the minimum child support award, based upon the following considerations:

1. Extraordinary medical, psychological, educational, or dental expenses.

2. Independent income of the child, not to include mon-

eys received by a child from supplemental security income.

3. The payment of support for a parent which regularly has been paid and for which there is a demonstrated need.

4. Seasonal variations in one or both parents' incomes or expenses.

5. The age of the child, taking into account the greater needs of older children.

6. Special needs, such as costs that may be associated with the disability of a child, that have traditionally been met within the family budget even though the fulfilling of those needs will cause the support to exceed the proposed guidelines.

7. Total available assets of the obligee, obligor, and the child.

8. The impact of the Internal Revenue Service dependency exemption and waiver of that exemption. The court may order the primary residential parent to execute a waiver of the Internal Revenue Service dependency exemption if the noncustodial parent is current in support payments.

9. When application of the child support guidelines requires a person to pay another person more than 55 percent of his or her gross income for a child support obligation for current support resulting from a single support order.

10. The particular shared parental arrangement, such as where the child spends a significant amount of time, but less than 40 percent of the overnights, with the noncustodial parent, thereby reducing the financial expenditures incurred by the primary residential parent; or the refusal of the noncustodial parent to become involved in the activities of the child.

11. Any other adjustment which is needed to achieve an equitable result which may include, but not be limited to, a reasonable and necessary existing expense or debt. Such expense or debt may include, but is not limited to, a reasonable and necessary expense or debt which the parties jointly incurred during the marriage.

(b) Whenever a particular shared parental arrangement provides that each child spend a substantial amount of time with each parent, the court shall adjust any award of child support, as follows:

1. In accordance with subsections (9) and (10), calculate the amount of support obligation apportioned to the noncustodial parent without including day care and health insurance costs in the calculation and multiply the amount by 1.5.

2. In accordance with subsections (9) and (10), calculate the amount of support obligation apportioned to the custodial parent without including day care and health insurance costs in the calculation and multiply the amount by 1.5.

3. Calculate the percentage of over-night stays the child spends with each parent.

4. Multiply the noncustodial parent's support obligation as calculated in subparagraph 1. by the percentage of the custodial parent's overnight stays with the child as calculated in subparagraph 3.

5. Multiply the custodial parent's support obligation as calculated in subparagraph 2. by the percentage of the noncustodial parent's overnight stays with the child as calculated in subparagraph 3.

6. The difference between the amounts calculated in subparagraphs 4 and 5. shall be the monetary transfer necessary between the custodial and noncustodial parents for the care of the child, subject to an adjustment for day care and health insurance expenses.

7. Pursuant to subsections (7) and (8), calculate the net amounts owed by the custodial and noncustodial parents for the expenses incurred for day care and health insurance coverage for the child. Day care shall be calculated without regard to the 25-percent reduction applied by subsection (7).

8. Adjust the support obligation owed by the custodial or noncustodial parent pursuant to subparagraph 6. by crediting or debiting the amount calculated in subparagraph 7. This amount represents the child support which must be exchanged between the custodial and noncustodial parents.

9. The court may deviate from the child support amount calculated pursuant to subparagraph 8. based upon the considerations set forth in paragraph (a), as well as the custodial parent's low income and ability to maintain the basic necessities of the home for the child, the likelihood that the noncustodial parent will actually exercise the visitation granted by the court, and whether all of the children are exercising the same shared parental arrangement.

10. For purposes of adjusting any award of child support under this paragraph, "substantial amount of time" means that the noncustodial parent exercises visitation at least 40 percent of the overnights of the year.

(c) A noncustodial parent's failure to regularly exercise court-ordered or agreed visitation not caused by the custodial parent which resulted in the adjustment of the amount of child support pursuant to subparagraph (a)10. or paragraph (b) shall be deemed a substantial change of circumstances for purposes of modifying the child support award. A modification pursuant to this paragraph shall be retroactive to the date the noncustodial parent first failed to regularly exercise court-ordered or agreed visitation.

(12)(a) A parent with a support obligation may have other children living with him or her who were born or adopted after the support obligation arose. If such subsequent children exist, the court, when considering an upward modification of an existing award, may disregard the income from secondary employment obtained in addition to the parent's primary employment if the court determines that the employment was obtained primarily to support the subsequent children.

(b) Except as provided in paragraph (a), the existence of such subsequent children should not as a general rule be considered by the court as a basis for disregarding the amount provided in the guidelines. The parent with a support obligation for subsequent children may raise the existence of such subsequent children as a justification for deviation from the guidelines. However, if the existence of such subsequent children is raised, the income of the other parent of the subsequent children shall be considered by the court in determining whether or not there is a basis for deviation from the guideline amount.

(c) The issue of subsequent children under paragraph (a) or paragraph (b) may only be raised in a proceeding for an upward modification of an existing award and may not be applied to justify a decrease in an existing award.

(13) If the recurring income is not sufficient to meet the needs of the child, the court may order child support to be paid from nonrecurring income or assets.

(14) Every petition for child support or for modification of child support shall be accompanied by an affidavit which shows the party's income, allowable deductions, and net income computed in accordance with this section. The affidavit shall be served at the same time that the petition is served. The respondent, whether or not a stipulation is entered, shall make an affidavit which shows the party's income, allowable deductions, and net income computed in accordance with this section. The respondent shall include his or her affidavit with the answer to the petition or as soon thereafter as is practicable, but in any case at least 72 hours prior to any hearing on the finances of either party.

(15) For purposes of establishing an obligation for support in accordance with this section, if a person who is receiving public assistance is found to be noncooperative as defined in s. 409.2572, the IV-D agency is authorized to submit to the court an affidavit attesting to the income of the custodial parent based upon information available to the IV-D agency.

(16) The Legislature shall review the guidelines established in this section at least every 4 years beginning in 1997.

(17) In an initial determination of child support, whether in a paternity action, dissolution of marriage action, or petition for support during the marriage, the court has discretion to award child support retroactive to the date when the parents did not reside together in the same household with the child, not to exceed a period of 24 months preceding the filing of the petition, regardless of whether that date precedes the filing of the petition. In determining the retroactive award in such cases, the court shall consider the following:

(a) The court shall apply the guidelines in effect at the time of the hearing subject to the obligor's demonstration of his or her actual income, as defined by subsection (2), during the retroactive period. Failure of the obligor to so demonstrate shall result in the court using the obligor's income at the time of the hearing in computing child support for the retroactive period.

(b) All actual payments made by the noncustodial parent to the custodial parent or the child or third parties for the benefit of the child throughout the proposed retroactive period.

(c) The court should consider an installment payment plan for the payment of retroactive child support.

Chapter 742
Determination of Parentage

742.011 Determination of paternity proceedings; jurisdiction.— Any woman who is pregnant or has a child, any man who has reason to believe that he is the father of a child, or any child may bring proceedings in the circuit court, in chancery, to determine the paternity of the child when paternity has not been established by law or otherwise.

742.031 Hearings; court orders for support, hospital expenses, and attorney's fee.—

(1) Hearings for the purpose of establishing or refuting the allegations of the complaint and answer shall be held in the chambers and may be restricted to persons, in addition to the parties involved and their counsel, as the judge in his or her discretion may direct. The court shall determine the issues of paternity of the child and the ability of the parents to support the child. Each party's social security number shall be recorded in the file containing the adjudication of paternity. If the court finds that the alleged father is the father of the child, it shall so order. If appropriate, the court shall order the father to pay the complainant, her guardian, or any other person assuming responsibility for the child moneys sufficient to pay reasonable attorney's fees, hospital or medical expenses, cost of confinement, and any other expenses incident to the birth of the child and to pay all costs of the proceeding. Bills for pregnancy, childbirth, and scientific testing are admissible as evidence without requiring third-party foundation testimony, and shall constitute prima facie evidence of amounts incurred for

such services or for testing on behalf of the child. The court shall order either or both parents owing a duty of support to the child to pay support pursuant to s. 61.30. The court hall issue, upon motion by a party, a temporary order requiring the provision of child support pursuant to s. 61.30 pending an administrative or judicial determination of parentage, if there is clear and convincing evidence of paternity on the basis of genetic tests or other evidence. The court may also make a determination as to the parental responsibility and residental care and custody of the minor children in accordance with chapter 61.

(2) If a judgment of paternity contains no explicit award of custody, the establishment of a support obligation or of visitation rights in one parent shall be considered a judgment granting primary residential care and custody to the other parent without prejudice. If a paternity judgment contains no such provisions, custody shall be presumed to be with the mother.

* * * * *

742.10 Establishment of paternity for children born out of wedlock.—

(1) This chapter provides the primary jurisdiction and procedures for the determination of paternity for children born out of wedlock. When the establishment of paternity has been raised and determined within an adjudicatory hearing brought under the statutes governing inheritance, or dependency under workers' compensation or similar compensation programs, or when an affidavit acknowledging paternity or a stipulation of paternity is executed by both parties and filed with the clerk of the court, or when an affidavit or notarized voluntary acknowledgment of paternity as provided for in s. 382.013 or s. 382.016 is executed by both parties, it shall constitute the establishment of paternity for purposes of this chapter. If no adjudicatory proceeding was held, a notarized voluntary acknowledgment of paternity shall create a rebuttable presumption, as defined by s. 90.304, of paternity and is subject to the right of any signatory to rescind the acknowledgment within 60 days of the date the acknowledgment was signed or the date of an administrative or judicial proceeding relating to the child, including a proceeding to establish a support order, in which the signatory is a party, whichever is earlier. Both parents are required to provide their social security numbers on any acknowledgment of paternity, consent affidavit, or stipulation of paternity. Except for affidavits under seal pursuant to ss. 382.015 and 382.016, the Office of Vital Statistics shall provide certified copies of affidavits to the Title IV-D agency upon request.

* * * * *

(4) After the 60-day period referred to in subsection (1), a signed voluntary acknowledgment of paternity shall constitute an establishment of paternity and may be challenged in court only on the basis of fraud, duress, or material mistake of fact, with the burden of proof upon the challenger, and under which the legal responsibilities, including child support obligations of any signatory arising from the acknowledgment may not be suspended during the challenge, except upon a finding of good cause by the court.

* * * * *

742.108 Criminal penalties for false statements of paternity.— Notwithstanding any other provision of law, any person who knowingly and willfully provides false information to the sheriff's office, other law enforcement agency, or governmental agency, or under oath regarding the paternity of a child in conjunction with an application for, or the receipt of, public assistance for a dependent child commits a misdemeanor of the second degree, punishable as provided in s. 775.082 or s. 775.083, in addition to remaining subject to any other civil or criminal penalties for perjury or making false statements which are applicable under other provisions of law.

742.12 Scientific testing to determine paternity.—

(1) In any proceeding to establish paternity, the court on its own motion may require the child, mother, and alleged fathers to submit to scientific tests that are generally acceptable within the scientific community to show a probability of paternity. The court shall direct that the tests be conducted by a qualified technical laboratory.

(2) In any proceeding to establish paternity, the court may, upon request of a party providing a sworn statement or written declaration as provided by s. 92.525(2) alleging paternity and setting forth facts establishing a reasonable possibility of the requisite sexual contact between the parties or providing a sworn statement or written declaration denying paternity and setting forth facts establishing a reasonable possibility of the nonexistence of sexual contact between the parties, require the child, mother, and alleged fathers to submit to scientific tests that are generally acceptable within the scientific community to show a probability of paternity. The court shall direct that the tests be conducted by a qualified technical laboratory.

(3) The test results, together with the opinions and conclusions of the test laboratory, shall be filed with the court. Any objection to the test results must be made in writing and must be filed with the court at least 10 days prior to the hearing. If no objection is filed, the test results shall be admitted into evidence without the need for predicate to be laid or third-party foundation testimony to be presented. Nothing in this paragraph prohibits a party from calling an outside expert witness to refute or support the testing procedure or results, or the mathematical theory on which they are based. Upon the entry of the order for scientific testing, the court must inform each person to be tested of the procedure and requirements for objecting to the test results and of the consequences of the failure to object.

(4) Test results are admissible in evidence and should be weighed

along with other evidence of the paternity of the alleged father unless the statistical probability of paternity equals or exceeds 95 percent. A statistical probability of paternity of 95 percent or more creates a rebuttable presumption, as defined by s. 90.304, that the alleged father is the biological father of the child. If a party fails to rebut the presumption of paternity which arose from the statistical probability of paternity of 95 percent or more, the court may enter a summary judgment of paternity. If the test results show the alleged father cannot be the biological father, the case shall be dismissed with prejudice.

(5) Subject to the limitations in subsection (3), if the test results or the expert analysis of the inherited characteristics is disputed, the court, upon reasonable request of a party, shall order that an additional test be made by the same laboratory or an independent laboratory at the expense of the party requesting additional testing.

(6) Verified documentation of the chain of custody of the blood or other specimens is competent evidence to establish the chain of custody.

(7) The fees and costs for scientific tests shall be paid by the parties in proportions and at times determined by the court unless the parties reach a stipulated agreement which is adopted by the court.

Chapter 787
Kidnapping; False Imprisonment; Luring or Enticing a Child; Custody Offenses

787.03 Interference with custody.—

(1) Whoever, without lawful authority, knowingly or recklessly takes or entices, or aids, abets, hires, or otherwise procures another to take or entice, any child 17 years of age or under or any incompetent person from the custody of the child or incompetent person's parent, his or her guardian, a public agency having the lawful charge of the child or incompetent person, or any other lawful custodian commits the offense of interference with custody and commits a felony of the third degree, punishable as provided in s. 775.082, s. 775.083, or s. 775.084.

(2) In the absence of a court order determining rights to custody or visitation with any child 17 years of age or under or with any incompetent person, any parent of the child or incompetent person, whether natural or adoptive, stepparent, legal guardian, or relative of such child or incompetent person who has custody thereof and who takes, detains, conceals, or entices away that child or incompetent person within or without the state, with malicious intent to deprive another person of his or her right to custody of the child or incompetent person, commits a felony of the third degree, punishable as provided in s. 775.082, s. 775.083, or s. 775.084.

(3) A subsequently obtained court order for custody or visitation does not affect application of this section.

(4) It is a defense that:

(a) The defendant reasonably believes that his or her action was necessary to preserve the child or the incompetent person from danger to his or her welfare.

(b) The defendant was the victim of an act of domestic violence or had reasonable cause to believe that his or her action was necessary to protect himself or herself from an act of domestic violence as defined in s. 741.28.

(c) The child or incompetent person was taken away at his or her own instigation without enticement and without purpose to commit a criminal offense with or against the child or incompetent person.

(5) Proof that a child was 17 years of age or under creates the presumption that the defendant knew the child's age or acted in reckless disregard thereof.

(6)(a) This section does not apply in cases where a spouse who is the victim of any act of domestic violence or who has reasonable cause to believe he or she is about to become the victim of any act of domestic violence, as defined in s. 741.28, or believes that his or her action was necessary to preserve the child or the incompetent person from danger to his or her welfare seeks shelter from such acts or possible acts and takes with him or her any child 17 years of age or younger.

(b) In order to gain the exemption conferred by paragraph (a), a person who takes a child pursuant to this subsection must:

1.Within 10 days after taking the child, make a report to the sheriff's office or state attorney's office for the county in which the child resided at the time he or she was taken, which report must include the name of the person taking the child, the current address and telephone number of the person and child, and the reasons the child was taken.

2.Within a reasonable time after taking the child, commence a custody proceeding that is consistent with the federal Parental Kidnapping Prevention Act, 28 U.S.C. s. 1738A, or the Uniform Child Custody Jurisdiction Act, ss. 61.1302-61.1348.

3. Inform the sheriff's office or state attorney's office for the county in which the child resided at the time he or she was taken of any change of address or telephone number of the person and child.

(c) Information provided to a sheriff or state attorney under paragraph (b) is confidential and exempt from s. 119.07(1) and s. 24(a), Art. I of the State Constitution. This paragraph is subject to the Open Government Sunset Review Act of 1995 in accordance with s. 119.15 and is repealed on October 2, 2005, unless reviewed and saved from repeal through reenactment by the Legislature before that date.

Chapter 856
Drunkenness; Open House Parties; Loitering; Prowling; Desertion

856.04 Desertion; withholding support; proviso.—

(1) Any man who shall in this state desert his wife and children, or either of them, or his wife where there are no children or child, or who shall willfully withhold from them or either of them, the means of support, or any mother, who shall desert her child or children, or who shall willfully withhold from them the means of support, shall be guilty of a felony of the third degree, punishable as provided in s. 775.082, s. 775.083, or s. 775.084. However, no husband shall be prosecuted under this section for the desertion of his wife, or for withholding from his wife the means of supporting her where there is existing, at the time of such desertion or withholding, such cause or causes as are recognized as ground or grounds for dissolution of marriage, by statute, in this state, if such person shall have provided for the support of his children, if there be any.

* * * * *

Family Law Rules of Procedure

The following is one of the more significant rules of the new Family Law Rules of Procedure. You would be well advised to review both the Florida Rules of Civil Procedure and the full Family Law Rules of Procedure.

RULE 12.285. MANDATORY DISCLOSURE

(a) Application.

(1) Scope. This rule shall apply to all proceedings within the scope of these rules except proceedings involving adoption, simplified dissolution, enforcement, contempt, injunctions for domestic or repeat violence, and uncontested dissolutions when the respondent is served by publication and does not file an answer. Additionally, no financial affidavit or other documents shall be required under this rule from a party seeking attorneys' fees, suit money, or costs, if the basis for the request is solely under section 57.105, Florida Statutes, or any successor statute. Except for the provisions as to financial affidavits and child support guidelines worksheets, any portion of this rule may be modified by order of the court or agreement of the parties.

(2) Original and Duplicate Copies. Unless otherwise agreed by the parties or ordered by the court, copies of documents required under this rule may be produced in lieu of originals. Originals, when available, shall be produced for inspection upon request. Parties shall not be required to serve duplicates of documents previously served.

(b) Time for Production of Documents.

(1) Temporary Financial Hearings. Any document required under this rule in any temporary financial relief proceeding shall be served on the other party for inspection and copying as follows.

(A) The party seeking relief shall serve the required documents on the other party with the notice of temporary financial hearing, unless the documents have been served under subdivision (b)(2) of this rule.

(B) The responding party shall serve the required documents on the party seeking relief on or before 5:00 p.m., 2 business days before the day of the temporary financial hearing if served by delivery or 7 days before the day of the temporary financial hearing if served by mail, unless the documents have been received previously by the party seeking relief under subdivision (b)(2) of this rule. A responding party shall be given no less than 12 days to serve the documents required under this rule, unless otherwise ordered by the court. If the 45-day period for exchange of documents provided for in subdivision (b)(2) of this rule will occur before the expiration of the 12 days, the provisions of subdivision (b)(2) control.

(2) Initial and Supplemental Proceedings. Any document required under this rule for any initial or supplemental proceeding shall be served on the other party for inspection and copying within 45 days of service of the initial pleading on the respondent.

(c) Disclosure Requirements for Temporary Financial Relief. In any proceeding for temporary financial relief heard within 45 days of the service of the initial pleading or within any extension of the time for complying with mandatory disclosure granted by the court or agreed to by the parties, the following documents shall be served on the other party:

(1) A financial affidavit in substantial conformity with Florida Family Law Rules of Procedure Form 12.902(b) if the party's gross annual income is less than $ 50,000, or Florida_Family Law Rules of Procedure Form 12.902(c) if the party's gross annual income is equal to or more than $ 50,000. This requirement cannot be waived by the parties. The affidavit also must be filed with the court.

(2) All federal and state income tax returns, gift tax returns, and intangible personal property tax returns filed by the party or on the party's behalf for the past year. A party may file a transcript of the tax return as provided by Internal Revenue Service Form 4506 in lieu of his or her individual federal income tax return for purposes of a temporary hearing.

(3) IRS forms W-2, 1099, and K-1 for the past year, if the income tax return for that year has not been prepared.

(4) Pay stubs or other evidence of earned income for the 3 months prior to service of the financial affidavit.

(d) Parties' Disclosure Requirements for Initial or Supplemental Proceedings. A party shall serve the following documents in any proceeding for an initial or supplemental request for permanent financial relief, including, but not limited to, a request for child support, alimony, equitable distribution of assets or debts, or attorneys' fees, suit money, or costs:

(1) A financial affidavit in substantial conformity with Florida Family Law Rules_of Procedure Form 12.902(b) if the

party's gross annual income is less than $ 50,000, or Florida_Family Law Rules of Procedure Form 12.902(c) if the party's gross annual income is equal to or more than $ 50,000, which requirement cannot be waived by the parties. The financial affidavits also must be filed with the court. A party may request, by using the Standard Family Law Interrogatories, or the court on its own motion may order, a party whose gross annual income is less than $ 50,000 to complete Florida Family Law Rules of Procedure Form 12.902(c).

(2) All federal and state income tax returns, gift tax returns, and intangible personal property tax returns filed by the party or on the party's behalf for the past 3 years.

(3) IRS forms W-2, 1099, and K-1 for the past year, if the income tax return for that year has not been prepared.

(4) Pay stubs or other evidence of earned income for the 3 months prior to service of the financial affidavit.

(5) A statement by the producing party identifying the amount and source of all income received from any source during the 3 months preceding the service of the financial affidavit required by this rule if not reflected on the pay stubs produced.

(6) All loan applications and financial statements prepared or used within the 12 months preceding service of that party's financial affidavit required by this rule, whether for the purpose of obtaining or attempting to obtain credit or for any other purpose.

(7) All deeds within the last 3 years, all promissory notes within the last 12 months, and all present leases, in which the party owns or owned an interest, whether held in the party's name individually, in the party's name jointly with any other person or entity, in the party's name as trustee or guardian for any other person, or in someone else's name on the party's behalf.

(8) All periodic statements from the last 3 months for all checking accounts, and from the last 12 months for all other accounts (for example, savings accounts, money market funds, certificates of deposit, etc.), regardless of whether or not the account has been closed, including those held in the party's name individually, in the party's name jointly with any other person or entity, in the party's name as trustee or guardian for any other person, or in someone else's name on the party's behalf.

(9) All brokerage account statements in which either party to this action held within the last 12 months or holds an interest including those held in the party's name individually, in the party's name jointly with any person or entity, in the party's name as trustee or guardian for any other person, or in someone else's name on the party's behalf.

(10) The most recent statement for any profit sharing, retirement, deferred compensation, or pension plan (for example, IRA, 401(k), 403(b), SEP, KEOGH, or other similar account) in which the party is a participant or alternate payee and the summary plan description for any retirement, profit sharing, or pension plan in which the party is a participant or an alternate payee. (The summary plan description must be furnished to the party on request by the plan administrator as required by 29 U.S.C. § 1024(b)(4).)

(11) The declarations page, the last periodic statement, and the certificate for all life insurance policies insuring the party's life or the life of the party's spouse, whether group insurance or otherwise, and all current health and dental insurance cards covering either of the parties and/or their dependent children.

(12) Corporate, partnership, and trust tax returns for the last 3 tax years if the party has an ownership or interest in a corporation, partnership, or trust greater than or equal to 30%.

(13) All promissory notes for the last 12 months, all credit card and charge account statements and other records showing the party's indebtedness as of the date of the filing of this action and for the last 3 months, and all present lease agreements, whether owed in the party's name individually, in the party's name jointly with any other person or entity, in the party's name as trustee or guardian for any other person, or in someone else's name on the party's behalf.

(14) All written premarital or marital agreements entered into at any time between the parties to this marriage, whether before or during the marriage. Additionally, in any modification proceeding, each party shall serve on the opposing party all written agreements entered into between them at any time since the order to be modified was entered.

(15) All documents and tangible evidence supporting the producing party's claim of special equity or nonmarital status of an asset or debt for the time period from the date of acquisition of the asset or debt to the date of production or from the date of marriage, if based on premarital acquisition.

(16) Any court orders directing a party to pay or receive spousal or child support.

(e) Duty to Supplement Disclosure; Amended Financial Affidavit.

(1) Parties have a continuing duty to supplement documents described in this rule, including financial affidavits,

whenever a material change in their financial status occurs.

(2) If an amended financial affidavit or an amendment to a financial affidavit is filed, the amending party also shall serve any subsequently discovered or acquired documents supporting the amendments to the financial affidavit.

(f) Sanctions. Any document to be produced under this rule that is served on the opposing party fewer than 24 hours before a nonfinal hearing or in violation of the court's pretrial order shall not be admissible in evidence at that hearing unless the court finds good cause for the delay. In addition, the court may impose other sanctions authorized by rule 12.380 as may be equitable under the circumstances. The court may also impose sanctions upon the offending lawyer in lieu of imposing sanctions on a party.

(g) Extensions of Time for Complying with Mandatory Disclosure. By agreement of the parties, the time for complying with mandatory disclosure may be extended. Either party also may file, at least 5 days before the due date, a motion to enlarge the time for complying with mandatory disclosure. The court shall grant the request for good cause shown.

(h) Objections to Mandatory Automatic Disclosure. Objections to the mandatory automatic disclosure required by this rule shall be served in writing at least 5 days prior to the due date for the disclosure or the objections shall be deemed waived. The filing of a timely objection, with a notice of hearing on the objection, automatically stays mandatory disclosure for those matters within the scope of the objection. For good cause shown, the court may extend the time for the filing of an objection or permit the filing of an otherwise untimely objection. The court shall impose sanctions for the filing of meritless or frivolous objections.

(i) Certificate of Compliance. All parties subject to automatic mandatory disclosure shall file with the court a certificate of compliance, Florida Family Law Rules of Procedure Form 12.932, identifying with particularity the documents which have been delivered and certifying the date of service of the financial affidavit and documents by that party.

(j) Child Support Guidelines Worksheet. If the case involves child support, the parties shall file with the court at or prior to a hearing to establish or modify child support a Child Support Guidelines Worksheet in substantial conformity with Florida Family Law Rules of Procedure Form 12.902(e). This requirement cannot be waived by the parties.

(k) Place of Production.

(1) Unless otherwise agreed by the parties or ordered by the court, all production required by this rule shall take place in the county where the action is pending and in the office of the attorney for the party receiving production. Unless otherwise agreed by the parties or ordered by the court, if a party does not have an attorney or if the attorney does not have an office in the county where the action is pending, production shall take place in the county where the action is pending at a place designated in writing by the party receiving production, served at least 5 days before the due date for production.

(2) If venue is contested, on motion by a party the court shall designate the place where production will occur pending determination of the venue issue.

(l) Failure of Defaulted Party to Comply. Nothing in this rule shall be deemed to preclude the entry of a final judgment when a party in default has failed to comply with this rule.

Appendix B: Worksheet

Table of Worksheets

KEY INFORMATION WORKSHEET

The Other Party:

Full legal name: ______________________________

Address: ______________________________

____

Phone: ______________________________

Social Security No.: ______________________________

Employer: ______________________________

Employment Address: ______________________________

____

Work Phone: ______________________________

Attorney: ______________________________

Address: ______________________________

____

Phone: ______________________________

Fax: ______________________________

The Child(ren):

Name: ______________________________

Address: ______________________________

____

Date of Birth: ______________________________

Social Security No.: ______________________________

The Court:

Case No.: ______________________________

Court Address: ______________________________

Office of the Clerk phone: ______________________________

Judge: ______________________________

Secretary/Judicial Assistant: ______________________________

Judge phone: ______________________________

WITNESS TESTIMONY WORKSHEET

PURPOSE OF WITNESS:

PART I

1. Please state your name and address.
2. Do you know the parties in this case?
3. How do you know them?

PART II

1. What is your occupation?
2. How long have you been in your current occupation?
3. Where are you employed?
4. How long have you been employed there?
5. Please describe your educational background, and employment history.

PART III

Appendix C: Forms

The following is a list of the forms found in this appendix. The form number may be found in the upper outside corner of the first page of the form. The number to the far right indicates the page in this book where the form begins. The information in brackets [] gives the form number used by the Supreme Court, and the month and year of the most recent version of the form as this book went to press.

For example, following the listing below for form 1, the Affidavit of Indigency, you will find the notation "[Form 12.902(a) (9/00)]." This means that the Affidavit of Indigency will be listed as "Form 12.902(a)" on the Florida Courts website, and that it was last revised in September 2000.) If you check the forms on the Florida Courts website (www.flcourts.org), this infomation will help you determine if a form in this book has been superseded. If there is no information in brackets, it means it is not a Supreme Court form.

Table of Forms

IN THE CIRCUIT COURT OF THE ______________________ JUDICIAL CIRCUIT,
IN AND FOR ______________________ COUNTY, FLORIDA

Case No.: ______________________
Division: ______________________

______________________,
Petitioner,

and

______________________,
Respondent.

AFFIDAVIT OF INDIGENCY

I, *{full legal name}* ______________________, being sworn, certify that the following statements are true:

I am financially insolvent and unable to pay the charges, costs, or fees otherwise payable by law to the clerk of the circuit court or sheriff in this civil action. I make this claim because:
[√ **one** only]
___ a. I am currently receiving public assistance in the amount of: $________ per ( ) week ( ) month. My public assistance case number is: ______________________. My financial affidavit,✎❑ Florida Family Law Rules of Procedure Form 12.902(b), is attached.
___ b. I am unable to pay those clerk's fees and costs because of indigency, based on facts contained in my Family Law Financial Affidavit,✎❑| Florida Family Law Rules of Procedure Form 12.902(b), which is attached.

I CERTIFY THAT NO PERSON HAS BEEN PAID OR PROMISED ANY PAYMENT OF ANY REMUNERATION BY ME FOR SERVICES PERFORMED ON MY BEHALF IN CONNECTION WITH THIS ACTION OR PROCEEDING.

I certify that a copy of this document was [√ **one** only] ( ) mailed ( ) faxed and mailed ( ) hand delivered to the person(s) listed below on *{date}* ______________________.

Other party or his/her attorney:
Name: ______________________
Address: ______________________
City, State, Zip: ______________________
Fax Number: ______________________

I understand that I am swearing or affirming under oath to the truthfulness of the claims made in this affidavit and that the punishment for knowingly making a false statement includes fines and/or imprisonment.

Dated: ______________________

____
Signature of Party
Printed Name: ______________________
Address: ______________________
City, State, Zip: ______________________

Telephone Number: ______________________________
Fax Number: ___________________________________

STATE OF FLORIDA
COUNTY OF ____________________

Sworn to or affirmed and signed before me on ______________ by ______________________________.

____
NOTARY PUBLIC or DEPUTY CLERK

____
[Print, type, or stamp commissioned name of notary or clerk.]

____ Personally known
____ Produced identification
Type of identification produced ________________________

IF A NONLAWYER HELPED YOU FILL OUT THIS FORM, HE/SHE MUST FILL IN THE BLANKS BELOW: [✍ fill in **all** blanks]
I, *{full legal name and trade name of nonlawyer}* ____,
a nonlawyer, located at *{street}* ______________________________, *{city}* ____________________,
{state} ____________________, *{phone}* __________________, helped *{name}* __________________,
who is the [√ **one** only] ___ petitioner **or** ___ respondent, fill out this form.

IN THE CIRCUIT COURT OF THE ______________________ JUDICIAL CIRCUIT,
IN AND FOR ______________________ COUNTY, FLORIDA

Case No.: ______________________
Division: ______________________

______________________,
Petitioner,

and

______________________,
Respondent.

FAMILY LAW FINANCIAL AFFIDAVIT (SHORT FORM)

(Under $50,000 Individual Gross Annual Income)

I, *{full legal name}* ______________________, being sworn, certify that the following information is true:

My Occupation: ______________ Employed by: ______________________

Business Address: ______________________

Pay rate: $ __________ ( ) every week ( ) every other week ( ) twice a month ( ) monthly ( ) other: ______
□ Check here if unemployed and explain on a separate sheet your efforts to find employment.

SECTION I. PRESENT MONTHLY GROSS INCOME:

All amounts must be MONTHLY. See the instructions with this form to figure out money amounts for anything that is NOT paid monthly. Attach more paper, if needed. Items included under "other" should be listed separately with separate dollar amounts.

1. Monthly gross salary or wages — 1. $__________
2. Monthly bonuses, commissions, allowances, overtime, tips, and similar payments — 2. __________
3. Monthly business income from sources such as self-employment, partnerships, close corporations, and/or independent contracts (gross receipts minus ordinary and necessary expenses required to produce income) (□ Attach sheet itemizing such income and expenses.) — 3. __________
4. Monthly disability benefits/SSI — 4. __________
5. Monthly Workers' Compensation — 5. __________
6. Monthly Unemployment Compensation — 6. __________
7. Monthly pension, retirement, or annuity payments — 7. __________
8. Monthly Social Security benefits — 8. __________
9. Monthly alimony actually received
   9a. From this case: $ ______
   9b. From other case(s): ______ Add 9a and 9b — 9. __________
10. Monthly interest and dividends — 10. __________
11. Monthly rental income (gross receipts minus ordinary and necessary expenses required to produce income) (□ Attach sheet itemizing such income and expense items.) — 11. __________
12. Monthly income from royalties, trusts, or estates — 12. __________
13. Monthly reimbursed expenses and in-kind payments to the extent that they reduce personal living expenses — 13. __________
14. Monthly gains derived from dealing in property (not including nonrecurring gains) — 14. __________
15. Any other income of a recurring nature (list source) ______________ — 15. __________
16. ______________________ — 16. __________

17. PRESENT MONTHLY GROSS INCOME (Add lines 1–16) **TOTAL:** **17. $**____________

PRESENT MONTHLY DEDUCTIONS:

18. Monthly federal, state, and local income tax (corrected for filing status and allowable dependents and income tax liabilities)
    a. Filing Status ________
    b. Number of dependents claimed ______ 18. $________
19. Monthly FICA or self-employment taxes 19. ________
20. Monthly Medicare payments 20. ________
21. Monthly mandatory union dues 21. ________
22. Monthly mandatory retirement payments 22. ________
23. Monthly health insurance payments (including dental insurance), excluding portion paid for any minor children of this relationship 23. ________
24. Monthly court-ordered child support actually paid for children from another relationship 24. ________
25. Monthly court-ordered alimony actually paid
    25a. from this case: $______
    25b. from other case(s): ______ Add 25a and 25b 25. ________

26. TOTAL DEDUCTIONS ALLOWABLE UNDER SECTION 61.30, FLORIDA STATUTES (Add lines 18 through 25) **TOTAL: 26. $**____________

PRESENT NET MONTHLY INCOME (Subtract line 26 from line 17) **27. $**____________

SECTION II. AVERAGE MONTHLY EXPENSES

A. HOUSEHOLD:

Mortgage or rent	$________
Property taxes	$________
Utilities	$________
Telephone	$________
Food	$________
Meals outside home	$________
Maintenance/Repairs	$________
Other: ________	$________

B. AUTOMOBILE

Gasoline	$________
Repairs	$________
Insurance	$________

C. CHILD(REN)'S EXPENSES

Day care	$________
Lunch money	$________
Clothing	$________
Grooming	$________
Gifts for holidays	$________
Medical/dental (uninsured)	$________
Other: ________	$________

D. INSURANCE

Medical/dental	$________
Child(ren)'s medical/dental	$________
Life	$________

Other: ________ $________

E. OTHER EXPENSES NOT LISTED ABOVE

Clothing $ ______________
Medical/Dental (uninsured) $ ______________
Grooming $ ______________
Entertainment $ ______________
Gifts $ ______________
Religious organizations $ ______________
Miscellaneous $ ______________
Other: ______________ $ ______________
______________ $ ______________
______________ $ ______________
______________ $ ______________
______________ $ ______________
______________ $ ______________
______________ $ ______________

F. PAYMENTS TO CREDITORS

CREDITOR:	MONTHLY PAYMENT
______________	$ ______________
______________	$ ______________
______________	$ ______________
______________	$ ______________
______________	$ ______________
______________	$ ______________
______________	$ ______________
______________	$ ______________
______________	$ ______________
______________	$ ______________
______________	$ ______________

28. TOTAL MONTHLY EXPENSES (add **ALL** monthly amounts in A through F above) **28.** $ ______________

SUMMARY

29. TOTAL PRESENT MONTHLY NET INCOME (from line 27 of SECTION I. INCOME) **29. $** ______________

30. TOTAL MONTHLY EXPENSES (from line 28 above) **30. $** ______________

31. SURPLUS (If line 29 is more than line 30, subtract line 30 from line 29. This is the amount of your surplus. Enter that amount here.) **31. $** ______________

32. (DEFICIT) (If line 30 is more than line 29, subtract line 29 from line 30. This is the amount of your deficit. Enter that amount here.) **32. ($** ______________**)**

SECTION III. ASSETS AND LIABILITIES

Use the nonmarital column only if this is a petition for dissolution of mG40

arriage and you believe an item is "nonmarital," meaning it belongs to only one of you and should not be divided. You should indicate to whom you believe the item(s) or debt belongs. (Typically, you will only use this column if property/debt was owned/owed by one spouse before the marriage. See the **"General Information for Self-Represented Litigants"** found at the beginning of these forms and section 61.075(1), Florida Statutes, for definitions of "marital" and "nonmarital" assets and liabilities.)

A. ASSETS:

DESCRIPTION OF ITEM(S). List a description of each separate item owned by you (and/or your spouse, if this is a petition for dissolution of marriage). √ the box next to any asset(s) which you are requesting the judge award to you.	Current Fair Market Value	Nonmarital (√ correct column)	
		husband	wife
☐ Cash (on hand)	$		
☐ Cash (in banks or credit unions)			
☐ Stocks, Bonds, Notes			
☐ Real estate: (Home)			
☐ (Other)			
☐ Automobiles			
☐ Other personal property			
☐ Retirement plans (Profit Sharing, Pension, IRA, 401(k)s, etc.)			
☐ Other			
☐			
☐			
☐			
☐			
☐			
☐			
☐ √ here if additional pages are attached.			
Total Assets (add column B)	$ ________		

B. LIABILITIES:

DESCRIPTION OF ITEM(S). List a description of each separate debt owed by you (and/or your spouse, if this is a petition for dissolution of marriage). √ the box next to any debt(s) for which you believe you should be responsible.	Current Amount Owed	Nonmarital (√ correct column)	
		husband	wife
☐ Mortgages on real estate	$		
☐ Auto loans			
☐			
☐ Charge/credit card accounts			
☐			
☐			
☐			
☐ Other			
☐			
☐			
☐			
☐			
☐			
☐			
☐ √ here if additional pages are attached.			
Total Debts (add column B)	$________		

C. CONTINGENT ASSETS AND LIABILITIES:

INSTRUCTIONS: If you have any **POSSIBLE assets** (income potential, accrued vacation or sick leave, bonus, inheritance, etc.) or **POSSIBLE liabilities** (possible lawsuits, future unpaid taxes, contingent tax liabilities, debts assumed by another), you must list them here.

Contingent Assets √ the box next to any contingent asset(s) which you are requesting the judge award to you.	Possible Value	Nonmarital (√ correct column)	
		husband	wife
☐	$		
☐			
Total Contingent Assets	$________		

Contingent Liabilities √ the box next to any contingent debt(s) for which you believe you should be responsible.	Possible Amount Owed	Nonmarital (√ correct column)	
		husband	wife
☐	$		
☐			
Total Contingent Liabilities	$ ________		

SECTION IV. CHILD SUPPORT GUIDELINES WORKSHEET

(✎☐Florida Family Law Rules of Procedure Form 12.902(e), Child Support Guidelines Worksheet, MUST be filed with the court at or prior to a hearing to establish or modify child support. This requirement cannot be waived by the parties.) [√ **one** only]

____ **A Child Support Guidelines Worksheet IS or WILL BE filed in this case.** This case involves the establishment or modification of child support.

____ **A Child Support Guidelines Worksheet IS NOT being filed in this case.** The establishment or modification of child support is not an issue in this case.

I certify that a copy of this document was [√ **one** only] ( ) mailed ( ) faxed and mailed ( ) hand delivered to the person(s) listed below on *{date}* ________________________________.

Other party or his/her attorney:
Name: ______________________________
Address: ______________________________
City, State, Zip: ______________________________
Fax Number: ______________________________

I understand that I am swearing or affirming under oath to the truthfulness of the claims made in this affidavit and that the punishment for knowingly making a false statement includes fines and/or imprisonment.

Dated: ______________________

____
Signature of Party
Printed Name: ______________________________
Address: ______________________________
City, State, Zip: ______________________________
Telephone Number: ______________________________
Fax Number: ______________________________

STATE OF FLORIDA
COUNTY OF ____________________

Sworn to or affirmed and signed before me on ____________ by ______________________.

____
NOTARY PUBLIC or DEPUTY CLERK

____
[Print, type, or stamp commissioned name of notary or deputy clerk.]

____ Personally known
____ Produced identification
Type of identification produced ____________________

IF A NONLAWYER HELPED YOU FILL OUT THIS FORM, HE/SHE MUST FILL IN THE BLANKS BELOW: [✍ fill in **all** blanks]

I, *{full legal name and trade name of nonlawyer}*__________________________________,
a nonlawyer, located at *{street}* ___________________________, *{city}* ________________,
{state} ____________________, *{phone}* ____________, helped *{name}* ________________,
who is the [√ **one** only] ___ petitioner **or** ___ respondent, fill out this form.

IN THE CIRCUIT COURT OF THE ____________________ JUDICIAL CIRCUIT,
IN AND FOR ____________________ COUNTY, FLORIDA

Case No.: ____________________
Division: ____________________

____________________,
Petitioner,

and

____________________,
Respondent.

FAMILY LAW FINANCIAL AFFIDAVIT
($50,000 or more Individual Gross Annual Income)

I, *{full legal name}* ____________________
________, being sworn, certify that the following information is true:

SECTION I. INCOME

1. Date of Birth: ____________________
2. Social Security Number: ____________________
3. My occupation is: ____________________
4. I am currently

[√ **all** that apply]

____ a. Unemployed

Describe your efforts to find employment, how soon you expect to be employed, and the pay you expect to receive: ____________________

____

____ b. Employed by: ____________________

Address: ____________________

City, State, Zip code: ____________________

Telephone Number: ____________________

Pay rate: $ __________ ( ) every week ( ) every other week ( ) twice a month

( ) monthly ( ) other: ____________________

If you are expecting to become unemployed or change jobs soon, describe the change you expect and why and how it will affect your income: ____________________

____

□ Check here if you currently have more than one job. List the information above for the second job(s) on a separate sheet and attach it to this affidavit.

____ c. Retired. Date of retirement: ____________________

Employer from whom retired: ____________________

Address: ______________________________

City, State, Zip code: ____________________ Telephone Number: __________

LAST YEAR'S GROSS INCOME: Your Income Other Party's Income *(if known)*

YEAR ______________ $ ______________ $ _____

PRESENT MONTHLY GROSS INCOME:

All amounts must be MONTHLY. See the instructions with this form to figure out money amounts for anything that is NOT paid monthly. Attach more paper, if needed. Items included under "other" should be listed separately with separate dollar amounts.

1. Monthly gross salary or wages 1. $__________
2. Monthly bonuses, commissions, allowances, overtime, tips, and similar payments 2. __________
3. Monthly business income from sources such as self-employment, partnerships, close corporations, and/or independent contracts (Gross receipts minus ordinary and necessary expenses required to produce income.) 3. __________
   (□ Attach sheet itemizing such income and expenses.) 4. __________
4. Monthly disability benefits/SSI 5. __________
5. Monthly Workers' Compensation 6. __________
6. Monthly Unemployment Compensation 7. __________
7. Monthly pension, retirement, or annuity payments 8. __________
8. Monthly Social Security benefits
9. Monthly alimony actually received
   9a. From this case: $ ________ 9. __________
   9b. From other case(s): ________ Add 9a and 9b 10. __________
10. Monthly interest and dividends
11. Monthly rental income (gross receipts minus ordinary and necessary expenses required to produce income) (□ Attach sheet itemizing such income and expense items.) 11. __________ 12. __________
12. Monthly income from royalties, trusts, or estates
13. Monthly reimbursed expenses and in-kind payments to the extent that they reduce personal living expenses (□ Attach sheet itemizing each item and amount.) 13. __________
14. Monthly gains derived from dealing in property (not including nonrecurring gains) 14. __________

Any other income of a recurring nature (identify source) 15. __________

15. ______________________________ 16. __________

16. ______________________________

17. PRESENT MONTHLY GROSS INCOME (Add lines 1–16) **TOTAL:** **17. $** ________

PRESENT MONTHLY DEDUCTIONS:

All amounts must be MONTHLY. See the instructions with this form to figure out money amounts for anything that is NOT paid monthly.

18. Monthly federal, state, and local income tax (corrected for filing status and allowable dependents and income tax liabilities)
    a. Filing Status ____________
    b. Number of dependents claimed __________ 18. $__________

19. Monthly FICA or self-employment taxes 19. ________
20. Monthly Medicare payments 20. ________
21. Monthly mandatory union dues 21. ________
22. Monthly mandatory retirement payments 22. ________
23. Monthly health insurance payments (including dental insurance), excluding portion paid for any minor children of this relationship 23. ________
24. Monthly court-ordered child support actually paid for children from another relationship 24. ________
25. Monthly court-ordered alimony actually paid
    25a. from this case: $______
    25b. from other case(s): ______ Add 25a and 25b 25. ________

26. TOTAL DEDUCTIONS ALLOWABLE UNDER SECTION 61.30, FLORIDA STATUTES (Add lines 18 through 25) **TOTAL: 26. $** ____________

27. PRESENT NET MONTHLY INCOME (Subtract line 26 from line 17) **27. $** ____________

SECTION II. AVERAGE MONTHLY EXPENSES

Proposed/Estimated Expenses. If this is a dissolution of marriage case **and** your expenses as listed below do not reflect what you actually pay currently, you should write "estimate" next to each amount that is estimated.

HOUSEHOLD:

1. Monthly mortgage or rent payments 1. $________
2. Monthly property taxes (if not included in mortgage) 2. ________
3. Monthly insurance on residence (if not included in mortgage) 3. ________
4. Monthly condominium maintenance fees and homeowner's association fees 4. ________
5. Monthly electricity 5. ________
6. Monthly water, garbage, and sewer 6. ________
7. Monthly telephone 7. ________
8. Monthly fuel oil or natural gas 8. ________
9. Monthly repairs and maintenance 9. ________
10. Monthly lawn care 10. ________
11. Monthly pool maintenance 11. ________
12. Monthly pest control 12. ________
13. Monthly misc. household 13. ________
14. Monthly food and home supplies 14. ________
15. Monthly meals outside home 15. ________
16. Monthly cable t.v. 16. ________
17. Monthly alarm service contract 17. ________
18. Monthly service contracts on appliances 18. ________
19. Monthly maid service 19. ________

Other:

20. ______________________________ 20. ________
21. ______________________________ 21. ________
22. ______________________________ 22. ________
23. ______________________________ 23. ________

24. ____ 24. ________

25. **SUBTOTAL** (add lines 1 through 24) **25. $** __________

AUTOMOBILE:

26. Monthly gasoline and oil 26. $________
27. Monthly repairs 27. ________
28. Monthly auto tags and emission testing 28. ________
29. Monthly insurance 29. ________
30. Monthly payments (lease or financing) 30. ________
31. Monthly rental/replacements 31. ________
32. Monthly alternative transportation (bus, rail, car pool, etc.) 32. ________
33. Monthly tolls and parking 33. ________
34. Other: ______________________________________ 34. ________

35. **SUBTOTAL** (add lines 26 through 34) **35. $**__________

MONTHLY EXPENSES FOR CHILDREN COMMON TO BOTH PARTIES:

36. Monthly nursery, babysitting, or day care 36. $ ________
37. Monthly school tuition 37. ________
38. Monthly school supplies, books, and fees 38. ________
39. Monthly after school activities 39. ________
40. Monthly lunch money 40. ________
41. Monthly private lessons or tutoring 41. ________
42. Monthly allowances 42. ________
43. Monthly clothing and uniforms 43. ________
44. Monthly entertainment (movies, parties, etc.) 44. ________
45. Monthly health insurance 45. ________
46. Monthly medical, dental, prescriptions (nonreimbursed only) 46. ________
47. Monthly psychiatric/psychological/counselor 47. ________
48. Monthly orthodontic 48. ________
49. Monthly vitamins 49. ________
50. Monthly beauty parlor/barber shop 50. ________
51. Monthly nonprescription medication 51. ________
52. Monthly cosmetics, toiletries, and sundries 52. ________
53. Monthly gifts from child(ren) to others (other children, relatives, teachers, etc.) 53. ________
54. Monthly camp or summer activities 54. ________
55. Monthly clubs (Boy/Girl Scouts, etc.) 55. ________
56. Monthly access expenses (for nonresidential parent) 56. ________
57. Monthly miscellaneous 57. ________

58. **SUBTOTAL** (add lines 36 through 57) **58. $**__________

MONTHLY EXPENSES FOR CHILD(REN) FROM ANOTHER RELATIONSHIP: (other than court-ordered child support)

59. ____ 59. $________

60. ______________________________ 60. __________
61. ______________________________ 61. __________
62. ______________________________ 62. __________

63. **SUBTOTAL** (add lines 59 through 62) **63. $**__________

MONTHLY INSURANCE:

64. Health insurance, excluding portion paid for any minor child(ren) of this relationship 64. $__________
65. Life insurance 65. __________
66. Dental insurance 66. __________

Other:

67. ______________________________ 67. __________
68. ______________________________ 68. __________

69. **SUBTOTAL** (add lines 64 through 68) **69. $**__________

OTHER MONTHLY EXPENSES NOT LISTED ABOVE:

70. Monthly dry cleaning and laundry 70. $__________
71. Monthly clothing 71. __________
72. Monthly medical, dental, and prescription (unreimbursed only) 72. __________
73. Monthly psychiatric, psychological, or counselor (unreimbursed only) 73. __________
74. Monthly non-prescription medications, cosmetics, toiletries, and sundries 74. __________
75. Monthly grooming 75. __________
76. Monthly gifts 76. __________
77. Monthly pet expenses 77. __________
78. Monthly club dues and membership 78. __________
79. Monthly sports and hobbies 79. __________
80. Monthly entertainment 80. __________
81. Monthly periodicals/books/tapes/CD's 81. __________
82. Monthly vacations 82. __________
83. Monthly religious organizations 83. __________
84. Monthly bank charges/credit card fees 84. __________
85. Monthly education expenses 85. __________

Other: (include any usual and customary expenses not otherwise mentioned in the items listed above)

86. ______________________________ 86. __________
87. ______________________________ 87. __________
88. ______________________________ 88. __________
89. ______________________________ 89. __________

90. **SUBTOTAL** (add lines 70 through 89) **90. $**__________

MONTHLY PAYMENTS TO CREDITORS: (only when payments are currently made by you on outstanding balances)

NAME OF CREDITOR(s):

91. ______________________________ 91. $__________
92. ______________________________ 92. __________
93. ______________________________ 93. __________
94. ______________________________ 94. __________

95. ____ 95. ________
96. ____ 96. ________
97. ____ 97. ________
98. ____ 98. ________
99. ____ 99. ________
100. ____ 100. ________
101. ____ 101. ________
102. ____ 102. ________
103. ____ 103. ________

104. **SUBTOTAL** (add lines 91 through 103) **104. $**__________

105. TOTAL MONTHLY EXPENSES:
(add lines 25, 35, 58, 63, 69, 90, and 104 of Section II, Expenses) **105. $** __________

SUMMARY

106. TOTAL PRESENT MONTHLY NET INCOME
(from line 27 of SECTION I. INCOME) **106. $**__________

107. TOTAL MONTHLY EXPENSES (from line 105 above) **107. $**__________

108. SURPLUS (If line 106 is more than line 107, subtract line 107 from line 106. This is the amount of your surplus. Enter that amount here.) **108. $**__________

109. (DEFICIT) (If line 107 is more than line 106, subtract line 106 from line 107. This is the amount of your deficit. Enter that amount here.) **109. ($**__________)

SECTION III. ASSETS AND LIABILITIES

A. ASSETS (This is where you list what you OWN.)

INSTRUCTIONS:

STEP 1: **In column A,** list a description of each separate item owned by you (and/or your spouse, if this is a petition for dissolution of marriage). Blank spaces are provided if you need to list more than one of an item.

STEP 2: If this is a petition for dissolution of marriage, check the box **in Column A** next to any item that you are requesting the judge award to you.

STEP 3: **In column B,** write what you believe to be the current fair market value of all items listed.

STEP 4: **Use column C only if this is a petition for dissolution of marriage and you believe an item is "nonmarital," meaning it belongs to only one of you and should not be divided.** You should indicate to whom you believe the item belongs. (Typically, you will only use Column C if property was owned by one spouse before the marriage. See the **"General Information for Self-Represented Litigants"** found at the beginning of these forms and section 61.075(1), Florida Statutes, for definitions of "marital" and "nonmarital" assets and liabilities.)

A ASSETS: DESCRIPTION OF ITEM(S) √ the box next to any asset(s) which you are requesting the judge award to you.	B Current Fair Market Value	C Nonmarital (√ correct column) husband	 wife
☐ Cash (on hand)	$		

A ASSETS: DESCRIPTION OF ITEM(S) √ the box next to any asset(s) which you are requesting the judge award to you.	B Current Fair Market Value	C Nonmarital (√ correct column) husband	 wife
☐ Cash (in banks or credit unions)			
☐			
☐ Stocks/Bonds			
☐			
☐			
☐ Notes (money owed to you in writing)			
☐			
☐			
☐ Money owed to you (not evidenced by a note)			
☐			
☐			
☐ Real estate: (Home)			
☐ (Other)			
☐			
☐			
☐			
☐			
☐			
☐ Business interests			
☐			
☐			
☐			
☐			
☐ Automobiles			
☐			
☐			
☐			
☐ Boats			
☐			
☐			
☐ Other vehicles			
☐			
☐			
☐ Retirement plans (Profit Sharing, Pension, IRA, 401(k)s, etc.)			
☐			
☐			

Florida Family Law Rules of Procedure Form 12.902(c), Family Law Financial Affidavit (9/00)

A ASSETS: DESCRIPTION OF ITEM(S) √ the box next to any asset(s) which you are requesting the judge award to you.	B Current Fair Market Value	C Nonmarital (√ correct column) husband	 wife
☐			
☐ Furniture & furnishings in home			
☐			
☐ Furniture & furnishings elsewhere			
☐			
☐ Collectibles			
☐			
☐ Jewelry			
☐			
☐ Life insurance (cash surrender value)			
☐			
☐			
☐ Sporting and entertainment (T.V., stereo, etc.) equipment			
☐			
☐			
☐			
☐			
☐ Other assets			
☐			
☐			
☐			
☐			
☐			
☐			
☐			
Total Assets (add column B)	$ ________		

B. LIABILITIES/DEBTS (This is where you list what you OWE.)

INSTRUCTIONS:

STEP 1: **In column A**, list a description of each separate debt owed by you (and/or your spouse, if this is a petition for dissolution of marriage). Blank spaces are provided if you need to list more than one of an item.

STEP 2: If this is a petition for dissolution of marriage, check the box **in Column A** next to any debt(s) for which you believe you should be responsible.

STEP 3: **In column B**, write what you believe to be the current amount owed for all items listed.

STEP 4: **Use column C only if this is a petition for dissolution of marriage and you believe an item is "nonmarital," meaning the debt belongs to only one of you and should not be divided.** You should indicate to whom you believe the debt belongs. (Typically, you will only use Column C if the debt was owed by one spouse before the marriage. See the **"General Information for Self-Represented Litigants"** found at the beginning of these forms and section 61.075(1), Florida Statutes, for definitions of "marital" and "nonmarital" assets and liabilities.)

A LIABILITIES: DESCRIPTION OF ITEM(S) √ the box next to any debt(s) for which you believe you should be responsible.	B Current Amount Owed	C Nonmarital (√ correct column) husband	 wife
☐ Mortgages on real estate: (Home)	$		
☐ (Other)			
☐			
☐			
☐ Charge/credit card accounts			
☐			
☐			
☐			
☐			
☐			
☐ Auto loan			
☐ Auto loan			
☐ Bank/Credit Union loans			
☐			
☐			
☐			
☐ Money you owe (not evidenced by a note)			
☐			
☐ Judgments			
☐			
☐ Other			
☐			
☐			
☐			
☐			
☐			
☐			
Total Debts (add column B)	$ ________		

C. NET WORTH (excluding contingent assets and liabilities)

Total Assets (enter total of Column B in Asset Table; Section A) $ ____________
Total Liabilities (enter total of Column B in Liabilities Table; Section B)$ ____________

TOTAL NET WORTH (Total Assets minus Total Liabilities)
(excluding contingent assets and liabilities) **$**____________

D. CONTINGENT ASSETS AND LIABILITIES

INSTRUCTIONS:

If you have any **POSSIBLE assets** (income potential, accrued vacation or sick leave, bonus, inheritance, etc.) or **POSSIBLE liabilities** (possible lawsuits, future unpaid taxes, contingent tax liabilities, debts assumed by another), you must list them here.

A Contingent Assets √ the box next to any contingent asset(s) which you are requesting the judge award to you.	B Possible Value	C Nonmarital (√ correct column)	
		husband	wife
☐	$		
☐			
☐			
☐			
☐			
Total Contingent Assets	$________		

A Contingent Liabilities √ the box next to any contingent debt(s) for which you believe you should be responsible.	B Possible Amount Owed	C Nonmarital (√ correct column)	
		husband	wife
☐	$		
☐			
☐			
☐			
☐			
Total Contingent Liabilities	$________		

E. Has there been any agreement between you and the other party that one of you will take responsibility for a debt and will hold the other party harmless from that debt? ( ) yes ( ) no

If yes, explain: ____

____

____

____

____

____

F. CHILD SUPPORT GUIDELINES WORKSHEET. ✎❑ Florida Family Law Rules of Procedure Form 12.902(e), Child Support Guidelines Worksheet, MUST be filed with the court at or prior to a hearing to establish or modify child support. This requirement cannot be waived by the parties.

[√ **one** only]

____ **A Child Support Guidelines Worksheet IS or WILL BE filed in this case.** This case involves the establishment or modification of child support.

____ **A Child Support Guidelines Worksheet IS NOT being filed in this case.** The establishment or modification of child support is not an issue in this case.

I certify that a copy of this financial affidavit was: ( ) mailed, ( ) faxed and mailed, or ( ) hand delivered to the person(s) listed below on *{date}* ______________________.

Other party or his/her attorney:
Name: ______________________
Address: ______________________
City, State, Zip: ______________________
Fax Number: ______________________

I understand that I am swearing or affirming under oath to the truthfulness of the claims made in this affidavit and that the punishment for knowingly making a false statement includes fines and/or imprisonment.

Dated: ______________________

____
Signature of Party
Printed Name: ______________________
Address: ______________________
City, State, Zip: ______________________
Telephone Number: ______________________
Fax Number: ______________________

STATE OF FLORIDA
COUNTY OF ______________________

Sworn to or affirmed and signed before me on ____________ by ______________________.

____
NOTARY PUBLIC or DEPUTY CLERK

____
[Print, type, or stamp commissioned name of notary or deputy clerk .]

____ Personally known
____ Produced identification
Type of identification produced ______________________

IF A NONLAWYER HELPED YOU FILL OUT THIS FORM, HE/SHE MUST FILL IN THE BLANKS BELOW: [✍ fill in **all** blanks]
I, *{full legal name and trade name of nonlawyer}* ______________________,
a nonlawyer, located at *{street}* ______________________, *{city}* ______________________,
{state} ______________________, *{phone}* ______________________, helped *{name}* ______________________,
who is the [√ **one** only] ___ petitioner **or** ___ respondent, fill out this form.

IN THE CIRCUIT COURT OF THE ______________________ JUDICIAL CIRCUIT,
IN AND FOR ______________________ COUNTY, FLORIDA

Case No.: ______________________
Division: ______________________

______________________________________,
Petitioner,

and

______________________________________,
Respondent.

UNIFORM CHILD CUSTODY JURISDICTION ACT (UCCJA) AFFIDAVIT

I, *{full legal name}* ______________________, being sworn, certify that the following statements are true:

1. The number of minor child(ren) subject to this proceeding is __________. The name, social security number, place of birth, birth date, and sex of each child; the present address, periods of residence, and places where each child has lived **within the past five (5) years**; and the name, present address, and relationship to the child of each person with whom the child has lived during that time are:

THE FOLLOWING INFORMATION IS TRUE ABOUT CHILD # __1__:

Child's Full Legal Name: ______________________ S.S. # ______________
Place of Birth: ______________ Date of Birth: ______________ Sex: ______________

Child's Residence for the past 5 years:

Dates (From/To)	Address (including city and state) where child lived	Name and present address of person child lived with	Relationship to child
____ /present*			
____/____			
____/____			
____/____			
____/____			
____/____			

*** If you are the petitioner in an injunction for protection against domestic violence case and you have filed Petitioner's Request for Confidential Filing of Address, ✎❑ Florida Supreme Court Approved Family Law Form 12.980(i), you should write "confidential" in any space on this form that would require you to enter the address where you are currently living.**

THE FOLLOWING INFORMATION IS TRUE ABOUT CHILD # ____:

Child's Full Legal Name: ______________________________ S.S. # ______________
Place of Birth: ______________ Date of Birth: ______________ Sex: ______________

Child's Residence for the past 5 years:

Dates (From/To)	Address (including city and state) where child lived	Name and present address of person child lived with	Relationship to child
_____/present			
_____/_____			
_____/_____			
_____/_____			
_____/_____			
_____/_____			

THE FOLLOWING INFORMATION IS TRUE ABOUT CHILD # ____:

Child's Full Legal Name: ______________________________ S.S. # ______________
Place of Birth: ______________ Date of Birth: ______________ Sex: ______________

Child's Residence for the past 5 years:

Dates (From/To)	Address (including city and state) where child lived	Name and present address of person child lived with	Relationship to child
_____/present			
_____/_____			
_____/_____			
_____/_____			
_____/_____			
_____/_____			

2. **Participation in custody proceeding(s):**

[√ **one** only]

____ I HAVE NOT participated as a party, witness, or in any capacity in any other litigation or custody proceeding in this or any other state, concerning custody of a child subject to this proceeding.

____ I HAVE participated as a party, witness, or in any capacity in any other litigation or custody

proceeding in this or another state, concerning custody of a child subject to this proceeding. Explain:
a. Name of each child: ______________________________
b. Type of proceeding: ______________________________
c. Court and state: ______________________________
d. Date of court order or judgment (if any): ______________________________

3. **Information about custody proceeding(s):**
[√ **one** only]
____ I HAVE NO INFORMATION of any custody proceeding pending in a court of this or any other state concerning a child subject to this proceeding.
___ I HAVE THE FOLLOWING INFORMATION concerning a custody proceeding pending in a court of this or another state concerning a child subject to this proceeding, other than set out in item 2. Explain:
a. Name of each child: ______________________________
b. Type of proceeding: ______________________________
c. Court and state: ______________________________
d. Date of court order or judgment (if any): ______________________________

4. **Persons not a party to this proceeding:**
[√ **one** only]
____ I DO NOT KNOW OF ANY PERSON not a party to this proceeding who has physical custody or claims to have custody or visitation rights with respect to any child subject to this proceeding.
____ I KNOW THAT THE FOLLOWING NAMED PERSON(S) not a party to this proceeding has (have) physical custody or claim(s) to have custody or visitation rights with respect to any child subject to this proceeding:
a. Name and address of person: ______________________________
____
( ) has physical custody ( ) claims custody rights ( ) claims visitation rights.
Name of each child: ______________________________
b. Name and address of person: ______________________________
____
( ) has physical custody ( ) claims custody rights ( ) claims visitation rights.
Name of each child: ______________________________
c. Name and address of person: ______________________________
____
( ) has physical custody ( ) claims custody rights ( ) claims visitation rights.
Name of each child: ______________________________

5. **Knowledge of prior child support proceedings:**
[√ **one** only]
____ The child(ren) described in this affidavit are NOT subject to existing child support order(s) in this or any state or territory.
____ The child(ren) described in this affidavit are subject to the following existing child support order(s):
a. Name of each child: ______________________________
b. Type of proceeding: ______________________________
c. Court and address: ______________________________
d. Date of court order/judgment (if any): ______________________________
e. Amount of child support paid and by whom: ______________________________

6. **I acknowledge that I have a continuing duty to advise this Court of any custody, visitation,**

child support, or guardianship proceeding (including dissolution of marriage, separate maintenance, child neglect, or dependency) concerning the child(ren) in this state or any other state about which information is obtained during this proceeding.

I certify that a copy of this document was [√ **one** only] ( ) mailed ( ) faxed and mailed ( ) hand delivered to the person(s) listed below on *{date}* ______________________.

Other party or his/her attorney:
Name: ______________________
Address: ______________________
City, State, Zip: ______________________
Fax Number: ______________________

I understand that I am swearing or affirming under oath to the truthfulness of the claims made in this affidavit and that the punishment for knowingly making a false statement includes fines and/or imprisonment.

Dated: ______________________

____
Signature of Party
Printed Name: ______________________
Address: ______________________
City, State, Zip: ______________________
Telephone Number: ______________________
Fax Number: ______________________

STATE OF FLORIDA
COUNTY OF ______________________

Sworn to or affirmed and signed before me on ______________ by ______________________.

____
NOTARY PUBLIC or DEPUTY CLERK

____
[Print, type, or stamp commissioned name of notary or clerk.]

____ Personally known
____ Produced identification
Type of identification produced ______________________

IF A NONLAWYER HELPED YOU FILL OUT THIS FORM, HE/SHE MUST FILL IN THE BLANKS BELOW: [✍ fill in **all** blanks]
I, *{full legal name and trade name of nonlawyer}* ______________________, a nonlawyer, located at *{street}* ______________________, *{city}* ______________________, *{state}* ______________________, *{phone}* ______________, helped *{name}* ______________________, who is the [√ **one** only] ___ petitioner **or** ___ respondent, fill out this form.

IN THE CIRCUIT COURT OF THE ______________________ JUDICIAL CIRCUIT,
IN AND FOR ______________________ COUNTY, FLORIDA

Case No.: ______________________
Division: ______________________

______________________,
Petitioner,

and

______________________,
Respondent.

CHILD SUPPORT GUIDELINES WORKSHEET

I, *{full legal name}* ______________________, certify that the following statements are true:

	FATHER	MOTHER	
1. PRESENT NET MONTHLY INCOME Enter the amount from line number 27, Section I of ✎❑ Florida Family Law Rules of Procedure Form 12.902(b) or (c), Financial Affidavit.	1a. $______	1b. $______	
2. COMBINED PRESENT NET MONTHLY INCOME Add 1a and 1b.			2. $______
3. BASIC MONTHLY OBLIGATION There is (are) *{number}* ______ minor child(ren) common to the parties. Using the amount on line 2, enter the appropriate amount from the child support guidelines chart.			3. $______
4. PERCENT OF FINANCIAL RESPONSIBILITY Divide the amount on line 1a by the amount on line 2 to get Father's percentage financial responsibility. Enter answer on line 4a.	4a. ______%		
Divide the amount on line 1b. by the amount on line 2 to get Mother's percentage financial responsibility. Enter answer on line 4b.		4b. ______%	
5. SHARE OF BASIC MONTHLY OBLIGATION Multiply the number on line 3 by the percent on line 4a to get Father's share of basic obligation. Enter answer on line 5a.	5a. $______		
Multiply the number on line 3 by the percent on line 4b to get Mother's share of basic obligation. Enter answer on line 5b.		5b. $______	

If the noncustodial parent does not exercise visitation at least 40 percent of the overnights in the year (146 overnights in the year) you should complete Nos. 6 through 9 and No. 17 below. If the noncustodial parent does exercise visitation at least 40 percent of the overnights in the year (146 overnights in the year), skip to No. 10 and complete Nos. 10 through 17 below.

6. TOTAL MONTHLY CHILD CARE COSTS

Child care costs should not exceed the level required to provide quality care from a licensed source for the child(ren). See section 61.30(7), Fla. Stat. for more information. 6. $________

7. PERCENTAGE OF CHILD CARE COSTS
Multiply the amount on line 6 by .75 (to determine 75% of the total child care costs). Enter answer on line 7. 7. $________

Multiply the number on line 4a by the amount on line 7 to get Father's share of the child care obligation. Enter answer on line 7a. 7a. $_______

Multiply the number on line 4b by the amount on line 7 to get Mother's share of the child care obligation. Enter answer on line 7b. 7b. $_______

8. TOTAL MONTHLY CHILD(REN)'S HEALTH INSURANCE COSTS
This is only amounts paid for insurance on the child(ren). Enter answer on line 8. 8. $________

Multiply the number on 4a by the amount on line 8 to get Father's share of the child(ren)'s health insurance obligation. Enter answer on line 8a. 8a. $_______

Multiply the number on 4b by the amount on line 8 to get Mother's share of the child(ren)'s health insurance obligation. Enter answer on line 8b. 8b. $_______

9. TOTAL MONTHLY OBLIGATION
Add lines 5a, 7a, and 8a to determine Father's total obligation. Enter answer on line 9a. 9a. $_______

Add lines 5b, 7b, and 8b to determine Mother's total obligation. Enter answer on line 9b. **Stop and continue to No. 17.** 9b. $______

Florida Family Law Rules of Procedure Form 12.902(e), Child Support Guidelines Worksheet (6/01)

10. SHARED PARENTING ADJUSTMENT

Multiply each line 5a and 5b by 1.5. Enter each answer on line 10a and 10b.

5a $________ 5b $________
1.5 1.5
10a. $______ 10b. $______

11. PERCENTAGE OF OVERNIGHT STAYS

The child(ren) spend(s)_______ Overnight stays with the father each year.

Using the number on the above line, multiply it by 100 and divide by 365. Enter this number on line 11a.

11a._______%

The child(ren) spend(s) _______ overnight stays with the mother each year.

Using the number on the above line, multiply it by 100 and divide by 365. Enter this number on line 11b.

11b. ______%

12. ADJUSTED FINANCIAL RESPONSIBILITY

Multiply the number on line 10a by the percent on line 11b to get father's financial responsibility. Enter answer on line 12a.

12a. _______

Multiply the number on line 10b by the percent on line 11a to get mother's financial responsibility. Enter answer on line12b.

12b. _______

13. TOTAL MONTHLY CHILD CARE COSTS

Calculate the net amount owed for the expenses incurred for day care. Child care costs should not exceed the level required to provide quality care from a licensed source for the child(ren). See section 61.30(7), Fla. Stat. for more information. Enter this amount on line 13. For purposes of calculating child support under this shared parenting arrangement, day care shall be calculated without regard to the 25% reduction.

13. $_________

Multiply the number on line 4a by the amount on line 13 to get the father's share of the child care obligation. Enter the answer on line 13a.

13a. $______

Multiply the number on line 4b by the amount on line13 to get the mother's share of the child care obligation. Enter the answer on line 13b.

13b. $______

14. TOTAL MONTHLY CHILD(REN)'S HEALTH INSURANCE COSTS

This is only amounts paid for insurance on the child(ren). Enter answer on line 14.

14. $_________

Multiply the number on line 4a by the amount on line 14 to get father's share of the child(ren)'s health insurance obligation. Enter answer on line 14a. 14a. $______

Multiply the number on line 4b by the amount on line 14 to get mother's share of the child(ren)'s health insurance obligation. Enter answer on line 14b. 14b. $______

15. TOTAL MONTHLY OBLIGATION

Add lines 12a, 13a, and 14a to determine father's total obligation. Enter answer on line 15a. 15a. $______

Add lines 12b, 13b, and 14b to determine mother's total obligation. Enter answer on line 15b. 15b. $______

16. MONETARY TRANSFER

Using the amounts on lines 15a and 15b, subtract the lesser number from the greater number. Enter the answer on line 16. If the number on line 15a is the lesser number, the amount on line 16 shall be paid to the father, subject to any direct payments for child care or health insurance expense. If the number on line 15b is the lesser number, the amount on line 16 shall be paid to the mother, subject to any direct payments for child or health insurance expense.

16. $______

17. ADJUSTMENTS TO GUIDELINES AMOUNT. If you or the other parent are requesting the Court to award a child support amount that is more or less than the child support guidelines, you must complete and file Motion to Deviate from Child Support Guidelines, ✎❑ Florida Supreme Court Approved Family Law Form 12.943.

[√ **one** only]

____ a. **Deviation from the guidelines amount is requested.** The Motion to Deviate from Child Support Guidelines, ✎❑ Florida Supreme Court Approved Family Law Form 12.943, is attached.

____ b. **Deviation from the guidelines amount is NOT requested.** The Motion to Deviate from Child Support Guidelines, ✎❑ Florida Supreme Court Approved Family Law Form 12.943, is not attached.

I certify that a copy of this document was [√ **one** only] ( ) mailed ( ) faxed and mailed ( ) hand delivered to the person(s) listed below on *{date}* ______________________.

Other party or his/her attorney:

Name: ______________________

Address: ______________________

City, State, Zip: ______________________

Fax Number: ______________________

Date: ______________________

____

Signature of Party

Printed Name: ______________________

Address: ______________________

City, State, Zip: ______________________

Telephone Number: ______________________

Fax Number: ______________________

STATE OF FLORIDA

COUNTY OF ______________________

Sworn to or affirmed and signed before me on ______________________ by ______________.

____

NOTARY PUBLIC or DEPUTY CLERK

____

[Print, type, or stamp commissioned name of notary or deputy clerk .]

____ Personally known
____ Produced identification
Type of identification produced ______________________

IF A NONLAWYER HELPED YOU FILL OUT THIS FORM, HE/SHE MUST FILL IN THE BLANKS BELOW: [✍ fill in **all** blanks]
I, *{full legal name and trade name of nonlawyer}* ______________________________,
a nonlawyer, located at *{street}* ______________________, *{city}* ______________,
{state} ______________________, *{phone}* ______________________, helped
{name} ____,
who is the [√ **one** only] ___ petitioner **or** ___ respondent, fill out this form.

IN THE CIRCUIT COURT OF THE ____________________ JUDICIAL CIRCUIT,
IN AND FOR ____________________ COUNTY, FLORIDA

Case No.: ____________________
Division: ____________________

____________________,
Petitioner,

and

____________________,
Respondent.

NOTICE OF SOCIAL SECURITY NUMBER

I, *{full legal name}* ____________________, certify that my social security number is ____________________, as required in section 61.052(7), sections 61.13(9) or (10), section 742.031(3), sections 742.032(1)–(3), and/or sections 742.10(1)–(2), Florida Statutes. My date of birth is ____________________.

[√ **one** only]

___ 1. This notice is being filed in a dissolution of marriage case in which the parties have **no** minor children in common.

___ 2. This notice is being filed in a paternity or child support case, or in a dissolution of marriage in which the parties have minor children in common. The minor child(ren)'s name(s), date(s) of birth, and social security number(s) is/are:

Name	**Birth date**	**Social Security Number**

{Attach additional pages if necessary.}

Disclosure of social security numbers shall be limited to the purpose of administration of the Title IV-D program for child support enforcement.

I understand that I am swearing or affirming under oath to the truthfulness of the claims made in this notice and that the punishment for knowingly making a false statement includes fines and/or imprisonment.

Dated: ______________________

____
Signature
Printed Name: ______________________
Address: ______________________
City, State, Zip: ______________________
Telephone Number: ______________________
Fax Number: ______________________

STATE OF FLORIDA
COUNTY OF ________

Sworn to or affirmed and signed before me on ____________ by ______________________.

____
NOTARY PUBLIC or DEPUTY CLERK

____
[Print, type, or stamp commissioned name of notary or clerk]

___ Personally known
___ Produced identification
Type of identification produced ______________________

IF A NONLAWYER HELPED YOU FILL OUT THIS FORM, HE/SHE MUST FILL IN THE BLANKS BELOW: [✍ fill in **all** blanks]

I, *{full legal name and trade name of nonlawyer}* ______________________, a nonlawyer, located at *{street}* ______________________, *{city}* ____________, *{state}* ________, *{phone}* ____________, helped *{name}* ______________________, who is the [√ **one** only] ___ petitioner **or** ___ respondent, fill out this form.

IN THE CIRCUIT COURT OF THE ______________ JUDICIAL CIRCUIT,
IN AND FOR ______________ COUNTY, FLORIDA

Case No.: ______________
Division: ______________

______________,
Petitioner,

and

______________,
Respondent.

ANSWER TO SUPPLEMENTAL PETITON

I, {full legal name} ______________, being sworn, certify that the following information is true:

1. I **agree** with ( ) Petitioner ( ) Respondent as to the allegations raised in the following numbered paragraphs in the Supplemental Petition and, therefore, **admit** those allegations: *{indicate section and paragraph number}* ______________.

2. I **disagree** with ( ) Petitioner ( ) Respondent as to the allegations in the following numbered paragraphs in the Supplemental Petition and, therefore, **deny** those allegations: *{indicate section and paragraph number}* ______________.

3. I currently am unable to admit or deny the following paragraphs due to lack of information: *{indicate section and paragraph number}* ______________.

4. A completed Financial Affidavit, ✎ ❑ Florida Family Law Form 12.901(d) or (e), is, or will be, filed.

5. A completed Notice of Social Security Number, ✎ ❑ Florida Family Law Form 12.901(J), is filed with this answer, if one has not been previously filed in this case.

[✔ **if** applies]

___ 6. This case involves custody or visitation with a minor child(ren), and a completed Uniform Child Custody Jurisdiction Act (UCCJA) Affidavit, ✎ ❑ Florida Family Law Form 12.901(f), is filed with this answer.

___ 7. This case involves child support, and a completed **Child Support Guidelines Worksheet**, ✎ ❑ Florida Family Law Form 12.901(g), is, filed or will be filed with the court.

I certify that a copy of this document was [✔ **one** only] ( ) mailed ( ) faxed and mailed ( ) hand delivered to the person(s) listed below on {date} ______________.

Petitioner/Respondent or his/her attorney:
Name: ______________
Address: ______________
City, State, Zip: ______________
Fax Number: ______________

I understand that I am swearing or affirming under oath to the truthfulness of the claims made in this answer and that the punishment for knowingly making a false statement includes fines and/or imprisonment.

Dated: ______________________________

____
Signature of Party
Printed name: ______________________________
Address: ______________________________
City, State, Zip: ______________________________
Telephone Number: ______________________________
Fax Number: ______________________________

STATE OF FLORIDA
COUNTY OF ______________________
Sworn to or affirmed and signed before me on ____________________ by ______________________________.

____
NOTARY PUBLIC—STATE OF FLORIDA

____
[Print, type, or stamp commissioned name of notary.]

____ Personally known
____ Produced identification
Type of identification produced ________________________

IF A NONLAWYER HELPED YOU FILL OUT THIS FORM, HE/SHE MUST FILL IN THE BLANKS BELOW: [✍ fill in **all** blanks]

I, *{full legal name and trade name of nonlawyer}* ______________________________, a nonlawyer, located at *{street}* ______________________________, *{city}* ______________________, *{state}* ________________, *{phone}* ________________, helped *{name}* ______________________________, who is the petitioner/respondent, fill out this form

CIVIL COVER SHEET

The civil cover sheet and the information contained herein neither replace nor supplement the filing and service of pleadings or other papers as required by law. This form is required for the use of the Clerk of Court for the purpose of reporting judicial workload data pursuant to Florida Statute 25.075.

NAME OF COURT: FAMILY LAW, CIRCUIT COURT

I. CASE STYLE

____

PETITIONER,

Case #: ____________________

vs.

Division: ____________________

____

RESPONDENT.

II. TYPE OF CASE

(Place an x in one box only. If the case fits more than one type of case, select the most definite.)

Domestic Relations	Torts	Other Civil
☐ Simplified dissolution	☐ Professional Malpractice	☐ Contracts
☐ Dissolution	☐ Products liability	☐ Condominium
☐ Support - IV-D	☐ Auto negligence	☐ Real property/ Mortgage foreclosure
☐ Support - Non IV-D	☐ Other negligence	☐ Eminent domain
☐ URESA - IV-D		☐ Other
☐ Domestic violence		
☐ Other domestic relations		

III. IS JURY TRIAL DEMANDED IN COMPLAINT? ☐ Yes ☒ No

DATE______________________________

____

SIGNATURE OF ATTORNEY OR PARTY INITIATING ACTION:

ADDRESS ____

____

PHONE:____

FINAL DISPOSITION FORM

This form is required for the use of the Clerk of Court for the purpose of reporting judicial workload data pursuant to Florida Statute 25.075.

NAME OF COURT: FAMILY LAW, CIRCUIT COURT

I. CASE STYLE

____
PETITIONER,

Case #: ____________________

vs.

Division: ____________________

____
RESPONDENT.

II. MEANS OF FINAL DISPOSTION (Place an "x" in one box only.)

- ☐ Dismissed Before Hearing
- ☐ Dismissed After Hearing
- ☐ Disposed by Default
- ☐ Disposed by Judge
- ☐ Disposed by Non-Jury Trial
- ☐ Disposed by Jury Trial
- ☐ Other

DATE______________________

____
SIGNATURE OF ATTORNEY OR PARTY INITIATING ACTION:

ADDRESS ______________________________
____

PHONE:______________________________

IN THE CIRCUIT COURT OF THE ______________________ JUDICIAL CIRCUIT,
IN AND FOR ______________________ COUNTY, FLORIDA

Case No.: ______________________
Division: ______________________

______________________,
Petitioner,

and

______________________,
Respondent.

PETITION FOR SUPPORT UNCONNECTED WITH DISSOLUTION OF MARRIAGE WITH DEPENDENT OR MINOR CHILD(REN)

I, *{full legal name}* ______________________________________, the [**one** only] ( ) Husband ( ) Wife, being sworn, certify that the following statements are true:

1. JURISDICTION
( ) Husband ( ) Wife ( ) Both live in Florida at the filing of this Petition for Support Unconnected with Dissolution of Marriage, which is filed pursuant to section 61.09, Florida Statutes.

2. Petitioner [**one** only] ( ) is ( ) is not a member of the military service.
Respondent [**one** only] ( ) is ( ) is not a member of the military service.

3. MARRIAGE HISTORY
Date of marriage: *{month, day, year}* ______________________
Place of marriage: *{city, state, country}* ______________________
Date of separation: *{month, day, year}* ______________________ (if approximate)

4. MINOR CHILD(REN)
[**all** that apply]
____ a. The wife is pregnant. The baby is due on: *{date}* ______________.
____ b. The minor (under 18) child(ren) common to both parties are:

Name	Place of Birth	Birth date	Sex

____ c. The minor child(ren) born or conceived during the marriage who are **not** common to both parties are:

Name	Place of Birth	Birth date	Sex

The birth father(s) of the above minor child(ren) is (are) *{name and address}* ______________

____

____ d. The child(ren) common to both parties who are 18 or older but who are dependent upon the parties due to a mental or physical incapacity are:

Name	Place of Birth	Birth date	Sex

5. A completed Notice of Social Security Number, □ □ Florida Supreme Court Approved Family Law Form 12.902(j), is filed with this petition.

6. A completed Family Law Financial Affidavit, □ □ Florida Family Law Rules of Procedure Form 12.902(b) or (c), is, or will be, filed.

7. A completed Child Support Guidelines Worksheet, □ □ Florida Family Law Rules of Procedure Form 12.902(e), is, or will be, filed.

SECTION I. SPOUSAL SUPPORT (ALIMONY)

[□ **one** only]

____ 1. Petitioner does not request spousal support (alimony) from Respondent at this time.

____ 2. Respondent has the ability to contribute to the maintenance of Petitioner and has failed to do so. Petitioner requests that the Court order Respondent to pay the following spousal support (alimony) and claims that he or she has a need for the support that he or she is requesting. Spousal support (alimony) is requested in the amount of $ ____________ every ( ) week ( ) other week ( ) month, beginning *{date}* _________, and continuing until *{date or event}* _______________
____.

Explain why the Court should order Respondent to pay and any specific request(s) for type of alimony (temporary, permanent, rehabilitative, and/or lump sum): ____________________
____
____
____
____
____
____
____

[□ **if** applies] ( ) Petitioner requests life insurance on Respondent's life, provided by Respondent, to secure such support.

SECTION II. CHILD SUPPORT

Respondent has the ability to contribute to the maintenance of his or her minor child(ren) and has failed to do so. Petitioner has custody of the minor child(ren) or the child(ren) has (have) primary residence with Petitioner.

[□ **all** that apply]

____ 1. Petitioner requests that the Court award child support as determined by Florida's child support guidelines, section 61.30, Florida Statutes.

____ 2. Petitioner requests that the Court award child support to be paid beyond the age of 18 years because:

____ a. the following child(ren), *{name(s)}* ______________________________,
is (are) dependent because of a mental or physical incapacity which began prior to the age of 18 *{explain}:* ______________________________
____
______________________________.

____ b. the following child(ren), *{name(s)}* ______________________________,
is (are) dependent in fact and is (are) in high school while he/she (they) are between the ages of 18 and 19; said child(ren) is (are) performing in good faith with reasonable expectation of graduation before the age of 19.

____ 3. Petitioner requests that medical/dental insurance coverage for the minor child(ren) be provided by: [**one** only]

____ a. Father.
____ b. Mother.

____ 4. Petitioner requests that uninsured medical/dental expenses for the child(ren) be paid: [**one** only]

____ a. by Father.
____ b. by Mother.
____ c. by Father and Mother each paying one-half.
____ d. according to the percentages in the Child Support Guidelines Worksheet, Florida Family Law Rules of Procedure Form 12.902(e).
____ e. Other *{explain}*: ______________________________
____
____

____ 5. Petitioner requests that life insurance to secure child support be provided by:

____ a. Father.
____ b. Mother.
____ c. Both.

SECTION III. OTHER RELIEF

____
____
____
____
____
____

SECTION IV. PETITIONER'S REQUEST (This section summarizes what you are asking the Court to include in the order for support.)

Petitioner requests that the Court enter an order establishing support **and**:
[**all** that apply]

____ a. awarding spousal support (alimony) as requested in Section I of this petition;
____ b. establishing child support for the minor child(ren) common to both parties, as requested in Section II of this petition;
____ c. awarding other relief as requested in Section III of this petition; and any other terms the Court deems necessary.

I understand that I am swearing or affirming under oath to the truthfulness of the claims made in this petition and that the punishment for knowingly making a false statement includes fines and/or imprisonment.

Dated: ____________________

____
Signature of Petitioner
Printed Name: ______________________________
Address: __________________________________
City, State, Zip: ____________________________
Telephone Number: __________________________
Fax Number: _______________________________

STATE OF FLORIDA
COUNTY OF ______________________

Sworn to or affirmed and signed before me on ______________ by ____________________.

____
NOTARY PUBLIC or DEPUTY CLERK

____
[Print, type, or stamp commissioned name of notary or clerk.]

____ Personally known
____ Produced identification
Type of identification produced ______________________

IF A NONLAWYER HELPED YOU FILL OUT THIS FORM, HE/SHE MUST FILL IN THE BLANKS BELOW: [fill in **all** blanks]
I, *{full legal name and trade name of nonlawyer}* ______________________________,
a nonlawyer, located at *{street}* ______________________, *{city}* ______________,
{state} ______________, *{phone}* ______________, helped *{name}* ______________,
who is the petitioner, fill out this form.

IN THE CIRCUIT COURT OF THE ________________________ JUDICIAL CIRCUIT,
IN AND FOR __________________________ COUNTY, FLORIDA

Case No.: __________________________
Division: __________________________

____________________________________,
Petitioner,

and

____________________________________,
Respondent.

JOINT PETITION TO MODIFY JUDGMENT DISSOLVING MARRIAGE

This request of the parties shows:

1. We, the parties in this action, were divorced on ______________________, _________. A copy of the final judgment dissolving marriage is attached.

2. We have agreed, and hereby stipulate, to a change in the terms of the judgment as indicated below, and request this court to issue an order so modifying our judgment:

❑ Child support shall be ❑ increased ❑ decreased to the sum of $_________________ per ____________________________________, on the same terms, methods, and conditions of payment as stated in the final judgment or most recent modification thereof.

❑ Primary parental responsibility/custody of the minor child(ren) shall be changed to the ❑ husband ❑ wife, until ____ ____, or until further order of this court.

❑ The non-custodial parent's visitation with the minor child(ren) shall be changed to:

❑ Alimony shall be be ❑ increased ❑ decreased to the sum of $_______________ per ________________________________, on the same terms, methods, and conditions of payment as stated in the final judgment or most recent modification thereof..

❑ Other agreed provisions:

3. We further agree that this/these modification(s) is/are to become effective immediately.

4. The modification(s) requested is/are in the best interest of the parties and our minor child(ren).

5. All other provisions of the final judgment, or any subsequest modification thereof, which are not in conflict with the changes indicated above shall remain in full force and effect.

DATED: ____________________________ DATED: ____________________________

____________________________ ____________________________
Signature Signature

Name ____________________________ Name ____________________________
Address __________________________ Address __________________________
__________________________ __________________________
Telephone No. ______________________ Telephone No. ______________________

IF A NONLAWYER HELPED YOU FILL OUT THIS FORM, HE/SHE MUST FILL IN THE BLANKS BELOW: [✍ fill in **all** blanks]

I, *{full legal name and trade name of nonlawyer}* ____,
a nonlawyer, located at *{street}* ______________________________.*{city}* ____________________,
{state} ______________, *{phone}* ____________________, helped *{name}* ____________________,
who is the petitioner/respondent, fill out this form.

IN THE CIRCUIT COURT OF THE ____________________ JUDICIAL CIRCUIT,
IN AND FOR ______________________ COUNTY, FLORIDA

Case No.: ______________________
Division: ______________________

______________________________,
Petitioner,

and

______________________________,
Respondent.

ORDER MODIFYING JUDGMENT DISSOLVING MARRIAGE

THIS CAUSE, having come before the court on the parties' Joint Petition to Modify Judgment Dissolving Marriage,

IT IS HEREBY ORDERED that:

❑ Child support shall be ❑ increased ❑ decreased to the sum of $______________ per ____________________________, on the same terms, methods, and conditions of payment as stated in the final judgment or most recent modification thereof..

❑ Primary parental responsibility/custody of the minor child(ren) shall be changed to the ❑ husband ❑ wife, until ______________________________________ ____________________________________, or until further order of this court.

❑ The non-custodial parent's visitation with the minor child(ren) shall be changed to:

❑ Alimony shall be be ❑ increased ❑ decreased to the sum of $_______________ per ________________________________, on the same terms, methods, and conditions of payment as stated in the final judgment or most recent modification thereof..

❑ Other provisions:

This order is effective immediately, and all other provisions of the final judgment, or any subsequest modification thereof, which are not in conflict with this order shall remain in full force and effect.

DATED: ____________________________

____
CIRCUIT JUDGE

Copies furnished to:

Husband or Attorney for Husband
Name ______________________________
Address ____________________________
____
Telephone No. ______________________

Wife or Attorney for Wife
Name ______________________________
Address ____________________________
____
Telephone No. ______________________

IN THE CIRCUIT COURT OF THE ____________________________ JUDICIAL CIRCUIT,
IN AND FOR ____________________________ COUNTY, FLORIDA

Case No.: ____________________________
Division: ____________________________

____,
Petitioner,

and

____,
Respondent.

SUPPLEMENTAL PETITION TO MODIFY CUSTODY OR VISITATION AND OTHER RELIEF

I, *{full legal name}* ____, being sworn, certify that the following information is true:

1. The parties to this action were granted a final judgment of ( ) dissolution of marriage ( ) paternity on *{date}* __________________. A copy of the final judgment and any modification(s) is attached.

2. Paragraph(s) ______________ of the ( ) final judgment or ( ) most recent modification thereof describes the present custody and/or visitation ordered.

3. Since the final judgment or last modification thereof, there has been a substantial change in circumstances, requiring a modification in custody or visitation. Those substantial changes are as follows: *{explain}* ____
____
____
____
____
____
____
____
____

4. I ask the Court to modify the ( ) custody ( ) visitation as follows: *{explain}* ______________
____
____
____
____
____
____
____

5. This modification is in the best interests of the child(ren) because: *{explain}* ________________
____

____

____

____

6. If the requested modification is granted, Petitioner requests that child support be modified, consistent with the modification of custody or visitation. A Child Support Guidelines Worksheet, □ □ Florida Family Law Rules of Procedure Form 12.902(e), is, or will be filed.

7. A completed Family Law Financial Affidavit, □ □ Florida Family Law Rules of Procedure Form 12.902(b) or (c), is, or will be, filed.

8. A completed Uniform Child Custody Jurisdiction Act (UCCJA) Affidavit, □ □ Florida Supreme Court Approved Family Law Form 12.902(d), is filed with this petition.

9. If not previously filed in this case, a completed Notice of Social Security Number, □ □ Florida Supreme Court Approved Family Law Form 12.902(j), is filed with this petition.

10. Other:____

____

____

I understand that I am swearing or affirming under oath to the truthfulness of the claims made in this petition and that the punishment for knowingly making a false statement includes fines and/or imprisonment.

Dated: ____________________________

____
Signature of Party
Printed Name: ______________________
Address: ___________________________
City, State, Zip: ____________________
Telephone Number: __________________
Fax Number: ________________________

STATE OF FLORIDA
COUNTY OF ______________________

Sworn to or affirmed and signed before me on ______________ by ________________________.

____
NOTARY PUBLIC or DEPUTY CLERK

____
[Print, type, or stamp commissioned name of notary or clerk.]

____ Personally known
____ Produced identification
Type of identification produced ______________________

IF A NONLAWYER HELPED YOU FILL OUT THIS FORM, HE/SHE MUST FILL IN THE BLANKS BELOW: [fill in **all** blanks]

I, *{full legal name and trade name of nonlawyer}* ____,
a nonlawyer, located at *{street}* _______________________________, *{city}* ____________________,
{state} ____________________, *{phone}* ________________, helped *{name}* ___________________,
who is the [**one** only] ___ petitioner or ___ respondent, fill out this form.

IN THE CIRCUIT COURT OF THE ____________________________ JUDICIAL CIRCUIT,
IN AND FOR ______________________________ COUNTY, FLORIDA

Case No.: ______________________________
Division: ______________________________

______________________________________,
Petitioner,

and

______________________________________,
Respondent.

SUPPLEMENTAL PETITION FOR MODIFICATION OF CHILD SUPPORT

I, *{full legal name}* ______________________________________, being sworn, certify that the following information is true:

1. The parties to this action were granted a final judgment ( ) of dissolution of marriage ( ) of paternity ( ) for support unconnected with a dissolution of marriage on *{date}* ______________. A copy of the final judgment and any modification(s) is attached.

2. Paragraph(s) ______________ of the ( ) final judgment or ( ) most recent modification thereof establishes the present child support at $ ____________ every ( ) week ( ) other week ( ) month, beginning on *{date}* __________________.

3. Since the final judgment or most recent modification thereof, there has been a substantial change in circumstances, requiring a modification in child support. This change in circumstance is as follows: *{explain}* ____
____
____
____
____
____
____
____
____

4. I ask the Court to modify child support as follows: *{explain}* ______________________________
____
____
____
____
____
____
____

5. This change is in the best interests of the child(ren) because: *{explain}* ____________________
____

____
____
____
____
____
____
____

6. A completed Family Law Financial Affidavit, Florida Family Law Rules of Procedure Form 12.902(b) or (c), is, or will be, filed.

7. If not previously filed in this case, a completed Notice of Social Security Number, Florida Supreme Court Approved Family Law Form 12.902(j), is filed.

8. A Child Support Guidelines Worksheet, Florida Family Law Rules of Procedure Form 12.902(e), is, or will be, filed.

9. Other: ____
____
____
____
____

I understand that I am swearing or affirming under oath to the truthfulness of the claims made in this petition and that the punishment for knowingly making a false statement includes fines and/or imprisonment.

Dated: ____________________________

____
Signature of Party
Printed Name: ____________________________
Address: ________________________________
City, State, Zip: __________________________
Telephone Number: ________________________
Fax Number: ______________________________

STATE OF FLORIDA
COUNTY OF ______________________

Sworn to or affirmed and signed before me on _______________ by ____________________________.

____
NOTARY PUBLIC or DEPUTY CLERK

____
[Print, type, or stamp commissioned name of notary or clerk.]

____ Personally known

____ Produced identification
Type of identification produced ________________________

IF A NONLAWYER HELPED YOU FILL OUT THIS FORM, HE/SHE MUST FILL IN THE BLANKS BELOW: [fill in **all** blanks]
I, *{full legal name and trade name of nonlawyer}* ____,
a nonlawyer, located at *{street}*_________________________________, *{city}* ___________________,
{state} ___________________, *{phone}* _________________, helped *{name}* ___________________,
who is the [**one** only] ___ petitioner **or** ___ respondent, fill out this form.

IN THE CIRCUIT COURT OF THE ______________________ JUDICIAL CIRCUIT,
IN AND FOR ______________________ COUNTY, FLORIDA

Case No.: ______________________
Division: ______________________

______________________,
Petitioner,

and

______________________,
Respondent.

SUMMONS: PERSONAL SERVICE ON AN INDIVIDUAL
ORDEN DE COMPARECENCIA: SERVICIO PERSONAL EN UN INDIVIDUO
CITATION: L'ASSIGNATION PERSONAL SUR UN INDIVIDUEL

TO/PARA/A: *{enter other party's full legal name}* ______________________,
{address(including city and state)/location for service} ______________________.

IMPORTANT

A lawsuit has been filed against you. You have **20 calendar days** after this summons is served on you to file a written response to the attached complaint/petition with the clerk of this circuit court, located at: *{street address}* ______________________.
A phone call will not protect you. Your written response, including the case number given above and the names of the parties, must be **filed** if you want the Court to hear your side of the case.

If you do not file your written response on time, you may lose the case, and your wages, money, and property may be taken thereafter without further warning from the Court. There are other legal requirements. You may want to call an attorney right away. If you do not know an attorney, you may call an attorney referral service or a legal aid office (listed in the phone book).

If you choose to file a written response yourself, at the same time you file your written response to the Court, you must also mail or take a copy of your written response to the party serving this summons at:
{Name and address of party serving summons} ______________________
______________________.

Copies of all court documents in this case, including orders, are available at the Clerk of the Circuit Court's office. You may review these documents, upon request.

You must keep the Clerk of the Circuit Court's office notified of your current address. (You may file Notice of Current Address, Florida Supreme Court Approved Family Law Form 12.915.) Future papers in this lawsuit will be mailed to the address on record at the clerk's office.

WARNING: Rule 12.285, Florida Family Law Rules of Procedure, requires certain automatic disclosure of documents and information. Failure to comply can result in sanctions,

including dismissal or striking of pleadings.

IMPORTANTE

Usted ha sido demandado legalmente. Tiene veinte (20) dias, contados a partir del recibo de esta notificacion, para contestar la demanda adjunta, por escrito, y presentarla ante este tribunal. Localizado en: ______________________________. Una llamada telefonica no lo protegera. Si usted desea que el tribunal considere su defensa, debe presentar su respuesta por escrito, incluyendo el numero del caso y los nombres de las partes interesadas. Si usted no contesta la demanda a tiempo, pudiese perder el caso y podria ser despojado de sus ingresos y propiedades, o privado de sus derechos, sin previo aviso del tribunal. Existen otros requisitos legales. Si lo desea, usted puede consultar a un abogado inmediatamente. Si no conoce a un abogado, puede llamar a una de las oficinas de asistencia legal que aparecen en la guia telefonica.

Si desea responder a la demanda por su cuenta, al mismo tiempo en que presente su respuesta ante el tribunal, usted debe enviar por correo o entregar una copia de su respuesta a la persona denominada abajo.

Si usted elige presentar personalmente una respuesta por escrito, en el mismo momento que usted presente su respuesta por escrito al Tribunal, usted debe enviar por correo o llevar una copia de su respuesta por escrito a la parte entregando esta orden de comparencencia a:

Nombre y direccion de la parte que entrega la orden de comparencencia: ______________________________

____.

Copias de todos los documentos judiciales de este caso, incluyendo las ordenes, estan disponibles en la oficina del Secretario de Juzgado del Circuito [Clerk of the Circuit Court's office]. Estos documentos pueden ser revisados a su solicitud.

Usted debe de manener informada a la oficina del Secretario de Juzgado del Circuito de su direccion actual. (Usted puede presentar ______ el Formulario: Ley de Familia de la Florida 12.915, [Florida Supreme Court Approved Family Law Form 12.915], Notificacion de la Direccion Actual [Notice of Current Address].) Los papelos que se presenten en el futuro en esta demanda judicial seran env ados por correo a la direccion que este registrada en la oficina del Secretario.

ADVERTENCIA: Regla 12.285 (Rule 12.285), de las Reglas de Procedimiento de Ley de Familia de la Florida [Florida Family Law Rules of Procedure], requiere cierta revelacion automatica de documentos e informacion. El incumplimient, puede resultar en sanciones, incluyendo la desestimacion o anulacion de los alegatos.

IMPORTANT

Des poursuites judiciaries ont ete entreprises contre vous. Vous avez 20 jours consecutifs a partir de la date de l'assignation de cette citation pour deposer une reponse ecrite a la plainte ci-jointe aupres de ce tribunal. Qui se trouve a: *{L'Adresse}* ______________________________. Un simple coup de telephone est insuffisant pour vous proteger; vous etes obliges de deposer votre reponse ecrite, avec mention du numero de dossier ci-dessus et du nom des parties nommees ici, si vous souhaitez que le tribunal entende votre cause. Si vous ne deposez pas votre reponse ecrite dans le delai requis, vous risquez de perdre la cause ainsi que votre salaire, votre argent, et vos biens peuvent etre saisis par la suite, sans aucun preavis ulterieur du tribunal. Il y a d'autres obligations juridiques et vous pouvez requerir les services immediats d'un avocat. Si vous ne connaissez pas d'avocat, vous pourriez telephoner a un service de reference d'avocats ou a un bureau d'assistance juridique (figurant a l'annuaire de telephones).

Si vous choisissez de deposer vous-meme une reponse ecrite, il vous faudra egalement, en meme temps que cette formalite, faire parvenir ou expedier une copie au carbone ou une photocopie de votre reponse ecrite a la partie qui vous depose cette citation.

Nom et adresse de la partie qui depose cette citation: ____

____

Les photocopies de tous les documents tribunals de cette cause, y compris des arrets, sont disponible au bureau du greffier. Vous pouvez revue ces documents, sur demande.

Il faut aviser le greffier de votre adresse actuelle. (Vous pouvez deposer □ □ Florida Supreme_Court Approved Family Law Form 12.915, Notice of Current Address.) Les documents de l'avenir de ce proces seront envoyer a l' adresse que vous donnez au bureau du greffier.

ATTENTION: La regle 12.285 des regles de procedure du droit de la famille de la Floride exige que l'on remette certains renseignements et certains documents •a la partie adverse. Tout refus de les fournir pourra donner lieu a des sanctions, y compris le rejet ou la suppression d'un ou de plusieurs actes de procedure.

THE STATE OF FLORIDA
TO EACH SHERIFF OF THE STATE: You are commanded to serve this summons and a copy of the complaint in this lawsuit on the above-named person.

DATED: ______________________________

CLERK OF THE CIRCUIT COURT

(SEAL)

By: ____
Deputy Clerk

IN THE CIRCUIT COURT OF THE ______________________ JUDICIAL CIRCUIT,
IN AND FOR ______________________ COUNTY, FLORIDA

Case No.: ______________________
Division: ______________________

______________________,
Petitioner,

and

______________________,
Respondent.

PROCESS SERVICE MEMORANDUM

TO: ( ) Sheriff of ______________ County, Florida; ______________ Division
( ) Private process server: ______________________
Please serve the *{name of document(s)}* ______________________
____
in the above-styled cause upon:
Party: *{full legal name}* ______________________
Address or location for service: ______________________
____
Work Address: ______________________
____

If the party to be served owns, has, and/or is known to have guns or other weapons, describe what type of weapon(s): ______________________

SPECIAL INSTRUCTIONS: ______________________
____
____
____

Dated: ______________ ______________________
Signature of Party
*Printed Name: ______________________
*Address: ______________________
*City, State, Zip: ______________________
*Telephone Number: ______________________
*Fax Number: ______________________

*** If this is a domestic violence case, do not enter this information if your address or telephone number need to be kept confidential for safety reasons; instead write "confidential" in the spaces provided and file Florida Supreme Court Approved Family Law Form 12.980(i), Petitioner's Request for Confidential Filing of Address.**

Florida Supreme Court Approved Family Law Form 12.910(b), Process Service Memorandum (9/00)

Fax Number: ____________________

IF A NONLAWYER HELPED YOU FILL OUT THIS FORM, HE/SHE MUST FILL IN THE BLANKS BELOW: [fill in **all** blanks]

I, *{full legal name and trade name of nonlawyer}* ____________________, a nonlawyer, located at *{street}* ____________________, *{city}* ____________________, *{state}* ____________________, *{phone}* ____________________, helped *{name}* ____________________, who is the petitioner, fill out this form.

IN THE CIRCUIT COURT OF THE ____________________ JUDICIAL CIRCUIT,
IN AND FOR ____________________ COUNTY, FLORIDA

Case No.: ____________________
Division: ____________________

____________________,
Petitioner,

and

____________________,
Respondent.

MEMORANDUM FOR CERTIFICATE OF MILITARY SERVICE

TO: ( ) U.S. Coast Guard Commander (CGPC-ADM-3), Coast Guard Personnel Command, 2100 2nd St., S.W., Room 1616, Washington, D. C. 20593

( ) AFPC MSIMDL, 550 C Street, W., Suite 50, Randolph AFB, TX 78150-4752

( ) BUPERS, PERS 02116, 2 Navy Annex, Washington, D. C. 20370-0216

( ) USMC-CMC, HQMC-MMSB-10, 2008 Elliot Road, Room 201, Quantico, VA 22134-5030

( ) Surgeon General, U.S. Public Health Service, Div. of Comm., Off. Personnel, 5600 Fishers Lane, Room 4-21, Rockville, MD 20857

( ) Army World Wide Locator, U.S. Army Enlisted Records and Evaluation Center, 8899 East 56th Street, Indianapolis, IN 46249-5301

RE: ____________________ ____________________
{Name of Respondent} *{Respondent's Social Security Number}*

This case involves a family matter. It is imperative that a determination be made whether the above- named individual, who has an interest in these proceedings, is presently in the military service of the United States, and the dates of induction and discharge, if any. This information is requested under section 581 of the Soldiers' and Sailors' Civil Relief Act of 1940, as amended. Please supply a verification as soon as possible. My check for $__________ for your search fee and a self-addressed, stamped envelope are enclosed.

Dated: ____________________

____
Signature of Petitioner
Printed Name: ____________________
Address: ____________________
City, State, Zip: ____________________
Telephone Number: ____________________

Florida Supreme Court Approved Family Law Form 12.912(a), Memorandum for Certificate of Military Service (9/00)

Fax Number: ___________________________

IF A NONLAWYER HELPED YOU FILL OUT THIS FORM, HE/SHE MUST FILL IN THE BLANKS BELOW: [fill in **all** blanks]

I, *{full legal name and trade name of nonlawyer}* ______________________________,
a nonlawyer, located at *{street}* ______________________, *{city}* ______________,
{state} ______________, *{phone}* ______________, helped *{name}* ______________,
who is the petitioner, fill out this form.

IN THE CIRCUIT COURT OF THE ______________________ JUDICIAL CIRCUIT,
IN AND FOR ______________________ COUNTY, FLORIDA

Case No.: ______________________
Division: ______________________

______________________,
Petitioner,

and

______________________,
Respondent.

NONMILITARY AFFIDAVIT

I, *{full legal name}* ______________________, being sworn, certify that the following information is true:

[all that apply]

____ 1. I know of my own personal knowledge that Respondent is not on active duty in the armed services of the United States.

____ 2. I have inquired of the armed services of the United States and the U.S. Public Health Service to determine whether the Respondent is a member of the armed services and am attaching certificates stating that Respondent is not now in the armed services.

I understand that I am swearing or affirming under oath to the truthfulness of the claims made in this affidavit and that the punishment for knowingly making a false statement includes fines and/or imprisonment.

DATED: ______________________

____
Signature of Petitioner
Printed Name: ______________________
Address: ______________________
City, State, Zip: ______________________
Telephone Number: ______________________
Fax Number: ______________________

STATE OF FLORIDA
COUNTY OF ______________________

Sworn to or affirmed and signed before me on ______________ by ______________________.

____
NOTARY PUBLIC or DEPUTY CLERK

Florida Supreme Court Approved Family Law Form 12.912(b), Nonmilitary Affidavit (9/00)

____

[Print, type, or stamp commissioned name of notary or clerk.]

____ Personally known

____ Produced identification

Type of identification produced ____________________________

IF A NONLAWYER HELPED YOU FILL OUT THIS FORM, HE/SHE MUST FILL IN THE BLANKS BELOW: [fill in **all** blanks]

I, *{full legal name and trade name of nonlawyer}* ____, a nonlawyer, located at *{street}* ____________________________________, *{city}* _______________________, *{state}* _______________________, *{phone}* ______________________, helped *{name}* _______________________, who is the petitioner, fill out this form.

IN THE CIRCUIT COURT OF THE ______________________________ JUDICIAL CIRCUIT,
IN AND FOR ______________________________ COUNTY, FLORIDA

Case No.: ______________________________
Division: ______________________________

______________________________,
Petitioner,

and

______________________________,
Respondent.

AFFIDAVIT OF DILIGENT SEARCH AND INQUIRY

I, *{full legal name}* ______________________________, being sworn, certify that the following information is true:

1. I have made diligent search and inquiry to discover the name and current residence of Respondent: *{Specify details of search}* **Refer to checklist below and identify all actions taken (any additional information included such as the date the action was taken and the person with whom you spoke is helpful) (attach additional sheet if necessary):**

[**all** that apply]

____ United States Post Office inquiry through Freedom of Information Act for current address or any relocations.

____ Last known employment of Respondent, including name and address of employer. You should also ask for any addresses to which W-2 Forms were mailed, and, if a pension or profit-sharing plan exists, then for any addresses to which any pension or plan payment is and/or has been mailed.

____ Unions from which Respondent may have worked or that governed particular trade or craft.

____ Regulatory agencies, including professional or occupational licensing.

____ Names and addresses of relatives and contacts with those relatives, and inquiry as to Respondent's last known address. You are to follow up any leads of any addresses where Respondent may have moved. Relatives include, but are not limited to: parents, brothers, sisters, aunts, uncles, cousins, nieces, nephews, grandparents, great-grandparents, former in-laws, stepparents, stepchildren.

____ Information about the Respondent's possible death and, if dead, the date and location of the death.

____ Telephone listings in the last known locations of Respondent's residence.

____ Internet at http://www.switchboard.com or other Internet people finder or the library checked for me.

____ Law enforcement arrest and/or criminal records in the last known residential area of Respondent.

____ Highway Patrol records in the state of Respondent's last known address.

____ Department of Motor Vehicle records in the state of Respondent's last known address.

____ Department of Corrections records in the state of Respondent's last known address.

____ Title IV-D (child support enforcement) agency records in the state of Respondent's last known address.

____ Hospitals in the last known area of Respondent's residence.

____ Utility companies, which include water, sewer, cable TV, and electric, in the last known area of Respondent's residence.

____ Letters to the Armed Forces of the U.S. and their response as to whether or not there is any information about Respondent. (See Memorandum for Certificate of Military Service, Florida

Supreme Court Approved Family Law Form 12.912(a).)

____ Tax Assessor's and Tax Collector's Office in the area where Respondent last resided.

____ Other: *{explain}* ____

____

____

____

____

2. The age of Respondent is [**one** only] ( ) known *{enter age}* ____________ **or** ( ) unknown.

3. **Respondent's current residence**

[**one** only]

____ a. Respondent's current residence is unknown to me.

____ b. Respondent's current residence is in some state or country other than Florida, and Respondent's last known address is: ____.

____

____ c. The Respondent, having residence in Florida, has been absent from Florida for more than 60 days prior to the date of this affidavit, or conceals him(her)self so that process cannot be served personally upon him or her, and I believe there is no person in the state upon whom service of process would bind this absent or concealed Respondent.

I understand that I am swearing or affirming under oath to the truthfulness of the claims made in this affidavit and that the punishment for knowingly making a false statement includes fines and/or imprisonment.

Dated: ____________________________

____
Signature of Petitioner
Printed Name: ______________________________
Address: ______________________________
City, State, Zip: ______________________________
Telephone Number: ______________________________
Fax Number: ______________________________

STATE OF FLORIDA
COUNTY OF ______________________

Sworn to or affirmed and signed before me on ______________ by ______________________.

____
NOTARY PUBLIC or DEPUTY CLERK

____
[Print, type, or stamp commissioned name of notary or clerk.]

____

____ Personally known
____ Produced identification
Type of identification produced ______________________

IF A NONLAWYER HELPED YOU FILL OUT THIS FORM, HE/SHE MUST FILL IN THE

BLANKS BELOW: [☐ fill in **all** blanks]
I, *{full legal name and trade name of nonlawyer}* ______________________________,
a nonlawyer, located at *{street}* ______________________________, *{city}* ______________,
{state} ______________, *{phone}* ______________, helped *{name}* ______________,
who is the petitioner, fill out this form.

NOTICE OF ACTION

TO: ___________________________________

YOU ARE HEREBY NOTIFIED that an action for modification of the judgment of dissolution of marriage has been filed against you and you are required to serve a copy of your written defenses, if any, to it on *{name of Petitioner}* ____________________________, the Petitioner, whose address is ____ ____, on or before ______________________________, and file the original with the clerk of this court before service on Petitioner or immediately thereafter. If you fail to do so, a default will be entered against you for the relief demanded in the petition.

WARNING: Rule 12.285, Florida Family Law Rules of Procedure, requires certain automatic disclosure of documents and information. Failure to comply can result in sanctions, including dismisssal or striking of pleadings.

WITNESS my hand and the seal of this court on ____________________________.

CLERK OF THE COURT

By ______________________________________
Deputy Clerk

IN THE CIRCUIT COURT OF THE _________________________ JUDICIAL CIRCUIT,
IN AND FOR _________________________ COUNTY, FLORIDA

Case No.: _________________________
Division: _________________________

________________________________,
Petitioner,

and

________________________________,
Respondent.

CERTIFICATE OF SERVICE

I certify that a copy of *{name of document(s)}* ________________________________
____
was [**one** only] ( ) mailed ( ) faxed and mailed ( ) hand delivered to the person listed below on *{date}* ______________________________.

Other party or his/her attorney:
Name: ____
Address: __________________________________
City, State, Zip: ____________________________
Fax Number: ______________________________

____
Signature of Party
Printed Name: ______________________________
Address: __________________________________
City, State, Zip: ____________________________
Telephone Number: __________________________
Fax Number: ______________________________

IF A NONLAWYER HELPED YOU FILL OUT THIS FORM, HE/SHE MUST FILL IN THE BLANKS BELOW: [fill in **all** blanks]
I, *{full legal name and trade name of nonlawyer}* ________________________________,
a nonlawyer, located at *{street}* ______________________________, *{city}* ____________________,
{state} ____________________, *{phone}* ____________________, helped *{name}* ____________________,
who is the [**one** only] ____ petitioner **or** ____ respondent, fill out this form.

Florida Supreme Court Approved Family Law Form 12.914, Certificate of Service (9/00)

IN THE CIRCUIT COURT OF THE ______________________ JUDICIAL CIRCUIT,
IN AND FOR ______________________ COUNTY, FLORIDA

Case No.: ______________________
Division: ______________________

______________________,
Petitioner,

and

______________________,
Respondent.

NOTICE OF CURRENT ADDRESS

I, *{full legal name}* ______________________, being sworn, certify that my current address is: *{street}* ______________________ *{City}* ______________________, *{State}* ______ *{Zip}* ______ *{Telephone No.}* ______________ *{Fax No.}* ______________.

I understand that I must keep the clerk's office notified of my current address and that all future papers in this lawsuit will be mailed to the address on record at the clerk's office.

I certify that a copy of this document was [**one** only] ( ) mailed ( ) faxed and mailed ( ) hand-delivered to the person(s) listed below on *{date}* ______________________.

Other party or his/her attorney:
Name: ______________________
Address: ______________________
City, State, Zip: ______________________
Fax Number: ______________________

Dated: ______________________ ______________________
Signature of Party

STATE OF FLORIDA
COUNTY OF ______________________
Sworn to or affirmed and signed before me on ______________ by ______________________.

____
NOTARY PUBLIC or DEPUTY CLERK

[Print, type, or stamp commissioned name of notary or clerk.]

____ Personally known

____ Produced identification

Type of identification produced ____________________________

IF A NONLAWYER HELPED YOU FILL OUT THIS FORM, HE/SHE MUST FILL IN THE BLANKS BELOW: [fill in **all** blanks]

I, *{full legal name and trade name of nonlawyer}* ____________________________________,
a nonlawyer, located at *{street}* ______________________________, *{city}* ___________________,
{state} __________________, *{phone}* ________________, helped *{name}* __________________,
who is the [**one** only] ___ petitioner **or** ___ respondent, fill out this form.

IN THE CIRCUIT COURT OF THE ______________________ JUDICIAL CIRCUIT,
IN AND FOR ______________________ COUNTY, FLORIDA

Case No.: ______________________
Division: ______________________

______________________,
Petitioner,

and

______________________,
Respondent.

MOTION FOR REFERRAL TO GENERAL MASTER

I, *{full legal name}* ______________________, request that the Court enter an order referring this case to a general master. The case should be referred to a general master on the following issues: *{explain}* ______________________
____
____
____
____

I certify that a copy of this document was [**one** only] ( ) mailed ( ) faxed and mailed ( ) hand delivered to the person(s) listed below on *{date}* ______________________.

Other party or his/her attorney:
Name: ______________________
Address: ______________________
City, State, Zip: ______________________
Fax Number: ______________________

Dated: ______________________

____
Signature of Party
Printed Name: ______________________
Address: ______________________
City, State, Zip: ______________________
Telephone Number: ______________________
Fax Number: ______________________

IF A NONLAWYER HELPED YOU FILL OUT THIS FORM, HE/SHE MUST FILL IN THE BLANKS BELOW: [fill in **all** blanks]
I, *{full legal name and trade name of nonlawyer}* ______________________,
a nonlawyer, located at *{street}* ______________________, *{city}* ______________________,
{state} ______________________, *{phone}* ______________________, helped *{name}* ______________________,
who is the [**one** only] ___ petitioner **or** ___ respondent, fill out this form.

Florida Family Law Rules of Procedure Form 12.920(a), Motion for Referral to General Master (9/00)

IN THE CIRCUIT COURT OF THE ____________________ JUDICIAL CIRCUIT,
IN AND FOR ____________________ COUNTY, FLORIDA

Case No.: ____________________
Division: ____________________

____________________,
Petitioner,

and

____________________,
Respondent.

ORDER OF REFERRAL TO GENERAL MASTER

THIS CASE IS REFERRED TO THE GENERAL MASTER on the following issues:

1. ____________________
2. ____________________
3. ____________________
4. ____________________

AND ANY OTHER MATTER RELATED THERETO.

IT IS FURTHER ORDERED that the above issues are referred to General Master *{name}* ____________________, for further proceedings, under rule 12.490 of the Florida Family Law Rules of Procedure and current administrative orders of the Court. Financial Affidavits, □ □ Florida Family Law Rules of Procedure Form 12.902(b) or (c), shall be filed in accordance with Florida Family Law Rule of Procedure 12.285. The General Master is authorized to administer oaths and conduct hearings, which may include taking of evidence, and shall file a report and recommendations that contain findings of fact, conclusions of law, and the name of the court reporter, if any.

The General Master shall assign a time for the proceedings as soon as reasonably possible after this referral is made and shall give notice to each of the parties either directly or by directing counsel or a party to file and serve a notice of hearing.

Counties within the State of Florida may have different rules. Please consult the ( ) Clerk of the Court ( ) Family Law Intake Staff ( ) other ____________________ relating to this procedure.

A REFERRAL TO A GENERAL MASTER REQUIRES THE CONSENT OF ALL PARTIES. YOU ARE ENTITLED TO HAVE THIS MATTER HEARD BY A JUDGE. IF YOU DO NOT WANT TO HAVE THIS MATTER HEARD BY THE GENERAL MASTER, YOU MUST FILE A WRITTEN OBJECTION TO THE REFERRAL WITHIN 10 DAYS OF THE TIME OF SERVICE OF THIS ORDER. IF THE TIME SET FOR THE HEARING IS LESS THAN 10 DAYS AFTER SERVICE OF THIS ORDER, THE OBJECTION MUST BE MADE BEFORE THE HEARING. IF THIS ORDER IS SERVED WITHIN THE FIRST 20 DAYS AFTER SERVICE OF PROCESS, THE TIME TO FILE AN OBJECTION IS EXTENDED TO THE TIME WITHIN WHICH A RESPONSIVE PLEADING IS DUE. FAILURE TO FILE A WRITTEN OBJECTION WITHIN THE APPLICABLE TIME PERIOD IS DEEMED TO BE A CONSENT TO THE REFERRAL.

Florida Family Law Rules of Procedure Form 12.920(b), Order of Referral to General Master (9/00)

If either party files a timely objection, this matter shall be returned to the undersigned judge with a notice stating the amount of time needed for hearing.

REVIEW OF THE REPORT AND RECOMMENDATIONS MADE BY THE GENERAL MASTER SHALL BE BY EXCEPTIONS AS PROVIDED IN RULE 12.490(f), FLORIDA FAMILY LAW RULES OF PROCEDURE. A RECORD, WHICH INCLUDES A TRANSCRIPT, MAY BE REQUIRED TO SUPPORT EXCEPTIONS.

YOU ARE ADVISED THAT IN THIS CIRCUIT:

____ a. electronic recording is provided by the court. A party may provide a court reporter at that party's expense.

____ b. a court reporter is provided by the court.

SHOULD YOU WISH TO SEEK REVIEW OF THE REPORT AND RECOMMENDATION MADE BY THE GENERAL MASTER, YOU MUST FILE EXCEPTIONS IN ACCORDANCE WITH RULE 12.490(f), FLORIDA FAMILY LAW RULES OF PROCEDURE. YOU WILL BE REQUIRED TO PROVIDE THE COURT WITH A RECORD SUFFICIENT TO SUPPORT YOUR EXCEPTIONS, OR YOUR EXCEPTIONS WILL BE DENIED. A RECORD ORDINARILY INCLUDES A WRITTEN TRANSCRIPT OF ALL RELEVANT PROCEEDINGS. THE PERSON SEEKING REVIEW MUST HAVE THE TRANSCRIPT PREPARED IF NECESSARY FOR THE COURT'S REVIEW.

ORDERED on ________________________.

____
CIRCUIT JUDGE

COPIES TO:
Petitioner (or his or her attorney)
Respondent (or his or her attorney)
General Master

IN THE CIRCUIT COURT OF THE ______________________________ JUDICIAL CIRCUIT,
IN AND FOR ______________________________ COUNTY, FLORIDA

Case No.: ______________________________
Division: ______________________________

______________________________,
Petitioner,

and

______________________________,
Respondent.

NOTICE OF HEARING BEFORE GENERAL MASTER

[fill in **all** blanks]
TO: ______________________________
____

There will be a hearing before General Master *{name of general master}* ____________________, on *{date}* ____________________, at *{time}* ____________ m., in Room __________ of the ______________ Courthouse, on the following issues: ____.

____________ hour(s)/ ______ minutes have been reserved for this hearing.
PLEASE GOVERN YOURSELF ACCORDINGLY.

If the matter before the General Master is a Motion for Civil Contempt/Enforcement, FAILURE TO APPEAR AT THE HEARING MAY RESULT IN THE COURT ISSUING A WRIT OF BODILY ATTACHMENT FOR YOUR ARREST. IF YOU ARE ARRESTED, YOU MAY BE HELD IN JAIL UP TO 48 HOURS BEFORE A HEARING IS HELD.

PLEASE GOVERN YOURSELF ACCORDINGLY.

This part to be filled out by the court or filled in with information you have obtained from the court: If you are a person with a disability who needs any accommodation in order to participate in this proceeding, you are entitled, at no cost to you, to the provision of certain assistance. Please contact *{name}* ____, *{address}* ______________________________, *{telephone}* ______________, within 2 working days of your receipt of this Notice of Hearing. If you are hearing or voice impaired, call TDD 1-800-955-8771.

SHOULD YOU WISH TO SEEK REVIEW OF THE REPORT AND RECOMMENDATION MADE BY THE GENERAL MASTER, YOU MUST FILE EXCEPTIONS IN ACCORDANCE WITH RULE 12.490(f), FLORIDA FAMILY LAW RULES OF PROCEDURE. YOU WILL BE REQUIRED TO PROVIDE THE COURT WITH A RECORD SUFFICIENT TO SUPPORT YOUR EXCEPTIONS, OR YOUR EXCEPTIONS WILL BE DENIED. A RECORD ORDINARILY INCLUDES A WRITTEN TRANSCRIPT OF ALL RELEVANT PROCEEDINGS.

Florida Family Law Rules of Procedure Form 12.920(c), Notice of Hearing Before General Master (9/00)

THE PERSON SEEKING REVIEW MUST HAVE THE TRANSCRIPT PREPARED IF NECESSARY FOR THE COURT'S REVIEW.

YOU ARE HEREBY ADVISED THAT IN THIS CIRCUIT:

____ a. electronic recording is provided by the court. A party may provide a court reporter at that party's expense.

____ b. a court reporter is provided by the court.

If you are represented by an attorney or plan to retain an attorney for this matter you should notify the attorney of this hearing.

If this matter is resolved, the moving party shall contact the General Master's Office to cancel this hearing.

I certify that a copy of this document was [**one** only] ( ) mailed ( ) faxed and mailed ( ) hand delivered to the person(s) listed below on *{date}* ______________________________.

Other party or his/her attorney:
Name: ______________________________
Address: ______________________________
City, State, Zip: ______________________________
Fax Number: ______________________________

Dated: ____________________

____
Signature of Party
Printed Name: ______________________________
Address: ______________________________
City, State, Zip: ______________________________
Telephone Number: ______________________________
Fax Number: ______________________________

IF A NONLAWYER HELPED YOU FILL OUT THIS FORM, HE/SHE MUST FILL IN THE BLANKS BELOW: [fill in **all** blanks]
I, *{full legal name and trade name of nonlawyer}* ______________________________, a nonlawyer, located at *{street}* ____________________, *{city}* ____________________, *{state}* ____________________, *{phone}* ____________________, helped *{name}* ,who is the [**one** only] ___ petitioner **or** ___ respondent, fill out this form.

IN THE CIRCUIT COURT OF THE ____________________________ JUDICIAL CIRCUIT,
IN AND FOR ____________________________ COUNTY, FLORIDA

Case No.: ______________________________
Division: ______________________________

______________________________________,
Petitioner,

and

______________________________________,
Respondent.

NOTICE OF HEARING (CHILD SUPPORT ENFORCEMENT HEARING OFFICER)

TO: *{name of other party}* ____

There will be a hearing before Child Support Enforcement Hearing Officer *{name}* ___________ ___________________________, on *{date}* _________________, at *{time}* ___________ m., in Room ____________ of the____ County Courthouse, on the following issues: ____ ____ ____.

____________ hour(s)/ ______ minutes have been reserved for this hearing.

If the matter before the Child Support Enforcement Hearing Officer is a Motion for Civil Contempt/Enforcement, **FAILURE TO APPEAR AT THE HEARING MAY RESULT IN THE COURT ISSUING A WRIT OF BODILY ATTACHMENT FOR YOUR ARREST. IF YOU ARE ARRESTED, YOU MAY BE HELD IN JAIL UP TO 48 HOURS BEFORE A HEARING IS HELD.**

This part to be filled out by the court or filled in with information you have obtained from the court:

If you are a person with a disability who needs any accommodation in order to participate in this proceeding, you are entitled, at no cost to you, to the provision of certain assistance. Please contact *{name}*____
*{address}*____ *{telephone}* ______________
within 2 working days of your receipt of this Notice of Hearing. If you are hearing or voice impaired, call TDD 1-800-955-8771.

If you are represented by an attorney or plan to retain an attorney for this matter, you should notify the attorney of this hearing.

If this matter is resolved, the moving party shall contact the hearing officer's office to cancel this hearing.

I certify that a copy of this document was [one only] ( ) mailed ( ) faxed and mailed ( ) hand delivered to the person(s) listed below on *{date}* ______________________________.

Other party or his/her attorney:
Name: ______________________________
Address: ______________________________
City, State, Zip: ______________________________
Fax Number: ______________________________

Dated: ____________________

____
Signature of Party
Printed Name: ______________________________
Address: ______________________________
City, State, Zip: ______________________________
Telephone Number: ______________________________
Fax Number: ______________________________

IF A NONLAWYER HELPED YOU FILL OUT THIS FORM, HE/SHE MUST FILL IN THE BLANKS BELOW: [fill in **all** blanks]

I, *{full legal name and trade name of nonlawyer}* ______________________________,
a nonlawyer, located at *{street}* ____________________, *{city}* ____________________,
{state} ____________________, *{phone}* ____________________, helped *{name}* ____________________,
who is the [**one** only] ___ petitioner **or** ___ respondent, fill out this form.

IN THE CIRCUIT COURT OF THE ____________________ JUDICIAL CIRCUIT,
IN AND FOR ______________________ COUNTY, FLORIDA

Case No.: ______________________
Division: ______________________

______________________________,
Petitioner,

and

______________________________,
Respondent.

MOTION TO SET FINAL HEARING / TRIAL

The ❑ Petitioner ❑ Respondent moves the court for an order setting this matter for:

❑ Uncontested final hearing ❑ Non-jury trial ❑ Status Conference

pursuant to Rule 1.440, Florida Rules of Civil Procedure, and states:

1. This matter is at issue and ready to set for final hearing/trial.

2. The estimated time necessary to conduct the final hearing/trial is ________________ ______________________.

DATED: ______________________

____
Signature
Printed name: ____________________________
Address: ________________________________
City, State, Zip: __________________________
Telephone Number: ________________________
Fax Number: ______________________________

IF A NONLAWYER HELPED YOU FILL OUT THIS FORM, HE/SHE MUST FILL IN THE BLANKS BELOW: [✍ fill in all blanks]

I, *{full legal name and trade name of nonlawyer}* ______________________________,
a nonlawyer, located at *{street}* ______________________, *{city}* ______________________,
{state} ____________, *{phone}* ______________, helped *{name}* ______________________,
who is the petitioner/respondent, fill out this form.

IN THE CIRCUIT COURT OF THE ____________________ JUDICIAL CIRCUIT,
IN AND FOR ____________________ COUNTY, FLORIDA

Case No.: ____________________
Division: ____________________

____________________________________,
Petitioner,
and

____________________________________,
Respondent.

ORDER SETTING MATTER FOR FINAL HEARING OR FOR STATUS CONFERENCE

The court having reviewed the file finds that:

_____ The time to file an answer has expired, and therefore,

IT IS ORDERED that:

This case is set for uncontested final hearing before Judge *{name of judge}* ____________________ ____________________, on *{date}* ____________________, ________, at *{time}* ____________, in Room ________ of the ____________________________________ Courthouse.

[✔ **one** only]

_____ If no answer has been filed, please bring your default order. You will also need to bring proof of residency, i.e., a residency witness, affidavit of residency, valid Florida driver's license, or valid Florida voter registration card.

_____ If an answer has been filed, this hearing will serve as a status conference.

The ( ) Petitioner ( ) Respondent, or attorney for the ( ) Petitioner ( ) Respondent, is required to notify all other parties immediately of this hearing.

FAILURE TO APPEAR MAY RESULT IN A DISMISSAL OF THIS CASE

DATED: ____________________

____
CIRCUIT JUDGE

This part to be filled in by court: In accordance with the Americans with Disabilities Act of 1990, persons needing a special accommodation to participate in this proceeding should contact ____________________ for proceedings in court or ____________________ at ______________ for out of court proceedings no later than 7 days before the proceeding. Telephone ______________ or ______________ for assistance. If hearing impaired, telephone (TDD) ____________________ for proceedings in court or Florida Relay Service 1-800-955-8771 for out of court proceedings.

cc:

Petitioner or their attorney (if represented)
Name ____________________
Address: ____________________
____
City State Zip
Telephone No. ____________________
Fax No. ____________________

Respondent of their attorney (if represented)
Name ____________________
Address: ____________________
____
City State Zip
Telephone No. ____________________
Fax No. ____________________

IF A NONLAWYER HELPED YOU FILL OUT THIS FORM TO GIVE TO THE JUDGE TO SIGN, THE NONLAWYER WHO HELPED YOU MUST FILL IN THE BLANKS BELOW: [✍ fill in **all** blanks]

I, *{full legal name and trade name of nonlawyer}* ____________________________________,
a nonlawyer, located at *{street}* ____________________.*{city}* ____________________,
{state} __________, *{phone}* ____________________, helped *{name}* ____________________,
who is the petitioner/respondent, fill out this form.

IN THE CIRCUIT COURT OF THE ______________________ JUDICIAL CIRCUIT,
IN AND FOR ______________________ COUNTY, FLORIDA

Case No.: ______________________
Division: ______________________

______________________________,
Petitioner,

and

______________________________,
Respondent.

MOTION FOR DEFAULT

TO THE CLERK OF THE CIRCUIT COURT:

PLEASE ENTER A DEFAULT AGAINST RESPONDENT WHO HAS FAILED TO RESPOND TO THE PETITION.

I certify that a copy of this document was [**one** only] ( ) mailed ( ) faxed and mailed ( ) hand delivered to the person(s) listed below on *{date}* ______________________.

Other party or his/her attorney:
Name: ______________________
Address: ______________________
City, State, Zip: ______________________
Fax Number: ______________________

Dated: ______________

____
Signature of Petitioner
Printed Name: ______________________
Address: ______________________
City, State, Zip: ______________________
Telephone Number: ______________________
Fax Number: ______________________

IF A NONLAWYER HELPED YOU FILL OUT THIS FORM, HE/SHE MUST FILL IN THE BLANKS BELOW: [fill in **all** blanks]
I, *{full legal name and trade name of nonlawyer}* ______________________,
a nonlawyer, located at *{street}* ______________________, *{city}* ______________,
{state} ______________, *{phone}* ______________, helped *{name}* ______________,
who is the petitioner, fill out this form.

IN THE CIRCUIT COURT OF THE ____________________________ JUDICIAL CIRCUIT,
IN AND FOR ____________________________ COUNTY, FLORIDA

Case No.: ______________________________
Division: ______________________________

______________________________________,
Petitioner,

and

______________________________________,
Respondent.

DEFAULT

A default is entered in this action against Respondent for failure to serve or file a response or any paper as is required by law.

Dated: ____________

CLERK OF THE CIRCUIT COURT

(SEAL)

By: ____
Deputy Clerk

I certify that a copy of this document was [**one** only] ( ) mailed ( ) faxed and mailed ( ) hand delivered to the person(s) listed below on *{date}* ______________________________________.

Other party or his/her attorney:

Name: ______________________________________
Address: ____________________________________
City, State, Zip: _______________________________
Fax Number: _________________________________

Dated: ____________________

____
Signature of Petitioner
Printed Name: ____________________________________
Address: ____
City, State, Zip: __________________________________
Telephone Number: _________________________________
Fax Number: ______________________________________

IF A NONLAWYER HELPED YOU FILL OUT THIS FORM, HE/SHE MUST FILL IN THE BLANKS BELOW: [fill in **all** blanks]
I, *{full legal name and trade name of nonlawyer}* ______________________________________,
a nonlawyer, located at *{street}* ______________________________, *{city}* ________________,
{state} ____________________, *{phone}* ____________________, helped *{name}* ________________,
who is the petitioner, fill out this form.

Florida Supreme Court Approved Family Law Form 12.922(b), Default (9/00)

IN THE CIRCUIT COURT OF THE ______________________ JUDICIAL CIRCUIT,
IN AND FOR ______________________ COUNTY, FLORIDA

Case No.: ______________________
Division: ______________________

______________________,
Petitioner,

and

______________________,
Respondent.

NOTICE OF HEARING (GENERAL)

[fill in **all** blanks]

TO: *{name of other party}* ______________________

There will be a hearing before Judge *{name}* ______________________,
on *{date}* ______________, at *{time}* __________ m., in Room ________ of the______________
Courthouse, on the following issues: ______________________
____
____.

__________ hour(s)/ _____ minutes have been reserved for this hearing.

This part to be filled out by the court or to be filled in with information you obtained from the court:
If you are a person with a disability who needs any accommodation in order to participate in this proceeding, you are entitled, at no cost to you, to the provision of certain assistance. Please contact *{name}* ______________________,
{address} ______________________, *{telephone}* __________,
within 2 working days of your receipt of this Notice of Hearing. If you are hearing or voice impaired, call TDD 1-800-955-8771.

If you are represented by an attorney or plan to retain an attorney for this matter, you should notify the attorney of this hearing.

If this matter is resolved, the moving party shall contact the judge's office to cancel this hearing.

I certify that a copy of this document was [**one** only] ( ) mailed ( ) faxed and mailed ( ) hand delivered to the person(s) listed below on *{date}* ______________________.

Other party or his/her attorney:
Name: ______________________
Address: ______________________
City, State, Zip: ______________________
Fax Number: ______________________

Dated: ____________________

____
Signature of Party
Printed Name: ____________________
Address: ____________________
City, State, Zip: ____________________
Telephone Number: ____________________
Fax Number: ____________________

IF A NONLAWYER HELPED YOU FILL OUT THIS FORM, HE/SHE MUST FILL IN THE BLANKS BELOW: [fill in **all** blanks]
I, *{full legal name and trade name of nonlawyer}* ____________________________________,
a nonlawyer, located at *{street}* ____________________, *{city}* ____________________,
{state} ____________________, *{phone}* ____________________, helped *{name}* ____________________,
who is the [**one** only] ___ petitioner **or** ___ respondent, fill out this form.

IN THE CIRCUIT COURT OF THE ______________________________ JUDICIAL CIRCUIT,
IN AND FOR ______________________________ COUNTY, FLORIDA

Case No.: ______________________________
Division: ______________________________

______________________________,
Petitioner,

and

______________________________,
Respondent.

NOTICE FOR TRIAL

Pursuant to rule 12.440, Florida Family Law Rules of Procedure, the party signing below states that the case is ready to be set for trial. The estimated time needed for the parties to present their cases is: *{hours}* ____________________.

I certify that a copy of this document was [one only] ( ) mailed ( ) faxed and mailed ( ) hand delivered to the person(s) listed below on *{date}* ______________________________.

Other party or his/her attorney:
Name: ______________________________
Address: ______________________________
City, State, Zip: ______________________________
Fax Number: ______________________________

Dated: ______________________________

____
Signature of Party
Printed Name: ______________________________
Address: ______________________________
City, State, Zip: ______________________________
Telephone Number: ______________________________
Fax Number: ______________________________

IF A NONLAWYER HELPED YOU FILL OUT THIS FORM, HE/SHE MUST FILL IN THE BLANKS BELOW: [fill in **all** blanks]
I, *{full legal name and trade name of nonlawyer}* ______________________________,
a nonlawyer, located at *{street}* ______________________________, *{city}* ____________________,
{state} ____________________, *{phone}* ____________________, helped *{name}* ____________________,
who is the [**one** only] ___ petitioner **or** ___ respondent, fill out this form.

IN THE CIRCUIT COURT OF THE ______________________________ JUDICIAL CIRCUIT,
IN AND FOR ______________________________ COUNTY, FLORIDA

Case No.: ______________________________
Division: ______________________________

____,
Petitioner,

and

____,
Respondent.

NOTICE OF SERVICE OF STANDARD FAMILY LAW INTERROGATORIES

I, *{full legal name}* ______________________________, have on *{date}* ____________, served upon *{name of person served}* ____, to be answered under oath within 30 days after service, the Standard Family Law Interrogatories for [**one** only]

( ) **Original or Enforcement Proceedings** ( ) **Modification Proceedings**

I am requesting that the following standard questions be answered: [**all** that apply]

____ 1	____ 2	____ 3	____ 4	____ 5	____ 6	____ 7
Background Information	Education	Employment	Assets	Liabilities	Miscellaneous	Long Form Affidavit

In addition, I am requesting that the attached *{#}* ____________ questions be answered.

I certify that a copy of this document was [**one** only] ( ) mailed ( ) faxed and mailed ( ) hand delivered to the person(s) listed below on *{date}* ______________________________.

Other party or his/her attorney:
Name: ______________________________
Address: ______________________________
City, State, Zip: ______________________________
Fax Number: ______________________________

Dated: ______________________

____
Signature of Party
Printed Name: ______________________________
Address: ______________________________
City, State, Zip: ______________________________
Telephone Number: ______________________________
Fax Number: ______________________________

IF A NONLAWYER HELPED YOU FILL OUT THIS FORM, HE/SHE MUST FILL IN THE BLANKS BELOW: [fill in **all** blanks]
I, *{full legal name and trade name of nonlawyer}* ______________________________,
a nonlawyer, located at *{street}* ______________________________, *{city}* ______________,

Florida Family Law Rules of Procedure Form 12.930(a), Notice of Service of Standard Family Law Interrogatories (9/00) *{state}* ______________________, *{phone}* ____________________, helped *{name}* _____________________, who is the [☐ **one** only] ___ petitioner **or** ___ respondent, fill out this form.

IN THE CIRCUIT COURT OF THE ______________________ JUDICIAL CIRCUIT,
IN AND FOR ______________________ COUNTY, FLORIDA

Case No.: ______________________
Division: ______________________

______________________,
Petitioner,

and

______________________,
Respondent.

STANDARD FAMILY LAW INTERROGATORIES
FOR ORIGINAL OR ENFORCEMENT PROCEEDINGS

TO BE COMPLETED BY THE PARTY SERVING THESE INTERROGATORIES

I am requesting that the following standard questions be answered: [**all** that apply]

____ 1	____ 2	____ 3	____ 4	____ 5	____ 6	____ 7
Background Information	Education	Employment	Assets	Liabilities	Miscellaneous	Long Form Affidavit

In addition, I am requesting that the attached *{#}* ____ questions be answered.

The answers to the following questions are intended to supplement the information provided in the Financial Affidavits, Florida Family Law Rules of Procedure Form 12.902(b) or (c). You should answer the group of questions indicated in the above shaded box. The questions should be answered in the blank space provided below each separately numbered question. If sufficient space is not provided, you may attach additional papers with the answers and refer to them in the space provided in the interrogatories. You should be sure to make a copy for yourself. Each question must be answered separately and as completely as the available information permits. All answers are to be made under oath or affirmation as to their truthfulness.

I, *{name of person answering interrogatories}* ______________________, being sworn, certify that the following information is true:

1. **BACKGROUND INFORMATION:**
   a. State your full legal name and any other name by which you have been known.
   b. State your present residence and telephone numbers.
   c. State your place and date of birth.

2. **EDUCATION:**

a. List all business, commercial, and professional licenses that you have obtained.

b. List all of your education including, but not limited to, vocational or specialized training, including the following:

(1) name and address of each educational institution.

(2) dates of attendance.

(3) degrees or certificates obtained or anticipated dates of same.

3. **EMPLOYMENT:**

a. For each place of your employment or self-employment during the last 3 years, state the following:

(1) name, address, and telephone number of your employer.

(2) dates of employment.

(3) job title and brief description of job duties.

(4) starting and ending salaries.

(5) name of your direct supervisor.

(6) all benefits received, including, for example, health, life, and disability insurance; expense account; use of automobile or automobile expense reimbursement; reimbursement for travel, food, or lodging expenses; payment of dues in any clubs or associations; and pension or profit sharing plans.

b. Other than as an employee, if you have been engaged in or associated with any business, commercial, or professional activity within the last 3 years that was not detailed above, state for each such activity the following:

(1) name, address, and telephone number of each activity.

(2) dates you were connected with such activity.

(3) position title and brief description of activities.

(4) starting and ending compensation.

(5) name of all persons involved in the business, commercial, or professional activity with you.

(6) all benefits and compensation received, including, for example, health, life, and disability insurance; expense account; use of automobile or automobile expense reimbursement; reimbursement for travel, food, or lodging expenses; payment of dues in any clubs or associations; and pension or profit sharing plans.

c. If you have been unemployed at any time during the last 3 years, state the dates of unemployment. If you have not been employed at any time in the last 3 years, give the information requested above in question 3.a for your last period of employment.

4. **ASSETS:**

a. **Real Estate.** State the street address, if any, and if not, the legal description of all real property that you own or owned during the last 3 years. For each property, state the following:

(1) the names and addresses of any other persons or entities holding any interest and their percentage of interest.

(2) the purchase price, the cost of any improvements made since it was purchased, and the amount of any depreciation taken.

(3) the fair market value on the date of your separation from your spouse.

(4) the fair market value on the date of the filing of the petition for dissolution of marriage.

b. **Tangible Personal Property.** List all items of tangible personal property that are owned by you or in which you have had any interest during the last 3 years including, but not limited to, motor vehicles, tools, furniture, boats, jewelry, art objects or other collections, and collectibles whose fair market value exceeds $100. For each item, state the following:

(1) the percentage and type interest you hold.

(2) the names and addresses of any other persons or entities holding any interest.

(3) the date you acquired your interest.

(4) the purchase price.

(5) the present fair market value.

(6) the fair market value on the date of your separation from your spouse.

(7) the fair market value on the date of the filing of the petition for dissolution of marriage.

c. **Intangible Personal Property.** Other than the financial accounts (checking, savings, money market, credit union accounts, or other such cash management accounts) listed in the answer to interrogatory 4.d below, list all items of intangible personal property that are owned by you or in which you have had any ownership interest (including closed accounts) within the last 3 years, including but not limited to, partnership and business interests (including good will), stocks, stock funds, mutual funds, bonds, bond funds, real estate investment trust, receivables, certificates of deposit, notes, mortgages, and debts owed to you by another entity or person. For each item, state the following:

(1) the percentage and type interest you hold.

(2) the names and addresses of any other persons or entities holding any interest and the names and addresses of the persons and entities who are indebted to you.

(3) the date you acquired your interest.

(4) the purchase price, acquisition cost, or loaned amount.

(5) the fair market value or the amounts you claim are owned by or owed to you:

(a) presently, at the time of answering these interrogatories.

(b) on the date of your separation from your spouse.

(c) on the date of the filing of the petition for dissolution of marriage.

You may comply with this interrogatory (4.c) by providing copies of all periodic (monthly, quarterly, semi-annual, or annual) account statements for each such account for the preceding 3 years. However, if the date of acquisition, the purchase price and the market valuations are not clearly reflected in the periodic statements which are furnished then these questions must be answered separately. You do not have to resubmit any periodic statements previously furnished under rule 12.285 (Mandatory Disclosure).

d. **Financial Accounts.** For all financial accounts (checking, savings, money market, credit union accounts, or other such cash management accounts) listed in your Financial Affidavit, in which you have had any legal or equitable interest, regardless of whether the interest is or was held in your own name individually, in your name with another person, or in any other name, give the following:

(1) name and address of each institution.

(2) name in which the account is or was maintained.

(3) account numbers.

(4) name of each person authorized to make withdrawals from the accounts.

(5) highest balance within each of the preceding 3 years.

(6) lowest balance within each of the preceding 3 years.

You may comply with this interrogatory (4.d) by providing copies of all periodic (monthly, quarterly, semi-annual, or annual) account statements for each such account for the preceding 3 years. You do not have to resubmit account statements previously furnished pursuant to rule 12.285 (Mandatory Disclosure).

e. **Closed Financial Accounts.** For all financial accounts (checking, savings, money market, credit union accounts, or other such cash management accounts) closed within the last 3 years, in which you have had any legal or equitable interest, regardless of whether the interest is or was held in your own name individually, in your name with another person, or in any other name, give the following:

(1) name and address of each institution.

(2) name in which the account is or was maintained.

(3) account numbers.

(4) name of each person authorized to make withdrawals from the accounts.

(5) date account was closed.

f. **Trust.** For any interest in an estate, trust, insurance policy, or annuity, state the following:

(1) If you are the beneficiary of any estate, trust, insurance policy, or annuity, give for each one the following:

(a) identification of the estate, trust, insurance policy, or annuity.

(b) the nature, amount, and frequency of any distributions of benefits.

(c) the total value of the beneficiaries' interest in the benefit.

(d) whether the benefit is vested or contingent.

(2) If you have established any trust or are the trustee of a trust, state the following:

(a) the date the trust was established.

(b) the names and addresses of the trustees.

(c) the names and addresses of the beneficiaries.

(d) the names and addresses of the persons or entities who possess the trust documents.

(e) each asset that is held in each trust, with its fair market value.

g. **Canceled Life Insurance Policies.** For all policies of life insurance within the preceding 3 years that you no longer hold, own, or have any interest in, state the following:

(1) name of company that issued the policy and policy number.

(2) name, address, and telephone number of agent who issued the policy.

(3) amount of coverage.

(4) name of insured.

(5) name of owner of policy.

(6) name of beneficiaries.

(7) premium amount.

(8) date the policy was surrendered.

(9) amount, if any, of monies distributed to the owner.

h. **Name of Accountant, Bookkeeper, or Records Keeper.** State the names, addresses, and telephone numbers of your accountant, bookkeeper, and any other persons who possess your financial records, and state which records each possesses.

i. **Safe Deposit Boxes, Lock Boxes, Vaults, Etc.** For all safe deposit boxes, lock boxes, vaults, or similar types of depositories, state the following:

(1) The names and addresses of all banks, depositories, or other places where, at any time during the period beginning 3 years before the initiation of the action, until the date of your answering this interrogatory, you did any of the following:

(a) had a safe deposit box, lock box, or vault.

(b) were a signatory or co-signatory on a safe deposit box, lock box, or vault.

(c) had access to a safe deposit box, lock box, or vault.

(d) maintained property.

(2) The box or identification numbers and the name and address of each person who has had access to any such depository during the same time period.

(3) All persons who have possession of the keys or combination to the safe deposit box, lock box, or vault.

(4) Any items removed from any safe deposit boxes, lock boxes, vaults, or similar types of depositories by you or your agent during that time, together with the present location and fair market value of each item.

(5) All items in any safe deposit boxes, lock boxes, vaults, or similar types of depositories and fair market value of each item.

5. **LIABILITIES:**

a. **Loans, Liabilities, Debts, and Other Obligations.** For all loans, liabilities, debts, and other obligations (other than credit cards and charge accounts) listed in your Financial Affidavit, indicate for each the following:

(1) name and address of the creditor.

(2) name in which the obligation is or was incurred.

(3) loan or account number, if any.

(4) nature of the security, if any.

(5) payment schedule.

(6) present balance and current status of your payments.

(7) total amount of arrearage, if any.

(8) balance on the date of your separation from your spouse.

(9) balance on the date of the filing of the petition for dissolution of marriage.

You may comply with this interrogatory (5.a) by providing copies of all periodic (monthly, quarterly, semi-annual, or annual) account statements for each such account for the preceding 3 years. You do not have to resubmit account statements previously furnished under rule 12.285 (Mandatory Disclosure).

b. **Credit Cards and Charge Accounts.** For all financial accounts (credit cards, charge accounts, or other such accounts) listed in your Financial Affidavit, in which you have had any legal or equitable interest, regardless of whether the interest is or was held in your own name individually, in your name with another person, or in any other name, give the following:

(1) name and address of the creditor.

(2) name in which the account is or was maintained.

(3) names of each person authorized to sign on the accounts.

(4) account numbers.

(5) present balance and current status of your payments.

(6) total amount of arrearage, if any.

(7) balance on the date of your separation from your spouse.

(8) balance on the date of the filing of the petition for dissolution of marriage.

(9) highest and lowest balance within each of the preceding 3 years.

You may comply with this interrogatory (5.b) by providing copies of all periodic (monthly quarterly, semi-annual, or annual) account statements for each such account for the preceding 3 years. You do not have to resubmit account statements previously furnished under rule 12.285 (Mandatory Disclosure).

c. **Closed Credit Cards and Charge Accounts.** For all financial accounts (credit cards, charge accounts, or other such accounts) closed with no remaining balance, within the last 3 years, in which you have had any legal or equitable interest, regardless of whether the interest is or was held in your own name individually, in your name with another person, or in any other name, give the following:

(1) name and address of each creditor.

(2) name in which the account is or was maintained.

(3) account numbers.

(4) names of each person authorized to sign on the accounts.

(5) date the balance was paid off.

(6) amount of final balance paid off.

You may comply with this interrogatory (5.c) by providing copies of all periodic (monthly, quarterly, semi-annual, or annual) account statements for each such account for the preceding 3 years. You do not have to resubmit account statements previously

furnished under rule 12.285 (Mandatory Disclosure).

6. **MISCELLANEOUS:**

a. If you are claiming a special equity in any assets, list the asset, the amount claimed as special equity, and all facts upon which you rely in your claim.

b. If you are claiming an asset or liability is nonmarital, list the asset or liability and all facts upon which you rely in your claim.

c. If the mental or physical condition of a spouse or child is an issue, identify the person and state the name and address of all health care providers involved in the treatment of that person for said mental or physical condition.

d. If custody of minor children is an issue, state why, and the facts that support your contention that you should be the primary residential parent or have sole parental responsibility of the child(ren).

7. **LONG FORM AFFIDAVIT:** If you filed the short form affidavit, Florida Family Law Rules of Procedure Form 12.902(b), and you were specifically requested in the Notice of Service of Standard Family Law Interrogatories to file the Long Form Affidavit, Form12.902(c), you must do so within the time to serve the answers to these interrogatories.

I certify that a copy of this document was [one only] ( ) mailed ( ) faxed and mailed ( ) hand delivered to the person(s) listed below on *{date}* ____________________.

Other party or his/her attorney:
Name: ____________________
Address: ____________________
City, State, Zip: ____________________
Fax Number: ____________________

I understand that I am swearing or affirming under oath to the truthfulness of the answers to these interrogatories and that the punishment for knowingly making a false statement includes fines and/or imprisonment.

Dated: ____________________

____
Signature of Party
Printed Name: ____________________
Address: ____________________
City, State, Zip: ____________________
Telephone Number: ____________________
Fax Number: ____________________

STATE OF FLORIDA
COUNTY OF ____________________

Sworn to or affirmed and signed before me on ______________ by ____________________.

____
NOTARY PUBLIC or DEPUTY CLERK

____
[Print, type, or stamp commissioned name of notary or clerk.]

____ Personally known
____ Produced identification
Type of identification produced ____________________

IF A NONLAWYER HELPED YOU FILL OUT THIS FORM, HE/SHE MUST FILL IN

THE BLANKS BELOW: [fill in **all** blanks]
I, *{full legal name and trade name of nonlawyer}* ______________________________,
a nonlawyer, located at *{street}* ______________________, *{city}* ______________,
{state} ______________, *{phone}* ______________, helped *{name}* ______________,
who is the [**one** only] ___ petitioner **or** ___ respondent, fill out this form.

IN THE CIRCUIT COURT OF THE ________________________ JUDICIAL CIRCUIT,
IN AND FOR ________________________ COUNTY, FLORIDA

Case No.: ________________________
Division: ________________________

________________________________,
Petitioner

and

________________________________,
Respondent.

STANDARD FAMILY LAW INTERROGATORIES
FOR MODIFICATION PROCEEDINGS

TO BE COMPLETED BY THE PARTY SERVING THESE INTERROGATORIES

I am requesting that the following standard questions be answered: [all that apply]

____ 1	____ 2	____ 3	____ 4	____ 5	____ 6	____ 7
Background Information	Education	Employment	Assets	Liabilities	Miscellaneous	Long Form Affidavit

In addition, I am requesting that the attached *{#}* ____ questions be answered.

The answers to the following questions are intended to supplement the information provided in the Financial Affidavits, Florida Family Law Rules of Procedure Form 12.902(b) or (c). You should answer the group of questions indicated in the above shaded box. The questions should be answered in the blank space provided below each separately numbered question. If sufficient space is not provided, you may attach additional papers with the answers and refer to them in the space provided in the interrogatories. You should be sure to make a copy for yourself. Each question must be answered separately and as completely as the available information permits. All answers are to be made under oath or affirmation as to their truthfulness.

I, *{name of person answering interrogatories}* ________________________________, being sworn, certify that the following information is true:

1. **BACKGROUND INFORMATION:**

   a. State your full legal name and any other name by which you have been known.

   b. State your present residence and telephone numbers.

   c. State your place and date of birth.

2. **EDUCATION:**

a. List all business, commercial, and professional licenses that you have obtained since the entry of the Final Judgment sought to be modified.

b. List all of your education since the entry of the Final Judgment sought to be modified including, but not limited to, vocational or specialized training, including the following:

(1) name and address of each educational institution.

(2) dates of attendance.

(3) degrees or certificates obtained or anticipated dates of same.

3. **EMPLOYMENT:**

a. For each place of your employment or self-employment since the entry of the Final Judgment sought to be modified, state the following:

(1) name, address, and telephone number of your employer.

(2) dates of employment.

(3) job title and brief description of job duties.

(4) starting and ending salaries.

(5) name of your direct supervisor.

(6) all benefits received, including, for example, health, life, and disability insurance; expense account; use of automobile or automobile expense reimbursement; reimbursement for travel, food, or lodging expenses; payment of dues in any clubs or associations; and pension or profit sharing plans.

b. Other than as an employee, if you have been engaged in or associated with any business, commercial, or professional activity since the entry of the Final Judgment sought to be modified that was not detailed above, state for each such activity the following:

(1) name, address, and telephone number of each activity.

(2) dates you were connected with such activity.

(3) position title and brief description of activities.

(4) starting and ending compensation.

(5) name of all persons involved in the business, commercial, or professional activity with you.

(6) all benefits and compensation received, including, for example, health, life, and disability insurance; expense account; use of automobile or automobile expense reimbursement; reimbursement for travel, food, or lodging expenses; payment of dues in any clubs or associations; and pension or profit sharing plans.

c. If you have been unemployed at any time since the entry of the Final Judgment sought to be modified, state the dates of unemployment. If you have not been employed at any time since the entry of the Final Judgment sought to be modified, give the information requested above in question 3.a for your last period of employment.

4. **ASSETS:**

a. **Real Estate.** State the street address, if any, and if not, the legal description of all real property that you own or owned during the last 3 years, or since the entry of the Final Judgment sought to be modified, if shorter. For each property, state the following:

(1) the names and addresses of any other persons or entities holding any interest and their percentage of interest.

(2) the present fair market value.

b. **Tangible Personal Property.** List all items of tangible personal property that are owned by you or in which you have had any interest during the last 3 years, or since the entry of the Final Judgment sought to be modified, if shorter, including, but not limited to, motor vehicles, tools, furniture, boats, jewelry, art objects or other collections, and collectibles whose fair market value exceeds $100. For each item, state the following:

(1) the percentage and type interest you hold.

(2) the names and addresses of any other persons or entities holding any interest.

(3) the present fair market value.

c. **Intangible Personal Property.** Other than the financial accounts (checking, savings, money market, credit union accounts, or other such cash management accounts) listed in the answer to interrogatory 4.d below, list all items of intangible personal property that are owned by you or in which you have had any ownership interest (including closed accounts) within the last 3 years, or since the entry of the Final Judgment sought to be modified, if shorter, including, but not limited to, partnership and business interests (including good will), stocks, stock funds, mutual funds, bonds, bond funds, real estate investment trusts, receivables, certificates of deposit, notes, mortgages, and debts owed to you by another entity or person. For each item, state the following:

(1) the percentage and type interest you hold.

(2) the names and addresses of any other persons or entities holding any interest and the names and addresses of the persons and entities who are indebted to you.

(3) the present fair market value or the amounts you claim are owned by or owed to you, at the time of answering these interrogatories.

You may comply with this interrogatory (4.c) by providing copies of all periodic (monthly, quarterly, semi-annual, or annual) account statements for each such account for the preceding 3 years, or since the entry of the Final Judgment sought to be modified, if shorter. However, if the date of acquisition, the purchase price, and the market valuations are not clearly reflected in the periodic statements which are furnished, then these questions must be answered separately. You do not have to resubmit any periodic statements previously furnished under rule 12.285 (Mandatory Disclosure).

d. **Financial Accounts.** For all financial accounts (checking, savings, money market, credit union accounts, or other such cash management accounts) listed in your Financial Affidavit, in which you have had any legal or equitable interest, regardless of whether the interest is or was held in your own name individually, in your name with another person, or in any other name, give the following:

(1) name and address of each institution.

(2) name in which the account is or was maintained.

(3) account numbers.

(4) names of each person authorized to make withdrawals from the accounts.

(5) highest balance within each of the preceding 3 years, or since the entry of the Final Judgment sought to be modified, if shorter.

(6) lowest balance within each of the preceding 3 years, or since the entry of the Final Judgment sought to be modified, if shorter.

You may comply with this interrogatory (4.d) by providing copies of all periodic (monthly, quarterly, semi-annual, or annual) account statements for each such account for the preceding 3 years, or since the entry of the Final Judgment sought to be modified, if shorter. You do not have to resubmit account statements previously furnished under rule 12.285 (Mandatory Disclosure).

e. **Closed Financial Accounts.** For all financial accounts (checking, savings, money market, credit union accounts, or other such cash management accounts) closed within the last 3 years, or since the entry of the Final Judgment sought to be modified, if shorter, in which you have had any legal or equitable interest, regardless of whether the interest is or was held in your own name individually, in your name with another person, or in any other name, give the:

(1) name and address of each institution.

(2) name in which the account is or was maintained.

(3) account numbers.

(4) name of each person authorized to make withdrawals from the accounts.

(5) date account was closed.

f. **Trust.** For any interest in an estate, trust, insurance policy, or annuity, state the following:

(1) if you are the beneficiary of any estate, trust, insurance policy, or annuity, give for each one the following:

(a) identification of the estate, trust, insurance policy, or annuity.

(b) the nature, amount, and frequency of any distributions of benefits.

(c) the total value of the beneficiaries' interest in the benefit.

(d) whether the benefit is vested or contingent.

(2) if you have established any trust or are the trustee of a trust, state the following:

(a) the date the trust was established.

(b) the names and addresses of the trustees.

(c) the names and addresses of the beneficiaries.

(d) the names and addresses of the persons or entities who possess the trust documents.

(e) each asset that is held in each trust, with its fair market value.

g. **Name of Accountant, Bookkeeper, or Records Keeper.** State the names, addresses, and telephone numbers of your accountant, bookkeeper, and any other persons who possess your financial records, and state which records each possesses.

5. **LIABILITIES:**

a. **Loans, Liabilities, Debts, and Other Obligations.** For all loans, liabilities, debts, and other obligations (other than credit cards and charge accounts) listed in your Financial Affidavit, indicate for each the following:

(1) name and address of the creditor.

(2) name in which the obligation is or was incurred.

(3) loan or account number, if any.

(4) nature of the security, if any.

(5) payment schedule.

(6) present balance and current status of your payments.

(7) total amount of arrearage, if any.

You may comply with this interrogatory (5.a) by providing copies of all periodic (monthly, quarterly, semi-annual, or annual) account statements for each such account for the preceding 3 years, or since the entry of the Final Judgment sought to be modified, if shorter. You do not have to resubmit account statements previously furnished under rule 12.285 (Mandatory Disclosure).

b. **Credit Cards and Charge Accounts.** For all financial accounts (credit cards, charge accounts, or other such accounts) listed in your Financial Affidavit, in which you have had any legal or equitable interest, regardless of whether the interest is or was held in your own name individually, in your name with another person, or in any other name, give the following:

(1) name and address of the creditor.

(2) name in which the account is or was maintained.

(3) name of each person authorized to sign on the accounts.

(4) account numbers.

(5) present balance and current status of your payments.

(6) total amount of arrearage, if any.

(7) highest and lowest balance within each of the preceding 3 years, or since the entry of the Final Judgment sought to be modified, if shorter.

You may comply with this interrogatory (5.b) by providing copies of all periodic (monthly, quarterly, semi-annual, or annual) account statements for each such account for the preceding 3 years, or since the entry of the Final Judgment sought to be modified, if shorter. You do not have to resubmit account statements previously furnished under rule 12.285 (Mandatory Disclosure).

c. **Closed Credit Cards and Charge Accounts.** As to all financial accounts (credit card, charge accounts, or other such accounts) closed with no remaining balance, within the last 3 years, or since the entry of the Final Judgment sought to be modified, if shorter, in which you have had any legal or equitable interest, regardless of whether the interest is or was held in your own name individually, in your name with another person, or in any other name, give the following:

(1) name and address of each creditor.

(2) name in which the account is or was maintained.

(3) account numbers.

(4) name of each person authorized to sign on the accounts.

(5) date the balance was paid off.

(6) amount of final balance paid off.

You may comply with this interrogatory (5.c) by providing copies of all periodic (monthly, quarterly, semi-annual, or annual) account statements for each such account for the preceding 3 years, or since the entry of the Final Judgment sought to be modified, if shorter. You do not have to resubmit account statements previously furnished under rule 12.285 (Mandatory Disclosure).

6. **MISCELLANEOUS:**

a. If you are claiming a diminished earning capacity since the entry of the Final Judgment sought to be modified as grounds to modify alimony or deviate from the child support established in your case, describe in detail how your earning capacity is lowered and state all facts upon which you rely in your claim. If unemployed, state how, why, and when you lost your job.

b. If you are claiming a change in a mental or physical condition since the entry of the Final Judgment sought to be modified as grounds to modify alimony or change the child support established in your case, describe in detail how your mental and/or physical capacity has changed and state all facts upon which you rely in your claim. Identify the change in your mental and/or physical capacity, and state the name and address of all health care providers involved in the treatment of this mental or physical condition.

c. If you are requesting a change in shared or sole parental responsibility, primary residency, the parenting schedule, or any combination thereof, for the minor child(ren), describe in detail the change in circumstances since the entry of the Final Judgment sought to be modified that you feel justify the requested change. State when the change of circumstances occurred, how the change of circumstances affects the child(ren), and why it is in the best interests of the child(ren) that the Court make the requested change. Attach your parenting schedule.

d. If you do not feel the requested change in shared or sole parental responsibility, primary residency, the parenting schedule, or any combination thereof, for the minor child(ren) is in their best interests, describe in detail any facts since the entry of the Final Judgment sought to be modified that you feel justify the Court denying the requested change. State, in your opinion, what change, if any, of the parenting arrangement is justified or agreeable to you and why it is in the best interests of the child(ren).

7. **LONG FORM AFFIDAVIT:** If you filed the short form affidavit, Florida Family Law Rules of Procedure Form 12.902(b), and you were specifically requested in the Notice of Service of Standard Family Law Interrogatories to file the Long Form Affidavit, Form 12.902(c), you must do so within the time to serve the answers to these interrogatories.

I certify that a copy of this document was [☐ **one** only] ( ) mailed ( ) faxed and mailed ( ) hand delivered to the person(s) listed below on *{date}* ________________________________.

Other party or his/her attorney:
Name: ________________________________
Address: ________________________________
City, State, Zip: ________________________________
Fax Number: ________________________________

I understand that I am swearing or affirming under oath to the truthfulness of the answers to these interrogatories and that the punishment for knowingly making a false statement includes fines and/or imprisonment.

Dated: ________________________

____
Signature of Party
Printed Name: ________________________________
Address: ________________________________
City, State, Zip: ________________________________
Telephone Number: ________________________________
Fax Number: ________________________________

STATE OF FLORIDA
COUNTY OF ____________________

Sworn to or affirmed and signed before me on ______________ by _________________________.

____
NOTARY PUBLIC or DEPUTY CLERK

____
[Print, type, or stamp commissioned name of notary or clerk.]

____ Personally known
____ Produced identification
Type of identification produced ______________________

IF A NONLAWYER HELPED YOU FILL OUT THIS FORM, HE/SHE MUST FILL IN THE BLANKS BELOW: [fill in **all** blanks]
I, *{full legal name and trade name of nonlawyer}* ______________________________________,
a nonlawyer, located at *{street}* ______________________________, *{city}* _________________,
{state} ___________________, *{phone}* ________________, helped *{name}* _________________,
who is the [**one** only] ___ petitioner **or** ___ respondent, fill out this form.

IN THE CIRCUIT COURT OF THE ______________________ JUDICIAL CIRCUIT,
IN AND FOR ______________________ COUNTY, FLORIDA

Case No.: ______________________
Division: ______________________

______________________,
Petitioner,

and

______________________,
Respondent.

NOTICE OF PRODUCTION FROM NONPARTY

TO: ______________________
{all parties}

YOU ARE NOTIFIED that, after **10 days** from the date of service of this notice, the undersigned will apply to the clerk of this Court for issuance of the attached subpoena directed to *{name of person, organization, or agency}* ______________________, who is not a party, to produce the items listed at the time and place specified in the subpoena. Objections to the issuance of this subpoena must be filed with the clerk of the circuit court within **10 days**.

I certify that a copy of this document was [**one** only] ( ) mailed ( ) faxed and mailed ( ) hand delivered to the person(s) listed below on *{date}* ______________________.

Other party or his/her attorney (if represented)	Other
Printed Name	Printed Name
Address	Address
City State Zip	City State Zip
Telephone (area code and number)	Telephone (area code and number)
Fax (area code and number)	Fax (area code and number)

Dated: ______________________

____
Signature of Party
Printed Name: ______________________
Address: ______________________
City, State, Zip: ______________________
Telephone Number: ______________________
Fax Number: ______________________

IF A NONLAWYER HELPED YOU FILL OUT THIS FORM, HE/SHE MUST FILL IN THE BLANKS BELOW: [fill in **all** blanks]
I, *{full legal name and trade name of nonlawyer}* ______________________,
a nonlawyer, located at *{street}* ______________________, *{city}* ______________________,
{state} ______________________, *{phone}* ______________________, helped *{name}* ______________________,
who is the [**one** only] ___ petitioner **or** ___ respondent, fill out this form.

Supreme Court Approved Family Law Form 12.931(a) Notice of Production from Nonparty (9/00)

IN THE CIRCUIT COURT OF THE ______________________ JUDICIAL CIRCUIT,
IN AND FOR ______________________ COUNTY, FLORIDA

Case No.: ______________________
Division: ______________________

______________________________,
Petitioner,

and

______________________________,
Respondent.

SUBPOENA FOR PRODUCTION OF DOCUMENTS FROM NONPARTY

THE STATE OF FLORIDA
TO: ____

YOU **MUST** go to *{place}* ______________________________, on *{date}* ____________, at *{time}* __________, a.m./p.m. and bring with you at that time and place the following: ____

____

____

____

____

These items will be inspected and may be copied at that time. You will not have to leave the original items.

You may obey this subpoena by providing readable copies of the items to be produced to the party **or** his/her attorney whose name appears on this subpoena on or before the scheduled date of production. You may condition the preparation of the copies upon payment in advance of the reasonable cost of preparation. If you mail or deliver the copies to the attorney whose name appears on this subpoena before the date indicated above, you do not have to appear in person.

You may be in contempt of court if you fail to: (1) appear as specified; (2) furnish the records instead of appearing as provided above; or (3) object to this subpoena.

You can only be excused by the person whose name appears on this subpoena and, unless excused by that person or the Court, you shall respond as directed.

Dated: ____________________

CLERK OF THE CIRCUIT COURT

(SEAL)

By: ______________________________
Deputy Clerk

This part to be filled out by the court or filled in with information you have obtained from the court: If you are a person with a disability who needs any accommodation in order to participate in this proceeding, you are entitled, at no cost to you, to the provision of certain assistance. Please contact
{name} ____,
{address} ______________________________, *{telephone}* ______________,
within 2 working days of your receipt of this subpoena. If you are hearing or voice impaired, call TDD 1-800-

955-8771.

I CERTIFY that I gave notice to every other party to this action of my intent to serve a subpoena upon a person who is not a party to this action directing that person to produce documents or things without deposition. I also certify that no objection under Florida Rule of Civil Procedure 1.351 has been received by the undersigned within 10 days of service of this notice, if service was by hand delivery or appropriate facsimile transmission, and within 15 days if service was by mail.

Dated: ____________________

____
Signature of Party
Printed Name: ______________________________
Address: ______________________________
City, State, Zip: ______________________________
Telephone Number: ______________________________
Fax Number: ______________________________

IF A NONLAWYER HELPED YOU FILL OUT THIS FORM, HE/SHE MUST FILL IN THE BLANKS BELOW: [fill in **all** blanks]
I, *{full legal name and trade name of nonlawyer}*______________________________,
a nonlawyer, located at *{street}*______________________________, *{city}* ____________________,
{state} ____________________, *{phone}* __________________, helped *{name}* ____________________,
who is the [**one** only] ___ petitioner **or** ___ respondent, fill out this form.

IN THE CIRCUIT COURT OF THE ______________________ JUDICIAL CIRCUIT,
IN AND FOR _______________________ COUNTY, FLORIDA

Case No.: ________________________
Division: ________________________

____________________________________,
Petitioner,

and

____________________________________,
Respondent.

SUBPOENA

THE STATE OF FLORIDA

TO:

YOU ARE HEREBY COMMANDED to appear before the Honorable ______________ ____________________________________, Judge of the Court, at the ____________________ County Courthouse in ______________________________, Florida, on _________________, ______, at ___________ ____.M., to testify in this action. If you fail to appear, you may be in contempt of court.

You are subpoenaed to appear by the attorneys or parties designated below, and unless excused from this subpoena by these attorneys or parties, or the court, you shall respond to this subpoena as directed.

DATED: ________________________

(SEAL)

Attorney or Party Requesting Subpoena

CLERK OF THE CIRCUIT COURT

Name: ___________________________
Address: ___________________________
____
Telephone No.: _____________________

By: _______________________________
Deputy Clerk

IN THE CIRCUIT COURT OF THE _____________________ JUDICIAL CIRCUIT,
IN AND FOR ______________________ COUNTY, FLORIDA

Case No.: _______________________
Division: _______________________

________________________________,
Petitioner,

and

________________________________,
Respondent.

SUBPOENA DUCES TECUM

THE STATE OF FLORIDA

TO:

YOU ARE HEREBY COMMANDED to appear before the Honorable _____________ ______________________________, Judge of the Court, at the ________________ County Courthouse in ___________________________, Florida, on ________________, ______, at __________ ____.M., to testify in this action, AND to bring the following items with you:

If you fail to appear, you may be in contempt of court.

You are subpoenaed to appear by the attorneys or parties designated below, and unless excused from this subpoena by these attorneys or parties, or the court, you shall respond to this subpoena as directed.

DATED: ______________________

(SEAL)

Attorney or Party Requesting Subpoena

CLERK OF THE CIRCUIT COURT

Name: ___________________________
Address: __________________________
____
Telephone No.: _____________________

By: ________________________________
Deputy Clerk

IN THE CIRCUIT COURT OF THE ____________________________ JUDICIAL CIRCUIT,
IN AND FOR ____________________________ COUNTY, FLORIDA

Case No.: ______________________________
Division: ______________________________

______________________________________,
Petitioner,

and

______________________________________,
Respondent.

CERTIFICATE OF COMPLIANCE WITH MANDATORY DISCLOSURE

I, *{full legal name}* ____, certify that I have complied with the mandatory disclosure required by Florida Family Law Rule 12.285 as follows:

1. FOR TEMPORARY FINANCIAL RELIEF, ONLY:

The date the following documents were served: ____.
[**all** that apply]

____ a. Financial Affidavit (Filing of a Financial Affidavit cannot be waived.)
( ) Florida Family Law Rules of Procedure Form 12.902(b) (short form)
( ) Florida Family Law Rules of Procedure Form 12.902(c) (long form)

___ b. ( ) All personal (1040) federal tax, gift tax, and intangible personal property tax returns for the preceding year; or
( ) Transcript of tax return as provided by IRS form 4506; or
( ) IRS forms W-2, 1099, and K-1 for the past year because the income tax return for the past year has not been prepared.

___ c. Pay stubs or other evidence of earned income for the 3 months before the service of the financial affidavit.

2. FOR INITIAL, SUPPLEMENTAL, AND PERMANENT FINANCIAL RELIEF:

The date the following documents were served: ____.
[**all** that apply]

____ a. Financial Affidavit (Filing of a Financial Affidavit cannot be waived.)
( ) Florida Family Law Rules of Procedure Form 12.902(b) (short form)
( ) Florida Family Law Rules of Procedure Form 12.902(c) (long form)

____ b. ( ) All personal (1040) federal and state tax income returns, gift tax returns, and intangible personal property tax returns for the preceding 3 years;
( ) IRS forms W-2, 1099, and K-1 for the past year because the income tax return for the past year has not been prepared.

___ c. Pay stubs or other evidence of earned income for the 3 months before the service of the financial affidavit.

____ d. A statement identifying the source and amount of all income for the 3 months before the service of the financial affidavit, if not reflected on the pay stubs produced.

____ e. All loan applications and financial statements prepared for any purpose or used for any purpose within the 12 months preceding the service of the financial affidavit.

____ f. All deeds to real estate in which I presently own or owned an interest within the past 3 years. All promissory notes in which I presently own or owned an interest within the last 12 months. All present leases in which I own an interest.

____ g. All periodic statements for the last 3 months for all checking accounts and for the last year for all savings accounts, money market funds, certificates of deposit, etc.

____ h. All brokerage account statements for the last 12 months.

____ i. Most recent statement for any pension, profit sharing, deferred compensation, or retirement plan (for example, IRA, 401(k), 403(b), SEP, KEOGH, etc.) and summary plan description for any such plan in which I am a participant or alternate payee.

___ j. The declarations page, the last periodic statement, and the certificate for any group insurance for all life insurance policies insuring my life or the life of my spouse.

____ k. All health and dental insurance cards covering either of me or my spouse and/or our dependent child(ren).

___ l. Corporate, partnership, and trust tax returns for the last 3 tax years, in which I have an ownership or interest greater than or equal to 30%.

____ m. All credit card and charge account statements and other records showing my(our) indebtedness as of the date of the filing of this action and for the prior 3 months. All promissory notes on which I presently owe or owed within the past year. All lease agreements I presently owe.

____ n. All premarital and marital agreements between the parties to this case.

____ o. If a modification proceeding, all written agreements entered into between the parties at any time since the order to be modified was entered.

____ p. All documents and tangible evidence relating to claims for special equity or nonmarital status of an asset or debt.

____ q. Any court order directing that I pay or receive spousal support (alimony) or child support.

I certify that a copy of this document was [**one** only] ( ) mailed ( ) faxed and mailed ( ) hand delivered to the person(s) listed below on *{date}* ______________________.

Other party or his/her attorney:
Name: ______________________
Address: ______________________
City, State, Zip: ______________________
Fax Number: ______________________

Dated: ______________________

____
Signature of Party
Printed Name: ______________________
Address: ______________________
City, State, Zip: ______________________
Telephone Number: ______________________
Fax Number: ______________________

IF A NONLAWYER HELPED YOU FILL OUT THIS FORM, HE/SHE MUST FILL IN THE BLANKS BELOW: [fill in **all** blanks]
I, *{full legal name and trade name of nonlawyer}* ______________________,
a nonlawyer, located at *{street}* ______________________, *{city}* ______________________,
{state} ______________________, *{phone}* ______________________, helped *{name}* ______________________,
who is the [**one** only] ___ petitioner **or** ___ respondent, fill out this form.

IN THE CIRCUIT COURT OF THE ____________________ JUDICIAL CIRCUIT,
IN AND FOR ____________________ COUNTY, FLORIDA

Case No.: ____________________
Division: ____________________

____________________,
Petitioner,

and

____________________,
Respondent.

MOTION FOR APPOINTMENT OF GUARDIAN AD LITEM

( ) Petitioner ( ) Respondent requests that the Court enter an order appointing a guardian ad litem with all powers, privileges, and responsibilities authorized in section 61.403, Florida Statutes, and states:

1. The following minor child(ren) is (are) subject to this proceeding:

Name	Birth date	Age	Sex	Location/Address
________	________	____	____	________
________	________	____	____	________
________	________	____	____	________
________	________	____	____	________
________	________	____	____	________

2. Verified allegations of child abuse or neglect as defined in section 39.01(2) or (45), Florida Statutes, ( ) HAVE ( ) HAVE NOT been made in this case.

3. The matters before the Court regarding the minor child(ren) are:
____ a. sole/shared parental responsibility
____ b. primary/secondary residential parent
____ c. visitation
____ d. other: ____________________

4. It is in the best interests of the minor child(ren) that a guardian ad litem be appointed to advance the best interests of the minor child(ren) because: ____________________
____
____
____
____
____

I certify that a copy of this document was [one only] ( ) mailed ( ) faxed and mailed ( ) hand delivered to the person(s) listed below on *{date}* ____________________.

Other party or his/her attorney:
Name: ____________________
Address: ____________________
City, State, Zip: ____________________
Fax Number: ____________________

Dated: ______________________________

____
Signature of Party
Printed Name: ________________________________
Address: ____________________________________
City, State, Zip: _____________________________
Telephone Number: ___________________________
Fax Number: _________________________________

IF A NONLAWYER HELPED YOU FILL OUT THIS FORM, HE/SHE MUST FILL IN THE BLANKS BELOW: [fill in **all** blanks]
I, *{full legal name and trade name of nonlawyer}* ____,
a nonlawyer, located at *{street}* _________________________________, *{city}* ___________________,
{state} ____________________, *{phone}* __________________, helped *{name}* ___________________,
who is the [**one** only] ___ petitioner **or** ___ respondent, fill out this form.

IN THE CIRCUIT COURT OF THE ______________________ JUDICIAL CIRCUIT,
IN AND FOR ______________________ COUNTY, FLORIDA

Case No.: ______________________
Division: ______________________

______________________,
Petitioner,

and

______________________,
Respondent.

ORDER APPOINTING GUARDIAN AD LITEM

Upon ( ) Petitioner's ( ) Respondent's ( ) Court's own motion to appoint guardian ad litem for the minor child(ren) herein and the Court finding that

____ a. verified allegations of child abuse or neglect as defined in section 39.01(2) or (45), Florida Statutes, have been made and are determined to be well-founded,

OR

____ b. it is otherwise in the best interests of the child(ren) that a guardian ad litem be appointed to advance the best interests of the minor child(ren) because: ______________________
____
____
____
______________________, it is thereupon

ORDERED as follows:

1. A guardian ad litem shall be appointed for the minor child(ren), *{name(s)}* ______________________
______________________,
now residing at *{street address}* ______________________.

2. The State of Florida Guardian ad Litem Program for the _____ JudicialCircuit shall assign a certified guardian ad litem for the minor child(ren). Upon filing of the Notice of Acceptance, the guardian ad litem can be served c/o Guardian ad Litem Program, *{address}* ______________________
______________________.

Pursuant to the State of Florida Guardian ad Litem Standards of Operation adopted by the Supreme Court of Florida, if the Guardian ad Litem Program is appointed in the absence of a well founded allegation of abuse or neglect, an automatic discharge by the Court will occur upon filing of a Motion to Discharge by the Program if the Program does not have sufficient volunteer and/or supervisory resources available to accommodate this appointment.

OR

{name} ______________________, an attorney in good standing with The Florida Bar, is appointed to serve as a private guardian ad litem for the above minor child(ren). The fees of the private guardian shall be paid by: ( ) Petitioner ( ) Respondent ( ) each party equally ( ) other, *{specify}* ______________________
______________________.

3. The guardian ad litem is a party to any judicial proceeding from the date of this order until the date of discharge and shall have all of the powers, privileges, and responsibilities authorized in section 61.403, Florida Statutes, to the extent necessary to advance the best interests of the minor child(ren).

4. The guardian ad litem must be provided with copies of all pleadings, notices, stipulations, and other documents filed in this action and is entitled to reasonable notice before any action affecting the child(ren) is taken by either of the parties, their counsel, or the Court. The guardian ad litem is entitled, through counsel, to be present at any depositions, hearings, or other proceedings concerning the minor child(ren).

5. The guardian ad litem may investigate the allegations of the pleadings affecting the minor child(ren), and after proper notice may interview witnesses or any other person having information concerning the welfare of the minor child(ren).

6. The guardian ad litem shall maintain any information received from any source described in section 61.403(2), Florida Statutes, as confidential and shall not disclose such information except in reports to the Court served upon both parties to this cause and their counsel, or as directed by the Court.

7. The parties, or any other person entrusted by the parties with the care of the minor child(ren) shall allow the guardian ad litem access to the minor child(ren) at reasonable times and locations and no person shall obstruct the guardian ad litem from the minor child(ren).

8. The guardian ad litem shall submit his or her recommendations to the Court regarding any stipulation or agreement, whether incidental, temporary, or permanent, which affects the interest or welfare of the minor child(ren), within 10 days after the date the stipulation or agreement is served upon the guardian ad litem.

9. The guardian ad litem shall file a written report with the Court, which may include recommendations and a statement of the wishes of the minor child(ren). The report must be filed and served on all parties at least 20 days prior to the hearing at which it will be presented unless the Court waives such time period. The guardian ad litem's report shall address the following areas, subject to any conditions ordered by this Court:

____ a. parental responsibility of child(ren);
____ b. residence of child(ren);
____ c. visitation, including times and locations;
____ d. appearance of child(ren) at depositions/hearings;
____ e. relocation;
____ f. best interests of child(ren) regarding scientific tests; and/or
____ g. other ____
____
____

This appointment is subject to the following conditions: ____________________
____
____
____
____
____

10. The guardian ad litem is automatically discharged without further order 30 days after the entry of a final order or judgment in this proceeding, unless otherwise ordered by the Court.

ORDERED on ________________________.

____
CIRCUIT JUDGE

COPIES TO:
Petitioner (or his or her attorney)
Respondent (or his or her attorney)
____ Guardian ad Litem Program
____ Other: ______________________________

IN THE CIRCUIT COURT OF THE __________________________ JUDICIAL CIRCUIT,
IN AND FOR ____________________________ COUNTY, FLORIDA

Case No.: ____________________________
Division: ____________________________

____________________________________,
Petitioner,

and

____________________________________,
Respondent.

MOTION TO DEVIATE FROM CHILD SUPPORT GUIDELINES

( ) Petitioner ( ) Respondent requests that the Court enter an order granting the following:

SECTION I
[**one** only]

____ a. **MORE** child support than the amount required by the child support guidelines. The Court should order MORE child support than the amount required by the child support guidelines because of:

[**all** that apply to your situation]
____ 1. Extraordinary medical, psychological, educational, or dental expenses;
____ 2. Seasonal variations in one or both parent's income;
____ 3. Age(s) of the child(ren), taking into consideration the greater needs of older child(ren);
____ 4. Special needs that have been met traditionally within the family budget even though the fulfilling of those needs will cause support to exceed the guidelines;
____ 5. The amount of time each child will spend with each parent under the shared parental arrangement;
____ 6. The direct and indirect financial expenses for each child as set forth in s. 61.30(11)(b)3, Florida Statutes;
____ 7. Total available assets of mother, father, and child(ren);
____ 8. Impact of IRS dependency exemption and waiver of that exemption;
____ 9. Residency of subsequently born or adopted child(ren) with the obligor, including consideration of the subsequent spouse's income;
____ 10. The comparative income of each parent, considering all relevant factors, as provided in s. 61.30(2)(a), Florida Statutes;
____ 11. The station in life of each parent and each child;
____ 12. The standard of living experienced by the entire family during the marriage;
____ 13. The financial status and ability of each parent; and/or
____ 14. Any other adjustment that is needed to achieve an equitable result, which may include reasonable and necessary expenses jointly incurred during the marriage.

Explain any items marked above: ____
____
____.

____ b. **LESS** child support than the amount required by the child support guidelines. The Court should order LESS child support than the amount required by the child support guidelines because of:

[**all** that apply to your situation]
____ 1. Extraordinary medical, psychological, educational, or dental expenses;
____ 2. Independent income of child(ren), excluding the child(ren)'s SSI income;
____ 3. Payment of both child support and spousal support to a parent that regularly has been paid and for which there is a demonstrated need;

____ 4. Seasonal variations in one or both parent's income;
____ 5. Age of the child(ren), taking into consideration the greater needs of older child(ren);
____ 6. The amount of time each child will spend with each parent under the shared parental arrangement;
____ 7. The direct and indirect financial expenses for each child as set forth in s. 61.30(11)(b), Florida Statutes;
____ 8. The comparative income of each parent, considering all relevant factors, as provided in s. 61.30(2)(a), Florida Statutes;
____ 9. Total available assets of obligee, obligor, and child(ren);
____ 10. Impact of IRS dependency exemption and waiver of that exemption;
____ 11. Application of the child support guidelines requires the obligor to pay more than 55% of gross income for a single support order;
____ 12. The station in life of each parent and each child;
____ 13. The standard of living experienced by the entire family during the marriage;
____ 14. The financial status and ability of each parent; and/or
____ 15. Any other adjustment that is needed to achieve an equitable result, which may include reasonable and necessary expenses jointly incurred during the marriage.

Explain any items marked above:____
____
____.

SECTION II. INCOME AND ASSETS OF CHILD(REN) COMMON TO BOTH PARTIES

List the total of any independent income or assets of the child(ren) common to both parties (income from Social Security, gifts, stocks/bonds, employment, trust fund(s), investment(s), etc.). Attach an explanation.

TOTAL VALUE OF ASSETS OF CHILD(REN) **$ __________**

TOTAL MONTHLY INCOME OF CHILD(REN) **$ __________**

SECTION III. EXPENSES FOR CHILD(REN) COMMON TO BOTH PARTIES

All amounts must be MONTHLY. See the instructions with this form to figure out money amounts for anything that is NOT paid monthly. Attach more paper, if needed. Items included under "other" should be listed separately with separate dollar amounts.

1. Monthly nursery, babysitting, or other child care 1. $ __________
2. Monthly after-school care 2. $ __________
3. Monthly school tuition 3. $ __________
4. Monthly school supplies, books, and fees 4. $ __________
5. Monthly after-school activities 5. $ __________
6. Monthly lunch money 6. $ __________
7. Monthly private lessons/tutoring 7. $ __________
8. Monthly allowance 8. $ __________
9. Monthly clothing 9. $ __________
10. Monthly uniforms 10. $ __________
11. Monthly entertainment (movies, birthday parties, etc.) 11. $ __________
12. Monthly health and dental insurance premiums 12. $ __________
13. Monthly medical, dental, prescription charges (unreimbursed) 13. $ __________
14. Monthly psychiatric/psychological/counselor (unreimbursed) 14. $ __________
15. Monthly orthodontic (unreimbursed) 15. $ __________
16. Monthly grooming 16. $ __________
17. Monthly non-prescription medications/cosmetics/toiletries/sundries 17. $ __________
18. Monthly gifts from children to others (other children, relatives, teachers, etc.) 18. $ __________
19. $ __________
19. Monthly camp or other summer activities 20. $ __________

20. Monthly clubs (Boy/Girl Scouts, etc.) or recreational fees 21. $ ____________
21. Monthly visitation expenses (for nonresidential parent) 22. $ ____________
Explain: ____
22. Monthly insurance (life, etc.) *{explain}*: ______________________

Other *{explain}*: 23. $ ____________
23. ____ 24. $ ____________
24. ____ 25. $ ____________
25. ____

26. TOTAL EXPENSES FOR CHILD(REN) COMMON TO BOTH PARTIES
(add lines 1 through 25) **26. $ ____________**

I have filed, will file, or am filing with this form the following additional documents:

1. Florida Family Law Family Law Financial Affidavit, Florida Family Law Rules of Procedure Form 12.902(b) or (c).

2. Child Support Guidelines Worksheet, Florida Family Law Rules of Procedure Form 12.902(e).

I certify that a copy of this document was [**one** only] ( ) mailed ( ) faxed and mailed ( ) hand delivered to the person(s) listed below on *{date}* ____________________________.

Other party or his/her attorney:
Name: ______________________________
Address: ______________________________
City, State, Zip: ______________________________
Fax Number: ______________________________

I understand that I am swearing or affirming under oath to the truthfulness of the claims made in this motion and that the punishment for knowingly making a false statement includes fines and/or imprisonment.

Dated: ____________________ ______________________________
Signature
Printed Name: ______________________________
Address: ______________________________
City, State, Zip: ______________________________
Telephone Number: ______________________________
Fax Number: ______________________________

STATE OF FLORIDA
COUNTY OF ____________________

Sworn to or affirmed and signed before me on ____________ by ______________________.

____
NOTARY PUBLIC or DEPUTY CLERK

____
[Print, type, or stamp commissioned name of notary or clerk.]

___ Personally known
___ Produced identification
Type of identification produced ____________________

IF A NONLAWYER HELPED YOU FILL OUT THIS FORM, HE/SHE MUST FILL IN THE BLANKS BELOW: [fill in **all** blanks]

I, *{full legal name and trade name of nonlawyer}*____________________________________,
a nonlawyer, located at *{street}*________________________________, *{city}* __________________,
{state} ____________________, *{phone}* ________________, helped *{name}* __________________,
who is the [**one** only] ___ petitioner **or** ___ respondent, fill out this form.

IN THE CIRCUIT COURT OF THE ______________________ JUDICIAL CIRCUIT,
IN AND FOR ______________________ COUNTY, FLORIDA

Case No.: ______________________
Division: ______________________

______________________,
Petitioner,

and

______________________,
Respondent.

MOTION FOR TESTIMONY AND ATTENDANCE OF MINOR CHILD(REN)

( ) Petitioner ( ) Respondent requests that the Court enter an order authorizing one or more of the actions listed below related to the following minor child(ren):

Name	Birth date	Age

[all that apply]

____ 1. Minor child(ren), *{name(s)}* ______________________, be subpoenaed to appear at hearing now scheduled for *{date}* ______________________.

____ 2. Minor child(ren), *{name(s)}* ______________________, attend deposition of *{name(s)}* ______________________ now scheduled for *{date}* ______________ at *{location}* ______________________.

____ 3. Minor child(ren)'s, *{name(s)}* ______________________, deposition be taken on *{date}* ______________ at *{location}* ______________________.

____ 4. Minor child(ren), *{name(s)}* ______________________, be brought to court to attend hearing now scheduled for *{date}* ______________ at *{location}* ______________________.

____ 5. Minor child(ren), *{name(s)}* ______________________, be brought to court to testify in a hearing now scheduled for *{date}* ______________ at *{location}* ______________________.

The Court should do this because: ______________________
____
____
____
____
____
______________________.

I certify that a copy of this document was [**one** only] ( ) mailed ( ) faxed and mailed ( ) hand delivered to the person(s) listed below on *{date}* ______________________.

Other party or his/her attorney:
Name: ______________________________
Address: ______________________________
City, State, Zip: ______________________________
Fax Number: ______________________________

Dated: ______________________________

____
Signature of Party
Printed Name: ______________________________
Address: ______________________________
City, State, Zip: ______________________________
Telephone Number: ______________________________
Fax Number: ______________________________

IF A NONLAWYER HELPED YOU FILL OUT THIS FORM, HE/SHE MUST FILL IN THE BLANKS BELOW: [fill in **all** blanks]
I, *{full legal name and trade name of nonlawyer}* ______________________________,
a nonlawyer, located at *{street}* ______________________________, *{city}* ______________________________,
{state} ______________________________, *{phone}* ______________________________, helped *{name}* ______________________________,
who is the [**one** only] ___ petitioner **or** ___ respondent, fill out this form.

IN THE CIRCUIT COURT OF THE ________________________ JUDICIAL CIRCUIT,
IN AND FOR ________________________ COUNTY, FLORIDA

Case No.: ________________________
Division: ________________________

________________________,
Petitioner,

and

________________________,
Respondent.

ORDER FOR TESTIMONY AND ATTENDANCE OF MINOR CHILD(REN)

Upon motion of ( ) Petitioner ( ) Respondent for testimony or attendance of minor child(ren) in these proceedings, and the Court finding that a showing of good cause has been made in support of the motion, it is

ORDERED that

[**all** that apply]

____ 1. Minor child(ren), *{name(s)}* ________________________,
be subpoenaed to appear at hearing now scheduled for *{date}* ________________________.

____ 2. Minor child(ren), *{name(s)}* ________________________,
attend deposition of *{name(s)}* ____________ now scheduled for *{date}* ____________
at *{location}* ________________________.

____ 3. Minor child(ren)'s, *{name(s)}* ________________________,
deposition be taken on *{date}* ____________ at *{location}* ________________________
________________________.

____ 4. Minor child(ren), *{name(s)}* ________________________,
be brought to court to attend hearing now scheduled for *{date}* ____________ at
{location} ________________________.

____ 5. Minor child(ren), *{name(s)}* ________________________,
be brought to court to testify in a hearing now scheduled for *{date}* ____________ at
{location} ________________________.

If the minor child or the person bringing the child is a person with a disability who needs any accommodation in order to participate in this proceeding, the child is entitled, at no cost, to the provision of certain assistance. Please contact *{name}* ________________________, *{address}* ________________________, *{telephone}* ____________, within 2 working days of your receipt of this order. If you are hearing or voice impaired, call TDD 1-800-955-8771.

Conditions or limitations concerning the minor child(ren), if any, include: ________________________
____
____
____
____
____
____
____
________________________.

ORDERED on ______________________.

____
CIRCUIT JUDGE

COPIES TO:
Petitioner (or his or her attorney)
Respondent (or his or her attorney)

IN THE CIRCUIT COURT OF THE ______________________ JUDICIAL CIRCUIT,
IN AND FOR ______________________ COUNTY, FLORIDA

Case No.: ______________________
Division: ______________________

______________________________________,
Petitioner,

and

______________________________________,
Respondent.

MOTION FOR CIVIL CONTEMPT/ENFORCEMENT

( ) Petitioner ( ) Respondent requests that the Court enter an order of civil contempt/enforcement against ( ) Petitioner ( ) Respondent in this case because:

1. A final judgment or order *{title of final judgment or order}* ______________________ in this case was entered on *{date}* ______________, by *{court, city, and state}* ______________________.

   ☐ Check here if the judgment or order is not from this Court and attach a copy.

2. This order of the Court required the other party in this case to do or not do the following: *{Explain what the other party was ordered to do or not do.}* ______________________

   ☐ Check here if additional pages are attached.

3. The other party in this case has willfully failed to comply with this order of the Court: *{Explain what the other party has or has not done.}* ______________________

   ☐ Check here if additional pages are attached.

4. I respectfully request that the Court issue an order holding the above-named person in civil contempt, if appropriate, and/or providing the following relief:

   ____ a. enforcing or compelling compliance with the prior order or judgment;
   ____ b. awarding a monetary judgment;
   ____ c. if a monetary judgment was included in the prior order, issuing a writ of execution or garnishment or other appropriate process;
   ____ d. awarding prejudgment interest;
   ____ e. requiring the other party to pay costs and fees in connection with this motion;
   ____ f. if the other party is found to be in civil contempt, ordering a compensatory fine;
   ____ g. if the other party is found to be in civil contempt, ordering a coercive fine;

____ h. if the other party is found to be in civil contempt, ordering incarceration of the other party;

____ i. issuing a writ of possession for real property, writ for possession of personal property, or other appropriate writ;

____ j. issuing a writ of bodily attachment if the other party fails to appear at the hearing set on this motion;

____ k. requiring the other party to make payments through the central governmental depository;

____ l. requiring the support payments to be automatically deducted from the other party's income or funds;

____ m. requiring the other party to seek employment;

____ n. awarding make-up visitation with minor child(ren) as follows *{explain}*: ____________
____
____
____
____
____; and

____ o. awarding other relief *{explain}*: ______________________________
____
____
____
____
____
____.

I certify that a copy of this document was [☐ one only] ( ) mailed ( ) faxed and mailed ( ) hand delivered to the person(s) listed below on *{date}* ______________________________.

Other party or his/her attorney:
Name: ______________________________
Address: ______________________________
City, State, Zip: ______________________________
Fax Number: ______________________________

I understand that I am swearing or affirming under oath to the truthfulness of the claims made above and that the punishment for knowingly making a false statement includes fines and/or imprisonment.

Dated: ______________________________

____
Signature of Party
Printed Name: ______________________________
Address: ______________________________
City, State, Zip: ______________________________
Telephone Number: ______________________________
Fax Number: ______________________________

STATE OF FLORIDA
COUNTY OF ______________________________

Sworn to or affirmed and signed before me on ____________________ by ____________________.

____

Florida Supreme Court Approved Family Law Form 12.960, Motion for Civil Contempt/Enforcement (9/00)

NOTARY PUBLIC or DEPUTY CLERK

____
[Print, type, or stamp commissioned name of notary or clerk.]

____ Personally known
____ Produced identification
Type of identification produced ____________________

IF A NONLAWYER HELPED YOU FILL OUT THIS FORM, HE/SHE MUST FILL IN THE BLANKS BELOW: [fill in **all** blanks]
I, *{full legal name and trade name of nonlawyer}*______________________________,
a nonlawyer, located at *{street}*____________________, *{city}* ______________,
{state} __________, *{phone}* ______________, helped *{name}* ____________________,
who is the [**one** only] ___ petitioner **or** ___ respondent, fill out this form.

Acknowledgement of Paternity

Statement of Father

I, ______________________________, being first sworn, on oath state:
(full legal name)

I am a resident of ______________________________ County, Florida.
(county)

I am the natural father of ______________________________,
(full legal name of child)

a ( ) male ( ) female child born to ______________________________,
(full legal name of mother)

on ____________________, in ______________________________,
(date of birth) (city)

______________________________ County, ____________________.
(county) (state)

The child's Social Security Number: ( ) is ____________________.

( ) has not yet been obtained.

No father was listed on the child's birth certificate.

I was not married to the mother of the above-named child at the time of the child's conception or at any subsequent time.

The child is not the legitimate child of any other man.

I am aware of my right to rescind this document within 60 days for any reason, and that after said 60-day period I may only rescind this document upon a showing of fraud, duress, or mistake of fact.

Date ____________________

____
Signature of Father

Social Security Number: ____________________

Statement of Mother

I, ______________________________, being first sworn, on oath state:
(full legal name)

I am a resident of ________________________________ County, Florida.
(county)

I am the natural mother of ______________________________________,
(full legal name of child)

a ( ) male ( ) female child born on _________________, in _______________,
(date of birth) (city)

____________________________ County, _________________________.
(county) (state)

The natural father of the child is ________________________________.
(full legal name of father)

No father was listed on the child's birth certificate.

I was not married at the time of the child's conception or at any subsequent time.

The child is not the legitimate child of any other man.

Date ____________________

____
Signature of Mother

Social Security Number: __________________

STATE OF FLORIDA

COUNTY OF _____________________

Sworn to or affirmed and signed before me on ________________________, by
____________________________ and ____________________________.

____
NOTARY PUBLIC

____
(Print, type, or stamp commissioned name of notary.)

____ Personally known

____ Produced identification

Type of identification produced _________________________

IN THE CIRCUIT COURT OF THE ______________________ JUDICIAL CIRCUIT,
IN AND FOR ______________________ COUNTY, FLORIDA

Case No.: ______________________
Division: ______________________

______________________,
Petitioner,

and

______________________,
Respondent.

PETITION TO DETERMINE PATERNITY AND FOR RELATED RELIEF

Petitioner, *{full legal name}* ______________________, being sworn, certifies that the following information is true:

This is an action for paternity and to determine custody, parental responsibility, and child support under chapter 742, Florida Statutes.

SECTION I.

1. Petitioner is the ( ) mother ( ) father of the following minor child(ren):

Name	Place of Birth	Birth date	Sex
(1) ____________	____________	____________	______
(2) ____________	____________	____________	______
(3) ____________	____________	____________	______
(4) ____________	____________	____________	______
(5) ____________	____________	____________	______
(6) ____________	____________	____________	______

2. Petitioner currently lives at: *{street address, city, state}* ______________________
______________________.

3. Respondent currently lives at: *{street address, city, state}* ______________________
______________________.

4. Both parties are over the age of 18, and neither is, nor has been within a 30-day period immediately prior to this date, a person in the military service of the United States as defined by the Amended Sailors' and Soldiers' Civil Relief Act of 1940.

5. Neither Petitioner nor Respondent is mentally incapacitated.

6. A completed **Uniform Child Custody Jurisdiction Act (UCCJA) Affidavit,** ✎❑ Florida Supreme Court Approved Family Law Form 12.902(d), is filed with this petition.

7. A completed **Notice of Social Security Number,** ✎❑ Florida Supreme Court Approved Family Law Form 12.902(j), is filed with this petition.

8. A completed **Family Law Financial Affidavit,** ✎❑ Florida Family Law Rules of Procedure Form

12.902(b) or (c), is, or will be, filed.

9. **Paternity Facts.**

[√ **one** only]

____ a. Paternity has previously been established as a matter of law.

____ b. The parties engaged in sexual intercourse with each other in the month(s) of *{list month(s) and year(s)}* ________________________________,
at *{city and state}* ________________________________.
As a result of the sexual intercourse, ( ) Petitioner ( ) Respondent conceived and gave birth to the minor child(ren) named in paragraph 1. ( ) Petitioner ( ) Respondent is the natural father of the minor child(ren). The mother ( ) was ( ) was not married at the time of the conception and/or birth of the minor child(ren) named in paragraph 1. If the mother was married, the name and address of her husband at the time of conception and/or birth is: ________________________________
________________________________.

SECTION II. CHILD CUSTODY, PARENTAL RESPONSIBILITY, AND VISITATION

1. The minor child(ren) currently reside(s) with ( ) Mother ( ) Father ( ) Other: *{explain}* ____
________________________________.

2. **Parental Responsibility.** It is in the child(ren)'s best interests that parental responsibility be:

[√ **one** only]

____ a. shared by both Father and Mother.

____ b. awarded solely to ( ) Father ( ) Mother. Shared parental responsibility would be detrimental to the child(ren) because: ________________________________
____
____
________________________________.

3. **Primary Residential Parent (Custody).** It is in the best interests of the child(ren) that the primary residential parent be ( ) Father ( ) Mother ( ) undesignated ( ) rotating because ________
____
____
________________________________.

4. **Visitation or Time Sharing.** Petitioner requests that the Court order

[√ **all** that apply]

____ a. no visitation.

____ b. limited visitation.

____ c. supervised visitation.

____ d. supervised or third-party exchange of child(ren).

____ e. visitation or time sharing as determined by the Court.

____ f. a visitation or time sharing schedule as follows:

Explain the requested visitation or time sharing schedule: ________________________________
____
____
____
____
____
____

Explain why this schedule is in the best interests of the child(ren): ________________________________

____

____

____

Has the above visitation or time sharing schedule been agreed to by the parties? ( ) yes ( ) no

5. The minor child(ren) should
[√ **only** one]
____ a. retain his/her (their) present name(s).
____ b. receive a change of name as follows:

present name(s)	be changed to
(1) ____________	(1) ____________
(2) ____________	(2) ____________
(3) ____________	(3) ____________
(4) ____________	(4) ____________
(5) ____________	(5) ____________
(6) ____________	(6) ____________

SECTION III. CHILD SUPPORT

[√ **all** that apply]

____ 1. Petitioner requests that the Court award child support as determined by Florida's child support guidelines, section 61.30, Florida Statutes. A completed **Child Support Guidelines Worksheet**, ✎❑ Florida Family Law Rules of Procedure Form 12.902(e), is, or will be, filed. Such support should be ordered retroactive to
[√ **one** only]
____ a. the date when the parents did not reside together in the same household with the child, not to exceed a period of 24 months before the date of filing of this petition.
____ b. the date of the filing of this petition.
____ c. other: *{date}* ________________. *{Explain}* ________________
____

____ 2. Petitioner requests that the Court award a child support amount that is more than or less than Florida's child support guidelines. Petitioner understands that a **Motion to Deviate from Child Support Guidelines**, ✎❑ Florida Supreme Court Approved Family Law Form 12.943, **must** be completed before the Court will consider this request.

____ 3. Petitioner requests that medical/dental insurance coverage for the minor child(ren) be provided by:
[√ **one** only]
____ a. Father.
____ b. Mother.

____ 4. Petitioner requests that uninsured medical/dental expenses for the child(ren) be paid by:
[√ **one** only]
____ a. Father.
____ b. Mother.
____ c. Father and Mother each pay one-half.
____ d. Father and Mother each pay according to the percentages in the **Child Support Guidelines Worksheet**, ✎❑Florida Family Law Rules of Procedure Form 12.902(e).

____ e. Other *{explain}*: ____
____
____.

____ 5. Petitioner requests that life insurance to secure child support be provided by:
[√ **one** only]
____ a. Father.
____ b. Mother.
____ c. Both.

____ 6. ( ) Petitioner ( ) Respondent ( ) Both has (have) incurred medical expenses in the amount of $__________ on behalf of the minor child(ren), including hospital and other expenses incidental to the birth of the minor child(ren). There should be an appropriate allocation or apportionment of these expenses.

____ 7. ( ) Petitioner ( ) Respondent ( ) Both has (have) received past public assistance for this (these) minor child(ren).

PETITIONER'S REQUEST

1. Petitioner requests a hearing on this petition and understands that he or she must attend the hearing.

2. Petitioner requests that the Court enter an order that:
[√ **all** that apply]
____ a. establishes paternity of the minor child(ren), ordering proper scientific testing, if necessary;
____ b. establishes parental responsibility, custody, and visitation of the minor child(ren);
____ c. awards child support, including medical/dental insurance coverage for the minor child(ren);
____ d. determines the appropriate allocation or apportionment of all expenses incidental to the birth of the child(ren), including hospital and medical expenses;
____ e. determines the appropriate allocation or apportionment of all other past, present, and future medical and dental expenses incurred or to be incurred on behalf of the minor child(ren);
____ f. changes the child(ren)'s name(s);
____ g. other relief as follows: ____
____
____
____; and
grants such other relief as may be appropriate and in the best interests of the minor child(ren).

I understand that I am swearing and affirming under oath to the truthfulness of the claims made in this petition and that the punishment for knowingly making a false statement includes fines and/or imprisonment.

Dated: ______________________

____
Signature of Petitioner
Printed Name: ______________________________
Address: ______________________________
City, State, Zip: ______________________________
Telephone Number: ______________________________
Fax Number: ______________________________

STATE OF FLORIDA

COUNTY OF ____________________

Sworn to or affirmed and signed before me on _______________ by ___________________________.

____
NOTARY PUBLIC or DEPUTY CLERK

____
[Print, type, or stamp commissioned name of notary or clerk.]

____ Personally known
____ Produced identification
Type of identification produced ________________________

IF A NONLAWYER HELPED YOU FILL OUT THIS FORM, HE/SHE MUST FILL IN THE BLANKS BELOW: [✍ fill in **all** blanks]
I, *{full legal name and trade name of nonlawyer}* ______________________________________,
a nonlawyer, located at *{street}* ______________________________, *{city}* ___________________,
{state} ___________________, *{phone}* _________________, helped *{name}* ___________________,
who is the petitioner, fill out this form.

IN THE CIRCUIT COURT OF THE ______________________ JUDICIAL CIRCUIT,
IN AND FOR ______________________ COUNTY, FLORIDA

Case No.: ______________________
Division: ______________________

______________________,
Petitioner,

and

______________________,
Respondent.

ANSWER TO PETITION TO DETERMINE PATERNITY AND FOR RELATED RELIEF

I, *{full legal name}* ______________________, Respondent, being sworn, certify that the following information is true:

1. I **agree** with Petitioner as to the allegations raised in the following numbered paragraphs in the Petition and, therefore, **admit** those allegations: *{indicate section and paragraph number}* ______________________.

2. I **disagree** with Petitioner as to the allegations raised in the following numbered paragraphs in the Petition and, therefore, **deny** those issues: *{indicate section and paragraph number}* ______________________.

3. I currently am unable to admit or deny the following paragraphs due to lack of information: *{indicate section and paragraph number}* ______________________.

4. A completed **Uniform Child Custody Jurisdiction Act (UCCJA) Affidavit,** ✎❑ Florida Supreme Court Approved Family Law Form 12.902(d), is filed with this petition.

5. A completed **Notice of Social Security Number,** ✎❑ Florida Supreme Court Approved Family Law Form 12.902(j), is filed with this petition.

6. A completed **Family Law Financial Affidavit,** ✎❑ Florida Family Law Rules of Procedure Form 12.902(b) or (c), is, or will be, filed.

I certify that a copy of this document was [√ **one** only] ( ) mailed ( ) faxed and mailed ( ) hand delivered to the person(s) listed below on *{date}* ______________________.

Petitioner or his/her attorney:
Name: ______________________
Address: ______________________
City, State, Zip: ______________________
Fax Number: ______________________

I understand that I am swearing or affirming under oath to the truthfulness of the claims made in this answer and that the punishment for knowingly making a false statement includes fines and/or imprisonment.

Dated: ____________________________

____
Signature of Respondent
Printed Name: ______________________________
Address: __________________________________
City, State, Zip: ____________________________
Telephone Number: __________________________
Fax Number: _______________________________

STATE OF FLORIDA
COUNTY OF ______________________

Sworn to or affirmed and signed before me on ________________ by ____________________________.

____
NOTARY PUBLIC or DEPUTY CLERK

____
[Print, type, or stamp commissioned name of notary or clerk.]

____ Personally known
____ Produced identification
Type of identification produced ________________________

IF A NONLAWYER HELPED YOU FILL OUT THIS FORM, HE/SHE MUST FILL IN THE BLANKS BELOW: [✍ fill in **all** blanks]
I, *{full legal name and trade name of nonlawyer}*____,
a nonlawyer, located at *{street}* ______________________________, *{city}* __________________,
{state} ___________________, *{phone}* __________________, helped *{name}* __________________,
who is the respondent, fill out this form.

IN THE CIRCUIT COURT OF THE ______________________ JUDICIAL CIRCUIT,
IN AND FOR ______________________ COUNTY, FLORIDA

Case No.: ______________________
Division: ______________________

______________________________,
Petitioner/Counterrespondent,
and

______________________________,
Respondent/Counterpetitioner.

**ANSWER TO PETITION AND COUNTERPETITION
TO DETERMINE PATERNITY AND FOR RELATED RELIEF**

I, *{full legal name}* ______________________________, Respondent, being sworn, certify that the following information is true:

ANSWER TO PETITION

1. I **agree** with Petitioner as to the allegations raised in the following numbered paragraphs in the Petition and, therefore, **admit** those allegations: *{indicate section and paragraph number}* ______________________________.

2. I **disagree** with Petitioner as to the allegations raised in the following numbered paragraphs in the Petition and, therefore, **deny** those issues: *{indicate section and paragraph number}* ______________________________.

3. I currently am unable to admit or deny the following paragraphs due to lack of information: *{indicate section and paragraph number}* ______________________________.

**COUNTERPETITION TO DETERMINE PATERNITY
AND FOR RELATED RELIEF**

SECTION I. PATERNITY

1. Respondent is the ( ) mother ( ) father of the following minor child(ren):

	Name	**Place of Birth**	**Birth date**	**Sex**
(1)	________	________	________	________
(2)	________	________	________	________
(3)	________	________	________	________
(4)	________	________	________	________
(5)	________	________	________	________
(6)	________	________	________	________

2. Petitioner currently lives at: *{street address, city, state}* ______________________________.

3. Respondent currently lives at: *{street address, city, state}* ________________________________
____.

4. Both parties are over the age of 18, and neither is, nor has been within a 30 day period immediately prior to this date, a person in the military service of the United States as defined by the Amended Sailors' and Soldiers' Civil Relief Act of 1940.

5. Neither Petitioner nor Respondent is mentally incapacitated.

6. A completed **Uniform Child Custody Jurisdiction Act (UCCJA) Affidavit,** ✎❑ Florida Supreme Court Approved Family Law Form 12.902(d), is filed with this counterpetition.

7. A completed **Notice of Social Security Number,** ✎❑ Florida Supreme Court Approved Family Law Form 12.902(j), is filed with this counterpetition.

8. A completed **Family Law Financial Affidavit,** ✎❑ Florida Family Law Rules of Procedure Form 12.902(b) or (c), is, or will be, filed.

9. **Paternity Facts.**
[√ **one** only]
____ a. Paternity has previously been established as a matter of law.
____ b. The parties engaged in sexual intercourse with each other in the month(s) of *{list month(s) and year(s)}* ____,
at *{city and state}* ____.
As a result of the sexual intercourse, ( ) Petitioner ( ) Respondent conceived and gave birth to the minor child(ren) named in paragraph 1. ( ) Petitioner ( ) Respondent is the natural father of the minor child(ren). The mother ( ) was ( ) was not married at the time of the conception and/or birth of the minor child(ren) named in paragraph 1. If the mother was married, the name and address of her husband at the time of conception and/or birth is: ________________________________
____.

SECTION II. CHILD CUSTODY, PARENTAL RESPONSIBILITY, AND VISITATION

1. The minor child(ren) currently reside(s) with ( ) Mother ( ) Father ( ) Other: *{explain}*______
____.

2. **Parental Responsibility.** It is in the child(ren)'s best interests that parental responsibility be:
[√ **one** only]
____ a. shared by both Father and Mother.
____ b. awarded solely to ( ) Father ( ) Mother. Shared parental responsibility would be detrimental to the child(ren) because: ____
____
____
____.

3. **Primary Residential Parent (Custody).** It is in the best interests of the child(ren) that the primary residential parent be ( ) Father ( ) Mother ( ) undesignated ( ) rotating because __________
____
____

____.

4. **Visitation or Time Sharing.** Respondent requests that the Court order:
[√ **all** that apply]
____ a. no visitation.
____ b. limited visitation.
____ c. supervised visitation.
____ d. supervised or third-party exchange of child(ren).
____ e. visitation or time sharing as determined by the Court.
____ f. a visitation or time sharing schedule as follows:
Explain the requested visitation or time sharing schedule: ______________________
____
____
____
____
____
____

Explain why this request is in the best interests of the child(ren): ______________
____
____
____
____
____

Has the above visitation or time sharing schedule been agreed to by the parties? ( ) yes ( ) no

5. The minor child(ren) should
[√ **only** one]
____ a. retain his/her (their) present name(s).
____ b. receive a change of name as follows:

present name(s)	be changed to
(1) ______________________	(1) ______________________
(2) ______________________	(2) ______________________
(3) ______________________	(3) ______________________
(4) ______________________	(4) ______________________
(5) ______________________	(5) ______________________
(6) ______________________	(6) ______________________

SECTION III. CHILD SUPPORT

[√ **all** that apply]
____ 1. Respondent requests that the court award child support as determined by Florida's child support guidelines, section 61.30, Florida Statutes. A completed **Child Support Guidelines Worksheet,** ✎❑ Florida Family Law Rules of Procedure Form 12.902(e), is, or will be, filed. Such support should be ordered retroactive to:
[√ **one** only]
____ a. the date when the parents did not reside together in the same household with the child, not to exceed a period of 24 months before the date of filing of this counterpetition.
____ b. the date of the filing of this petition.

____ c. other: *{date}* ________________. *{Explain}* ________________________________
____

____ 2. Respondent requests that the Court award a child support amount that is more than or less than Florida's child support guidelines. Respondent understands that a **Motion to Deviate from Child Support Guidelines**, ✎❑ Florida Supreme Court Approved Family Law Form 12.943, **must** be completed before the Court will consider this request.

____ 3. Respondent requests that medical/dental insurance coverage for the minor child(ren) be provided by:
[√ **one** only]
____ a. Father.
____ b. Mother.

____ 4. Respondent requests that uninsured medical/dental expenses for the child(ren) be paid by:
[√ **one** only]
____ a. Father.
____ b. Mother.
____ c. Father and Mother each pay one-half.
____ d. Father and Mother each pay according to the percentages in the **Child Support Guidelines Worksheet**, ✎❑ Florida Family Law Rules of Procedure Form 12.902(e).
____ e. Other *{explain}*: ____
____
____.

____ 5. Respondent requests that life insurance to secure child support be provided by:
[√ **one** only]
____ a. Father.
____ b. Mother.
____ c. Both.

____ 6. ( ) Petitioner ( ) Respondent ( ) Both has (have) incurred medical expenses in the amount of $__________ on behalf of the minor child(ren), including hospital and other expenses incidental to the birth of the minor child(ren). There should be an appropriate allocation or apportionment of these expenses.

____ 7. ( ) Petitioner ( ) Respondent ( ) Both has (have) received past public assistance for this (these) minor child(ren).

RESPONDENT'S REQUEST

1. Respondent requests a hearing on this petition and understands that he or she must attend the hearing.

2. Respondent requests that the Court enter an order that:

[√ **all** that apply]
____ a. establishes paternity of the minor child(ren), ordering proper scientific testing, if necessary;
____ b. establishes parental responsibility, custody, and visitation of the minor child(ren);
____ c. awards child support, including medical/dental insurance coverage, for the minor child(ren);

____ d. determines the appropriate allocation or apportionment of all expenses incidental to the birth of the child(ren), including hospital and medical expenses;

____ e. determines the appropriate allocation or apportionment of all other past, present, and future medical and dental expenses incurred or to be incurred on behalf of the minor child(ren);

____ f. changes the child(ren)'s name(s); and

____ g. other relief as follows: ____
____
____
____; and

grants such other relief as may be appropriate and in the best interests of the minor child(ren).

I certify that a copy of this document was [√ **one** only] ( ) mailed ( ) faxed and mailed ( ) hand delivered to the person(s) listed below on *{date}* ______________________________.

Petitioner or his/her attorney:
Name: ______________________________
Address: ______________________________
City, State, Zip: ______________________________
Fax Number: ______________________________ **I understand that I am swearing or affirming under oath to the truthfulness of the claims made in this answer and counterpetition and that the punishment for knowingly making a false statement includes fines and/or imprisonment.**

Dated: ______________________

____
Signature of Respondent/Counterpetitioner
Printed Name: ______________________
Address: ______________________
City, State, Zip: ______________________
Telephone Number: ______________________
Fax Number: ______________________

STATE OF FLORIDA
COUNTY OF ______________________

Sworn to or affirmed and signed before me on ______________ by ______________________.

____
NOTARY PUBLIC or DEPUTY CLERK

____
[Print, type, or stamp commissioned name of notary or clerk.]

____ Personally known
____ Produced identification
Type of identification produced ______________________

IF A NONLAWYER HELPED YOU FILL OUT THIS FORM, HE/SHE MUST FILL IN THE BLANKS BELOW: [✍ fill in **all** blanks]
I, *{full legal name and trade name of nonlawyer}* ______________________________,
a nonlawyer, located at *{street}* ______________________, *{city}* ______________,
{state} ______________, *{phone}* ______________, helped *{name}* ______________,
who is the respondent, fill out this form.

IN THE CIRCUIT COURT OF THE ____________________ JUDICIAL CIRCUIT,
IN AND FOR ____________________ COUNTY, FLORIDA

Case No.: ____________________
Division: ____________________

____________________,
Petitioner,

and

____________________,
Respondent.

MOTION FOR SCIENTIFIC PATERNITY TESTING

( ) Petitioner ( ) Respondent certifies that the following information is true:

1. At this time, other than testimony, very little or no substantial proof of paternity or nonpaternity is available in this action.

2. I request, under section 742.12, Florida Statutes, that the Court enter an order for appropriate scientific testing of the biological samples of Petitioner and Respondent and the minor child(ren) listed below, so that a determination of paternity of the minor child(ren) can be made to a reasonable degree of medical certainty:

	Name	Birth date
(1)		
(2)		
(3)		
(4)		
(5)		
(6)		

3. I request that the costs of the scientific testing initially be borne by ( ) Petitioner ( ) Respondent ( ) both Petitioner and Respondent.

I certify that a copy of this document was [√ **one** only] ( ) mailed ( ) faxed and mailed ( ) hand delivered to the person(s) listed below on *{date}* ____________________.

( ) Petitioner ( ) Respondent or his/her attorney:
Name: ____________________
Address: ____________________
City, State, Zip: ____________________
Fax Number: ____________________

Dated: ____________________

____
Signature of Party
Printed Name: ____________________
Address: ____________________
City, State, Zip: ____________________

Telephone Number: ______________________
Fax Number: ______________________

STATE OF FLORIDA
COUNTY OF ______________

Sworn to or affirmed and signed before me on ____________ by ______________________.

____
NOTARY PUBLIC or DEPUTY CLERK

____
[Print, type, or stamp commissioned name of notary or clerk.]

___ Personally known
___ Produced identification
Type of identification produced ______________

IF A NONLAWYER HELPED YOU FILL OUT THIS FORM, HE/SHE MUST FILL IN THE BLANKS BELOW: [✍ fill in **all** blanks]
I, *{full legal name and trade name of nonlawyer}* ______________________,
a nonlawyer, located at *{street}* ______________________, *{city}* ______________,
{state} ______________, *{phone}* ______________, helped *{name}* ______________,
who is the [√ **one** only] ___ petitioner **or** ___ respondent, fill out this form.

IN THE CIRCUIT COURT OF THE ______________________ JUDICIAL CIRCUIT,
IN AND FOR ______________________ COUNTY, FLORIDA

Case No.: ______________________
Division: ______________________

______________________,
Petitioner,

and

______________________,
Respondent.

ORDER ON MOTION FOR SCIENTIFIC PATERNITY TESTING

This cause having come to be heard on *{date}* ____________, upon a motion/stipulation for scientific paternity testing, and the Court having been fully advised in the premises, it is therefore FOUND:

1. That the Court has jurisdiction over the parties and subject matter of this action.

2. [√ **one** only]

____ a. That the natural mother of the dependent child(ren) at issue was not married to any individual at the time of conception or birth of the child(ren).

____ b. That the natural mother of the dependent child(ren) at issue was married to an individual other than the alleged father at the time of conception or birth of said child(ren); however, a court order has determined that said individual is not the child(ren)'s father.

It is therefore ORDERED:

1. The above motion is GRANTED.

2. Petitioner, Respondent, and the minor child(ren) shall appear for the purpose of appropriate scientific paternity testing:

[√ **one** only]

____ a. immediately.

____ b. at ________ a.m./p.m. on *{date}* ____________ at *{location}* ____________________.

____ c. at a time and place to be specified by the Florida Department of Revenue. Appropriate scientific paternity testing on Petitioner, Respondent, and the minor child(ren) shall be in *{city}* ______________________, Florida, with at least 30 days advance written notice. If the Florida Department of Revenue fails to notify the party(ies), the party(ies) shall contact the Florida Department of Revenue for further instructions.

3. The costs of the scientific paternity testing shall be assessed ( ) at a later date ( ) against Petitioner ( ) against Respondent ( ) Other *{explain}* ______________________________.

4. The test results, together with the opinions and conclusions of the test laboratory, shall be filed with the Court. Any objection to the test results must be made in writing and must be filed with the Court at least 10 days before the hearing. If no objection is filed, the test results shall be admitted into evidence with no further predicate. Nothing in this paragraph prohibits a party from calling an outside

expert witness to refute or support the testing procedure or results or the mathematical theory on which they are based.

5. Test results are admissible in evidence and should be weighed along with other evidence of the paternity of the alleged father unless the statistical probability of paternity equals or exceeds 95 percent. A statistical probability of 95 percent or more creates a rebuttable presumption that the alleged father is the biological father of the child(ren). If the party fails to rebut the presumption of paternity, the Court may enter a summary judgment of paternity. If the test results show the alleged father cannot be the biological father, the case shall be dismissed with prejudice.

6. The Court reserves jurisdiction over the parties and the subject matter of this action to enforce the terms and provisions of this and all previous orders as well as to enter such other orders as may be just.

ORDERED on ______________________.

____

CIRCUIT JUDGE

COPIES TO:
Petitioner (or his or her attorney)
Respondent (or his or her attorney)
____ Other: ______________________________________.

I CERTIFY the foregoing is a true and correct copy of the original as it appears on file in the office of the Clerk of the Circuit Court of_________________ County, Florida, and that I have furnished copies of this order as indicated above.

CLERK OF THE CIRCUIT COURT

(SEAL)

By: ____
Deputy Clerk

IN THE CIRCUIT COURT OF THE ______________________ JUDICIAL CIRCUIT,
IN AND FOR ______________________ COUNTY, FLORIDA

Case No.: ______________________
Division: ______________________

______________________,
Petitioner,

and

______________________,
Respondent.

FINAL JUDGMENT OF PATERNITY

This cause came before the Court upon a Petition to Determine Paternity and for Related Relief, under chapter 742, Florida Statutes. The Court having reviewed the file and heard the testimony, makes these findings of fact and reaches these conclusions of law:

1. The Court has jurisdiction of the subject matter and the parties.

2. **Paternity.** [√ **one** only] ( ) By operation of law, ( ) The Court finds that *{full legal name}* ______________________________, is the natural and biological father of the minor child(ren), listed below:

The parties' dependent or minor child(ren) is (are):

Name	Birth date

SECTION I. CUSTODY OF AND VISITATION WITH DEPENDENT OR MINOR CHILD(REN)

1. **Jurisdiction.** The Court has jurisdiction to determine custody of and visitation with the parties' minor child(ren) listed in paragraph 2 above.

2. **Parental Responsibility for the Minor Child(ren).**

[√ **one** only]

___ a. **Not adjudicated.** Since no request for relief was made in this action, parental responsibility of the minor child(ren) is governed by sections 742.031 and 744.301, Florida Statutes.

___ b. The parties shall have **shared parental responsibility** for the parties' minor child(ren). ( ) Mother ( ) Father shall have **primary residential responsibility** of the minor child(ren) and the other parent shall have secondary residential responsibility, as set forth in paragraph 3 below. **OR** The primary residential parent shall be ( ) undesignated ( ) rotating with time sharing for the ( ) Mother ( ) Father as set forth in paragraph 4 below.

___ c. ( ) Mother ( ) Father shall have **sole parental responsibility** for the parties' minor child(ren).

Shared parental responsibility would be detrimental to the child(ren) at this time because: ________
____
____
____

The other parent shall have visitation with the parties' minor child(ren) as set forth in paragraph 3 below.

3. **Secondary Residential Responsibility, Visitation or Time Sharing with Minor Child(ren).** The parent granted secondary residential responsibility, visitation, or time sharing shall have:

[√ **one** only]

____ a. **reasonable visitation or time sharing** with the parties' minor child(ren) after reasonable notice and as agreed to by the parties, subject to any limitations in paragraph 5 below. The Court reserves jurisdiction to set a specific schedule.

____ b. the following **specified visitation or time sharing** with the parties' minor child(ren), subject to any limitations set out in paragraph 5 below: *{specify days and times}* ________________
____
____
____
____
____
____
____
____
____
____
____

____ c. **no contact** with the parties' minor child(ren) until further order of the Court, due to the existing conditions that are detrimental to the welfare of the minor child(ren). *{explain}* ____________
____
____

4. **Limitations on Parental Responsibility, Visitation and Time Sharing.** Neither parent shall take the child(ren) from the custody of the other parent or any child care provider or other person entrusted by the other parent with the care of the child(ren) without the agreement of the other parent during the other parent's time of parental responsibility or visitation. The above reasonable (paragraph 3.a. above) or specified (paragraph 3.b. above) visitation shall be:

[√ **if** applies]

____ a. **supervised by a responsible adult** who is mutually agreeable to the parties. If the parties cannot agree, the supervising adult shall be: *{name}* ____________________________.

____ b. at the **supervised visitation** center located at: *{address}* ____________________
____

and shall be subject to the available times and rules of the supervised visitation center. The cost of such visits shall be paid by ( ) Mother ( ) Father ( ) Both.

5. **Communication Arrangements for Secondary Parenting, Visitation, and Time Sharing with Child(ren).**

[√ **if** applies]

____ The parties' communications to arrange visitation or time sharing and discuss issues relating to the child(ren) (if shared parenting or visitation is provided in paragraph 2 above) are restricted as follows:

( ) telephone, ( ) fax, e-mail, or letter, ( ) A responsible person shall coordinate the visitation or time sharing arrangements of the minor child(ren). If the parties cannot agree, the responsible person shall be: *{name}* ______________________________
( ) other conditions for arrangements or discussions: *{explain}* ______________________________
____
____
____
____

6. **Exchange of Minor Child(ren).** The exchange of the minor child(ren) shall be on time as scheduled and as agreed to by the parties. The following conditions, if checked below, shall also apply.

[√ **all** that apply]

____ a. The parties shall exchange the child(ren) at the following location(s): ______________________________
____
____
______________________________.

____ b. The parent granted secondary parenting, visitation, or time sharing shall not get out of the vehicle, and the other parent shall not approach the vehicle, during the time the child(ren) are exchanged.

____ c. A responsible person shall conduct all exchanges of the child(ren). Neither parent shall accompany the responsible person when that person is transferring the child(ren) from one parent to the other. If the parties' cannot agree, the responsible person shall be: *{name}* ______________________________

____ d. Other conditions for exchange of the child(ren) are as follows: ______________________________
____
____
____
____
____

____ 7. **Injunction Prohibiting Removing the Child(ren).** The Court hereby prohibits and enjoins the ( ) Mother ( ) Father ( ) Both from permanently removing the minor child(ren) from the ( ) State of Florida ( ) *{specify}* ______________________________
____
without a court order or the written consent of the other party.

____ 8. **Other Provisions Relating to the Minor Child(ren).**
____
____
____
____
____
____
____
____
____

SECTION II. CHILD SUPPORT

1. The Court finds that there is a need for child support and that the ( ) Mother ( ) Father (hereinafter Obligor) has the present ability to pay child support. The amounts in the **Child Support Guidelines**

Worksheet, ✎❐ Florida Family Law Rules of Procedure Form 12.902(e), filed by the ( ) Mother ( ) Father are correct **OR** the Court makes the following findings: The Mother's net monthly income is $__________, (Child Support Guidelines ____%). The Father's net monthly income is $__________, (Child Support Guidelines ______%). Monthly child care costs are $__________. Monthly health/dental insurance costs are $__________.

2. **Amount.** Obligor shall be obligated to pay child support in the amount of $__________ per month payable ( ) in accordance with Obligor's employer's payroll cycle, and in any event at least once a month ( ) other *{explain}*: ______________________________
____
beginning *{date}* __________, and continuing until

( ) the youngest of the minor child(ren) reaches the age of 18, become(s) emancipated, marries, dies, or otherwise becomes self-supporting **OR** one of the minor children reaches the age of 18, become(s) emancipated, marries, dies, or otherwise becomes self-supporting and either party files a supplemental petition to modify child support and the court enters such an order.
OR
( ) *{date/event}* ____,
{explain} ____.

If the child support ordered deviates from the guidelines by more than 5%, the factual findings which support that deviation are: ______________________________
____
____

3. **Arrearage/Retroactive Child Support.**
[√ **if** applies]
____ a. There is no retroactive child support or arrearage at the time of this Final Judgment.
____ b. ( ) Mother ( ) Father ( ) both has (have) incurred medical expenses in the amount of $ __________ on behalf of the minor child(ren), including hospital and other expenses incidental to the birth of the minor child(ren). Petitioner shall pay ____%, Respondent shall pay ____%, which shall be paid as follows: ( ) added to arrearage in paragraph c below ( ) other *{explain}* __________
____
____ c. The ( ) Mother ( ) Father shall pay to the other party the child support arrearage of:
$__________ for retroactive child support, as of *{date}* ______________.
$__________ for previously ordered unpaid child support, as of *{date}* ______________.
$__________ for previously incurred medical expenses.
The total of $________ in child support arrearage shall be repaid at the rate of $__________ per month, payable ( ) in accordance with Obligor's employer's payroll cycle, and in any event at least once a month ( ) other *{explain}* ______________________________
____,
beginning *{date}* ______________, until paid in full including statutory interest.

4. **Insurance.**
[√ **all** that apply]
____ a. **Health/Dental Insurance.** ( ) Mother ( ) Father shall be required to maintain ( ) health ( ) dental insurance coverage for the parties' minor child(ren), so long as reasonably available. The

party providing coverage shall be required to convey insurance cards demonstrating said coverage to the other party. **OR** ( ) Health ( ) dental insurance is not reasonably available at this time.

____ b. Reasonable and necessary **uninsured medical/dental/prescription drug costs** for the minor child(ren) shall be assessed as follows:

( ) Shared equally by both parents.

( ) Prorated according to the child support guideline percentages.

( ) Other *{explain}*: ____

____.

As to these uninsured medical/dental/prescription drug expenses, the party who incurs the expense shall submit request for reimbursement to the other party within 30 days, and the other party, within 30 days of receipt, shall submit the applicable reimbursement for that expense, according to the schedule of reimbursement set out in this paragraph.

5. **Life Insurance (to secure payment of support).** To secure the child support obligations in this judgment, ( ) Mother ( ) Father ( ) each party shall maintain life insurance coverage, in an amount of at least $__________, on ( ) his life ( ) her life ( ) his/her life naming the ( ) minor child(ren) as the beneficiary(ies) ( ) primary residential parent as the beneficiary as Trustee for the minor child(ren), so long as reasonably available. The obligation to maintain the life insurance coverage shall continue until the youngest child turns 18, becomes emancipated, marries, dies, or otherwise becomes self-supporting.

6. **IRS Income Tax Exemption(s).** The party granted primary residential responsibility or sole parental responsibility of the minor child(ren) shall have the benefit of any tax exemption(s) for the child(ren), **OR**, if checked here, ( ) assignment of any tax exemption(s) for the child(ren) shall be as follows:

____

____.

Further, each party shall execute any and all IRS forms necessary to effectuate the provisions of this paragraph.

7. **Other provisions relating to child support:** ________________________________

____

____

SECTION III. METHOD OF PAYMENT

Obligor shall pay court-ordered child support/alimony and arrears, if any, as follows:

1. **Central Governmental Depository.**

[√ **if** applies]

____ a. Obligor shall pay court-ordered support directly to the Central Governmental Depository in *{name}* ____________________ County, along with any depository service charge.

____ b. Both parties have requested and the court finds that it is in the best interests of the child(ren) that support payments need not be directed through the Central Governmental Depository. However, either party may subsequently apply to the depository pursuant to section 61.13(1)(d)3, Florida Statutes, to require payments through the Central Governmental Depository.

2. **Income Deduction.**

[√ **if** applies]

___ a. **Immediate.** Obligor shall pay through income deduction, pursuant to a separate Income Deduction Order which shall be effective immediately. Obligor is individually responsible for paying this support obligation until all of said support is deducted from Obligor's income. Until support payments are deducted from Obligor's paycheck, Obligor is responsible for making timely payments directly to the Central Governmental Depository or the Obligee, as previously set forth in this order.

___ b. **Deferred.** Income deduction is ordered this day, but it shall not be effective until a delinquency of $__________, or, if not specified, an amount equal to one month's obligation occurs. Income deduction is not being implemented immediately based on the following findings: Income deduction is **not** in the best interests of the child(ren) because: *{explain}* ______________________________
____
____,

AND

there is proof of timely payment of a previously ordered obligation without an income deduction order in cases of modification,

AND

( ) there is an agreement by the Obligor to advise the central governmental depository of any change in payor and health insurance **OR** ( ) there is a signed written agreement providing an alternative arrangement between the Obligor and the Obligee.

3. **Bonus/one-time payments.** ( ) All ( ) _________ % ( ) No income paid in the form of a bonus or other similar one-time payment, up to the amount of any arrearage or the remaining balance thereof owed pursuant to this order, shall be forwarded to Obligee pursuant to the payment method prescribed above.

4. **Other provisions relating to method of payment.** ______________________________
____
____

SECTION IV. CHILD(REN)'S NAME(S)

___ a. There shall be **no change** to the child(ren)'s name(s).

___ b. It is in the child(ren)'s best interests that the child(ren)'s

present name(s)	shall be changed to
(1) ____________________	(1) ____________________
(2) ____________________	(2) ____________________
(3) ____________________	(3) ____________________
(4) ____________________	(4) ____________________
(5) ____________________	(5) ____________________
(6) ____________________	(6) ____________________

by which the minor child(ren) shall hereafter be known.

SECTION V. ATTORNEY FEES, COSTS, AND SUIT MONEY

___ 1. ( ) Petitioner's ( ) Respondent's request(s) for attorney fees, costs, and suit money is (are) denied because ______________________________
____.

___ 2. The Court finds there is a need for and an ability to pay attorney fees, costs, and suit money. ( ) Petitioner ( ) Respondent is hereby ordered to pay to the other party $__________ in attorney fees, and $__________ in costs. The Court further finds that the attorney fees awarded are based on the reasonable rate of $____________ per hour and ____________ reasonable hours. Other provisions relating to attorney fees, costs, and suit money are as follows: ________________

____

____

3. The costs of the scientific paternity testing shall be assessed ( ) against Petitioner ( ) against Respondent ( ) Other *{explain}* ____.

SECTION VI. OTHER PROVISIONS

1. **Other Provisions.** ____

____

____

____

____

____

2. The Court reserves jurisdiction to modify and enforce this Final Judgment.

ORDERED on ______________________.

____

CIRCUIT JUDGE

COPIES TO:
Petitioner (or his or her attorney)
Respondent (or his or her attorney)
Central Governmental Depository
____ Other: ______________________________________

I CERTIFY the foregoing is a true copy of the original as it appears on file in the office of the Clerk of the Circuit Court of ____________ County, Florida, and that I have furnished copies of this order as indicated above.

CLERK OF THE CIRCUIT COURT

(SEAL)

By: ______________________________
Deputy Clerk

IN THE CIRCUIT COURT OF THE ________________________ JUDICIAL CIRCUIT,
IN AND FOR ________________________ COUNTY, FLORIDA

Case No.: ____________________
Division: ____________________

________________________________,
Petitioner,

and

________________________________,
Respondent.

SUPPLEMENTAL FINAL JUDGMENT MODIFYING PARENTAL RESPONSIBILITY/VISITATION

This cause came before this Court on a Supplemental Petition for Modification of Parental Responsibility and Visitation. The Court, having reviewed the file, heard the testimony, and being otherwise fully advised, makes these findings of fact and reaches these conclusions of law:

SECTION I. FINDINGS

1. The Court has jurisdiction over the subject matter and the parties.

2. The last order establishing or modifying parental responsibility or visitation was entered on *{date}* ______________.

3. There has been a substantial change in circumstances of the parties since the entry of the last order, specifically: ____
____
____
____
____
____

4. It is in the best interests of the minor child(ren) that the current parental responsibility/visitation order be changed because: ____
____
____
____
____
____

SECTION II. CUSTODY OF AND VISITATION WITH DEPENDENT OR MINOR CHILD(REN)

1. **Jurisdiction.** The Court has jurisdiction to determine custody of and visitation with the parties' minor child(ren) listed in paragraph 2 below.

2. **The parties' dependent or minor child(ren) is (are):**

Name	Birth date

3. **Parental Responsibility for the Minor Child(ren).**

[√ **one** only]

____ a. The parties shall have **shared parental responsibility** for the parties' minor child(ren). ( ) Mother ( ) Father shall have **primary residential responsibility** of the minor child(ren) and the other parent shall have secondary residential responsibility, as set forth in paragraph 4 below. **OR** The primary residential parent shall be ( ) undesignated ( ) rotating with time sharing for the ( ) Mother ( ) Father as set forth in paragraph 4 below.

____ b. ( ) Mother ( ) Father shall have **sole parental responsibility** for the parties' minor child(ren). Shared parental responsibility would be detrimental to the child(ren) at this time because:
____
____
____.

The other parent shall have visitation with the parties' minor child(ren) as set forth in paragraph 4 below.

4. **Secondary Residential Responsibility, Visitation, or Time Sharing with Minor Child(ren).** The parent granted secondary residential responsibility, visitation, or time sharing shall have:

[√ **one** only]

____ a. **reasonable visitation or time sharing** with the parties' minor child(ren) after reasonable notice and as agreed to by the parties, subject to any limitations in paragraph 5 below. The Court reserves jurisdiction to set a specific schedule.

____ b. the following **specified visitation or time sharing** with the parties' minor child(ren), subject to any limitations set out in paragraph 5 below: *{specify days and times}* ______________
____
____
____
____
____
____
____
____

____ c. **no contact** with the parties' minor child(ren) until further order of the Court, due to the existing conditions that are detrimental to the welfare of the minor child(ren). *{explain}* ______________
____

____

5. **Limitations on Parental Responsibility, Visitation or Time Sharing.** Neither parent shall take the child(ren) from the custody of the other parent or any child care provider or other person entrusted by the other parent with the care of the child(ren) without the agreement of the other parent during the other parent's time of parental responsibility or visitation. The above reasonable (paragraph 4.a. above) or specified (paragraph 4.b. above) visitation shall be:

[√ **if** applies]

___ a. **supervised by a responsible adult** who is mutually agreeable to the parties. If the parties cannot agree, the supervising adult shall be: *{name}* ______________________________.

___ b. at the **supervised visitation center** located at: *{address}* ______________________________ ______________________________, subject to the available times and rules of the supervised visitation center. The cost of such visits shall be paid by ( ) Mother ( ) Father ( ) Both.

6. **Communication Arrangements for Secondary Parenting, Visitation, or Time Sharing with Child(ren).**

[√ **if** applies]

___ The parties' communications to arrange visitation or time sharing and discuss issues relating to the child(ren) (if shared parenting or visitation is provided in paragraph 3 above) are restricted as follows: ( ) telephone, ( ) fax, e-mail, or letter, ( ) A responsible person shall coordinate the visitation or time sharing arrangements of the minor child(ren). If the parties cannot agree, the responsible person shall be: *{name}* ______________________________

( ) other conditions for arrangements or discussions: *{explain}* ______________________________
____
____
____

7. **Exchange of Minor Child(ren).** The exchange of the minor child(ren) shall be on time as scheduled and as agreed to by the parties. The following conditions, if checked below, shall also apply.

[√ **all** that apply]

___ a. The parties shall exchange the child(ren) at the following location(s): ______________________________
____
____
______________________________.

___ b. The parent granted secondary parenting, visitation, or time sharing shall not get out of the vehicle, and the other parent shall not approach the vehicle, during the time the child(ren) are exchanged.

___ c. A responsible person shall conduct all exchanges of the child(ren). Neither parent shall accompany the responsible person when that person is transferring the child(ren) from one parent to the other. If the parties' cannot agree, the responsible person shall be: *{name}* ______________________________

___ d. Other conditions for exchange of the child(ren) are as follows: ______________________________
____
____
____
____
____

___ 8. **Injunction Prohibiting Removing the Child(ren).** The Court hereby prohibits and enjoins the

( ) Mother ( ) Father ( ) Both from permanently removing the minor child(ren) from the ( ) State of Florida ( ) other *{specify}* ______________________________

____

without a court order or the written consent of the other party.

___ 9. **Other Provisions Relating to the Minor Child(ren).**

____

____

____

____

____

____

____

____

____

SECTION III. CHILD SUPPORT

1. **Modification of Child Support.**

[√ one only]

___ a. The modification of parental responsibility or visitation entered above does not necessitate a modification of child support. The previous order or final judgment establishing or modifying child support shall remain in effect.

___ b. The Court finds that there is a need for modification of child support and that the ( ) Mother ( ) Father (hereinafter Obligor) has the present ability to pay child support. The amounts in the Child Support Guidelines Worksheet, ✎❒ Florida Family Law Rules of Procedure Form 12.902(e), filed by the ( ) Mother ( ) Father are correct **OR** the Court makes the following findings: The Mother's net monthly income is $____, (Child Support Guidelines _%). The Father's net monthly income is $____________, (Child Support Guidelines ___%). Monthly child care costs are $___________. Monthly health/dental insurance costs are $__________.

2. **Amount.** Obligor shall be obligated to pay child support in the amount of $___________, per month payable ( ) in accordance with Obligor's employer's payroll cycle, and in any event at least once a month ( ) other *{explain}*: ______________________________

______________________________,

beginning *{date}* ________________, and continuing until

( ) the youngest of the minor child(ren) reaches the age of 18, become(s) emancipated, marries, dies, or otherwise becomes self-supporting **OR** one of the minor children reaches the age of 18, become(s) emancipated, marries, dies, or otherwise becomes self-supporting and either party files a supplemental petition to modify child support and the court enters such an order.

OR

( ) *{date/event}* ______________________________,
{explain} ______________________________.

If the child support ordered deviates from the guidelines by more than 5%, the factual findings which

support that deviation are: ____
____
____

3. **Arrearage/Retroactive Child Support.**
[√ **one** only]
____ a. There is no child support arrearage at the time of this Supplemental Final Judgment.
____ b. The ( ) Mother ( ) Father shall pay to the other party the child support arrearage of: $__________ for retroactive child support, as of *{date}* ____________________. $_________ for previously ordered unpaid child support, as of *{date}* ________________. The total of $_________ in child support arrearage shall be repaid in the amount of $___________, per month payable ( ) in accordance with Obligor's employer's payroll cycle, and in any event at least once a month ( ) other *{explain}* ____
____
beginning *{date}* __________________, until paid in full including statutory interest.

4. **Insurance.**
[√ **all** that apply]
____ a. **Health/Dental Insurance.** ( ) Mother ( ) Father shall be required to maintain ( ) health ( ) dental insurance coverage for the parties' minor child(ren), so long as reasonably available. The party providing coverage shall be required to convey insurance cards demonstrating said coverage to the other party. **OR** ( ) Health ( ) dental insurance is not reasonably available at this time.
____ b. Reasonable and necessary **uninsured medical/dental/prescription drug costs** for the minor child(ren) shall be assessed as follows:
( ) Shared equally by both parents.
( ) Prorated according to the child support guideline percentages.
( ) Other *{explain}*: ____
____
As to these uninsured medical/dental/prescription drug expenses, the party who incurs the expense shall submit a request for reimbursement to the other party within 30 days, and the other party, within 30 days of receipt, shall submit the applicable reimbursement for that expense, according to the schedule of reimbursement set out in this paragraph.

5. **Life Insurance (to secure payment of support).** To secure the child support obligations in this judgment, ( ) Petitioner ( ) Respondent ( ) Each party shall maintain life insurance coverage, in an amount of at least $_____, on ( ) his life ( ) her life ( ) his/her life naming the ( ) minor child(ren) as the beneficiary(ies) ( ) primary residentialparent as the beneficiary as Trustee for the minor child(ren), so long as reasonably available. The obligation to maintain the life insurance coverage shall continue until the first of the parties' minor children reaches the age of 18 or until one of the parties' children becomes emancipated, marries, dies, otherwise becomes self-supporting, at which time the amount of life insurance shall be recomputed.

6. **IRS Income Tax Exemption(s).** The party granted primary residential responsibility or sole parental responsibility of the minor child(ren) shall have the benefit of any tax exemption(s) for the child(ren), **OR**, if checked here, ( ) assignment of any tax exemption(s) for the child(ren) shall be as follows: ____
____.
Further, each party shall execute any and all IRS forms necessary to effectuate the provisions of this

paragraph.

7. **Other provisions relating to child support:** ____
____
____

SECTION IV. METHOD OF PAYMENT

Obligor shall pay court-ordered child support and arrears, if any, as follows:

1. **Central Governmental Depository.**

[√ **if** applies]

____ a. Obligor shall pay court-ordered support directly to the Central Governmental Depository in *{name of county}* ______________________ County, along with any depository service charge.

____ b. Both parties have requested and the court finds that it is in the best interests of the child(ren) that support payments need not be directed through the Central Governmental Depository. However, either party may subsequently apply to the depository pursuant to section 61.13(1)(d)3, Florida Statutes, to require payments through the Central Governmental Depository.

2. **Income Deduction.**

[√ **if** applies]

___ a. **Immediate.** Obligor shall pay through income deduction, pursuant to a separate Income Deduction Order which shall be effective immediately. Obligor is individually responsible for paying this support obligation until all of said support is deducted from Obligor's income. Until support payments are deducted from Obligor's paycheck, Obligor is responsible for making timely payments directly to the Central Governmental Depository or the Obligee, as previously set forth in this order.

___ b. **Deferred.** Income deduction is ordered this day, but it shall not be effective until a delinquency of $____________, or, if not specified, an amount equal to one month's obligation occurs. Income deduction is not being implemented immediately based on the following findings: Income deduction is **not** in the best interests of the child(ren) because: *{explain}* ______________________________
____
____,

AND

there is proof of timely payment of a previously ordered obligation without an income deduction order,

AND

( ) there is an agreement by the Obligor to advise the central governmental depository of any change in payor and health insurance **OR** ( ) there is a signed written agreement providing an alternative arrangement between the Obligor and the Obligee.

3. **Bonus/one-time payments.** ( ) All ( ) _________% ( ) No income paid in the form of a bonus or other similar one-time payment, up to the amount of any arrearage or the remaining balance thereof owed pursuant to this order, shall be forwarded to Obligee pursuant to the payment method prescribed above.

4. **Other provisions relating to method of payment.** ______________________________________
____
____

SECTION V. ATTORNEY FEES, COSTS, AND SUIT MONEY

___ 1. ( ) Petitioner's ( ) Respondent's request(s) for attorney fees, costs, and suit money is (are) denied because ____
____.

___ 2. The Court finds there is a need for and an ability to pay attorney fees, costs, and suit money. ( ) Petitioner ( ) Respondent is hereby ordered to pay to the other party $________ in attorney fees, and $________ in costs. The Court further finds that the attorney fees awarded are based on the reasonable rate of $____________ per hour and ___________ reasonable hours. Other provisions relating to attorney fees, costs, and suit money are as follows: ______________________________
____
____

SECTION VI. OTHER

1. **Other Provisions.** ____
____
____
____
____

2. The Court reserves jurisdiction to modify and enforce this Supplemental Final Judgment.

3. Unless specifically modified by this supplemental final judgment, the provisions of all final judgments or orders in effect remain the same.

ORDERED on ______________________.

____
CIRCUIT JUDGE

COPIES TO:
Petitioner (or his or her attorney)
Respondent (or his or her attorney)
Central Governmental Depository
Other: ______________________________

Florida Supreme Court Approved Family Law Form 12.993(a), Supplemental Final Judgment Modifying Parental Responsibility/Visitation (9/00)

IN THE CIRCUIT COURT OF THE ______________________ JUDICIAL CIRCUIT,
IN AND FOR ______________________ COUNTY, FLORIDA

Case No.: ______________________
Division: ______________________

______________________,
Petitioner,

and

______________________,
Respondent.

SUPPLEMENTAL FINAL JUDGMENT MODIFYING CHILD SUPPORT

This cause came before this Court on a Supplemental Petition for Modification of Child Support. The Court, having heard the testimony and reviewed the file and financial affidavits of the parties and being otherwise fully advised, makes these findings of fact and reaches these conclusions of law:

SECTION I. FINDINGS

1. The Court has jurisdiction over the subject matter and the parties.

2. **The parties' dependent or minor child(ren) is (are):**

Name	**Birth date**

3. The last order awarding or modifying child support was entered on *{date}* ______________.

4. There has been a substantial change in circumstances of the parties since the entry of the last order, specifically: ____
____
____
____
____
____

5. It is in the best interests of the minor child(ren) that the current child support order be changed because: ____
____
____
____
____
____.

SECTION II. CHILD SUPPORT

1. The Court finds that there is a need for modification of child support and that the ( ) Mother ( ) Father (hereinafter Obligor) has the present ability to pay child support. The amounts in the Child Support Guidelines Worksheet, ✎❒ Florida Family Law Rules of Procedure Form 12.902(e), filed by the ( ) Mother ( ) Father are correct **OR** the Court makes the following findings: The Mother's net monthly income is $__________, (Child Support Guidelines ________%). The Father's net monthly income is $__________, (Child Support Guidelines ____________%). Monthly child care costs are $________. Monthly health/dental insurance costs are $ ______________________.

2. **Amount.** Obligor shall be obligated to pay child support in the amount of $ __________, per month payable ( ) in accordance with Obligor's employer's payroll cycle, and in any event at least once a month ( ) other *{explain}*: ____
____,
beginning *{date}* ____________________, and continuing until

   ( ) the youngest of the minor child(ren) reaches the age of 18, become(s) emancipated, marries, dies, or otherwise becomes self-supporting **OR** one of the minor children reaches the age of 18, become(s) emancipated, marries, dies, or otherwise becomes self-supporting and either party files a supplemental petition to modify child support and the court enters such an order.

   OR

   ( ) *{date/event}* ____,
   {explain} ____.

   If the child support ordered deviates from the guidelines by more than 5%, the factual findings which support that deviation are: ____
   ____
   ____

3. **Arrearage/Retroactive Child Support.**
[√ **one** only]
____ a. There is no child support arrearage at the time of this Supplemental Final Judgment.
____ b. The ( ) Mother ( ) Father shall pay to the other party the child support arrearage of: $__________ for retroactive child support, as of *{date}* __________________. $_________ for previously ordered unpaid child support, as of *{date}* ______________________________.
The total of $______________ in child support arrearage shall be repaid in the amount of $____________, per month payable ( ) in accordance with his or her employer's payroll cycle, and in any event at least once a month ( ) other *{explain}*______________________________
____
beginning *{date}* ______________________, until paid in full including statutory interest.

4. **Insurance.**
[√ **all** that apply]
____ a. **Health/Dental Insurance.** ( ) Mother ( ) Father shall be required to maintain ( ) health

( ) dental insurance coverage for the parties' minor child(ren), so long as reasonably available. The party providing coverage shall be required to convey insurance cards demonstrating said coverage to the other party. **OR** ( ) Health ( ) Dental insurance is not reasonably available at this time.

____ b. Reasonable and necessary **uninsured medical/dental/prescription costs** for the minor child(ren) shall be assessed as follows:

( ) Shared equally by both parents.

( ) Prorated according to the child support guideline percentages.

( ) Other *{explain}*: ____

____

As to these uninsured medical/dental/prescription expenses, the party who incurs the expense shall submit a request for reimbursement to the other party within 30 days, and the other party, within 30 days of receipt, shall submit the applicable reimbursement for that expense, according to the schedule of reimbursement set out in this paragraph.

5. **Life Insurance (to secure payment of support).** To secure the child support obligations in this judgment, ( ) Mother ( ) Father ( ) Each party shall maintain life insurance coverage, in an amount of at least $________________, on ( ) his life ( ) her life ( ) his/her life naming the ( ) minor child(ren) as the beneficiary(ies) ( ) primary residential parent as the beneficiary as Trustee for the minor child(ren), so long as reasonably available. The obligation to maintain the life insurance coverage shall continue until the first of the parties' minor children reaches the age of 18 or until one of the parties' children becomes emancipated, marries, dies, otherwise becomes self-supporting, at which time the amount of life insurance coverage shall be recomputed.

6. **IRS Income Tax Exemption(s).** The party granted primary residential responsibility or sole parental responsibility of the minor child(ren) shall have the benefit of any tax exemption(s) for the child(ren), **OR**, if checked here, ( ) assignment of any tax exemption(s) for the child(ren) shall be as follows:

____

____.

Further, each party shall execute any and all IRS forms necessary to effectuate the provisions of this paragraph.

7. **Other provisions relating to child support:** ____

____

____

SECTION III. METHOD OF PAYMENT

1. **Central Governmental Depository.**

[√ **if** applies]

____ a. Obligor shall pay court-ordered support directly to the Central Governmental Depository in *{name of county}* ________________________ County, along with any depository service charge.

____ b. Both parties have requested and the court finds that it is in the best interests of the child(ren) that support payments need not be directed through the Central Governmental Depository. However, either party may subsequently apply to the depository pursuant to section 61.13(1)(d)3, Florida Statutes, to require payments through the Central Governmental Depository.

2. **Income Deduction.**

[√ **if** applies]

___ a. **Immediate.** Obligor shall pay through income deduction, pursuant to a separate Income Deduction Order which shall be effective immediately. Obligor is individually responsible for paying this support obligation until all of said support is deducted from Obligor's income. Until support payments are deducted from Obligor's paycheck, Obligor is responsible for making timely payments directly to the Central Governmental Depository or the Obligee, as previously set forth in this order.

___ b. **Deferred.** Income deduction is ordered this day, but it shall not be effective until a delinquency of $__________, or, if not specified, an amount equal to one month's obligation occurs. Income deduction is not being implemented immediately based on the following findings: Income deduction is **not** in the best interests of the child(ren) because: *{explain}* ______________________________
____
____,

AND

there is proof of timely payment of a previously ordered obligation without an income deduction order,

AND

( ) there is an agreement by the Obligor to advise the central governmental depository of any change in payor and health insurance **OR** ( ) there is a signed written agreement providing an alternative arrangement between the Obligor and the Obligee.

3. **Bonus/one-time payments.** ( ) All ( ) __________% ( ) No income paid in the form of a bonus or other similar one-time payment, up to the amount of any arrearage or the remaining balance thereof owed pursuant to this order, shall be forwarded to Obligee pursuant to the payment method prescribed above.

4. **Other provisions relating to method of payment.** ______________________________
____
____

SECTION IV. ATTORNEY FEES, COSTS, AND SUIT MONEY

___ 1. ( ) Petitioner's ( ) Respondent's request(s) for attorney fees, costs, and suit money is (are) denied because ____
____.

___ 2. The Court finds there is a need for and an ability to pay attorney fees, costs, and suit money. ( ) Petitioner ( ) Respondent is hereby ordered to pay to the other party $________ in attorney fees, and $________ in costs. The Court further finds that the attorney fees awarded are based on the reasonable rate of $________________ per hour and ________ reasonable hours. Other provisions relating to attorney fees, costs, and suit money are as follows: ______________________
____
____

SECTION V. OTHER

1. **Other Provisions.** ____
____
____
____
____
____

2. The Court reserves jurisdiction to modify and enforce this Supplemental Final Judgment.

3. Unless specifically modified by this supplemental final judgment, the provisions of all final judgment or orders in effect remain the same.

ORDERED on ________________________.

____
CIRCUIT JUDGE

COPIES TO:
Petitioner (or his or her attorney)
Respondent (or his or her attorney)
Central Governmental Depository
Other: __________________________________

IN THE CIRCUIT COURT OF THE ______________________________ JUDICIAL CIRCUIT,
IN AND FOR ______________________________ COUNTY, FLORIDA

Case No.: ____________________
Division: ____________________

______________________________,
Petitioner,

and

______________________________,
Respondent.

FINAL JUDGMENT FOR SUPPORT UNCONNECTED WITH DISSOLUTION OF MARRIAGE WITH DEPENDENT OR MINOR CHILD(REN)

This cause came before this Court on a Petition for Support Unconnected with Dissolution of Marriage under section 61.09, Florida Statutes. The Court, having reviewed the file and heard the testimony, makes these findings of fact and reaches these conclusions of law:

1. The Court has jurisdiction over the subject matter and the parties.

2. Petitioner has custody of the following minor child(ren) common to the parties or the child(ren) has (have) primary residence with Petitioner.

Name	**Birth date**

SECTION I. ALIMONY

1. ( ) The Court denies the request(s) for alimony. **OR**
( ) The Court finds that there is a need for alimony and that Respondent has/had the ability to support Petitioner and has failed to do so. Respondent (hereinafter Obligor) has the present ability to pay alimony as follows:

[√ **all** that apply]

___ a. **Permanent Periodic.** Obligor shall pay permanent periodic alimony to Obligee in the amount of $__________ per month, payable ( ) in accordance with Obligor's employer's payroll cycle, and in any event, at least once a month ( ) other *{explain}* ______________________________
____
beginning *{date}* ______________________. This alimony shall continue until modified by court order, the death of either party, or remarriage of Obligee, whichever occurs first.

___ b. **Lump Sum.** Obligor shall pay lump sum alimony to Obligee in the amount of $__________.
This amount shall be paid as follows: ______________________________
____

____

____ c. **Rehabilitative.** Obligor shall pay rehabilitative alimony to Obligee in the amount of $________ per month, payable ( ) in accordance with Obligor's employer's payroll cycle, and in any event, at least once a month ( ) other *{explain}* ____ beginning *{date}* ________________. This rehabilitative alimony shall continue until modified by court order, the death of either party or until *{date/event}* ______________________________, whichever occurs first. The rehabilitative plan presented demonstrated the following: __________
____
____

____ d. **Retroactive.** Obligor shall pay retroactive alimony in the amount of $________________ for the period of *{date}* ________________, through *{date}* ________________, which shall be paid pursuant to paragraph 3 below.

2. **Reasons for ( ) Awarding ( ) Denying Alimony.** The Court has considered all of the following in awarding/denying alimony:

a. The standard of living established during the marriage;

b. The duration of the marriage;

c. The age and the physical and emotional condition of each party;

d. The financial resources of each party, the nonmarital and the marital assets and liabilities distributed to each;

e. The contribution of each party to the marriage, including, but not limited to, services rendered in homemaking, child care, education, and career building of the other party; and

f. All sources of income available to either party.

Additionally, the Court has considered the following factors in reaching its decision: __________
____
____
____
____
____

□ Check here if additional pages are attached.

3. **Arrearage/Retroactive Alimony.**

[√ **one** only]

____ a. There is no alimony arrearage at the time of this Final Judgment.

____ b. Respondent shall pay to Petitioner the alimony arrearage of: $__________ for retroactive alimony, as of *{date}* ______________. $__________ for previously ordered unpaid alimony, as of *{date}* ________________. The total of $__________ in alimony arrearage shall be repaid in the amount of $__________ per month, payable ( ) in accordance with Obligor's employer's payroll cycle, and in any event, at least once a month ( ) other *{explain}* ______________________________
____
beginning *{date}* ________________, until paid in full including statutory interest.

4. **Insurance.**

[√ **all** that apply]

____ a. **Health Insurance.** ( ) Petitioner ( ) Respondent shall be required to pay health insurance premiums for the other party not to exceed $__________ per month. Further, ( ) Petitioner ( ) Respondent shall pay any reasonable and necessary uninsured medical costs for the other party not to exceed $____________ per year. As to these uninsured medical expenses, the party who is entitled to reimbursement of the uninsured medical expense shall submit a request for reimbursement to the other party within 30 days, and the other party shall, within 30 days after receipt, submit the applicable reimbursement for that expense.

____ b. **Life Insurance (to secure payment of support).** To secure the alimony obligations set forth in this judgment, Obligor shall maintain life insurance coverage on his/her life naming Obligee as the sole irrevocable beneficiary, so long as reasonably available. This insurance shall be in the amount of at least $____________________ and shall remain in effect until the obligation for alimony terminates.

5. **Other provisions relating to alimony:** ____
____
____
____.

SECTION II. CHILD SUPPORT

1. The Court finds that there is a need for child support and that the ( ) Mother ( ) Father (hereinafter Obligor) has the present ability to pay child support. The amounts in the Child Support Guidelines Worksheet, ✎❒ Florida Family Law Rules of Procedure Form 12.902(e), filed by the ( ) Mother ( ) Father are correct **OR** the Court makes the following findings: The Mother's net monthly income is $____, (Child Support Guidelines ______%). The Father's net monthly income is $____________, (Child Support Guidelines ________%). Monthly child care costs are $________. Monthly health/dental insurance costs are $_______________.

2. **Amount.** Obligor shall be obligated to pay child support in the amount of $_______________, per month payable ( ) in accordance with Obligor's employer's payroll cycle, and in any event at least once a month ( ) other *{explain}:* ____
____,
beginning *{date}* ____________________, and continuing

( ) until the first of the parties' minor children reaches the age of 18 or until one of the parties' children becomes emancipated, marries, dies, otherwise becomes self-supporting, at which time the child support shall be recomputed under the then-current Child Support Guidelines

OR

( ) until *{date/event}* ____,
{explain} ____.

If the child support ordered deviates from the guidelines by more than 5%, the factual findings which support that deviation are: ____
____
____

3. **Arrearage/Retroactive Child Support.**
[√ **one** only]
____ a. There is no child support arrearage at the time of this Final Judgment.
____ b. The ( ) Mother ( ) Father shall pay to the other party the child support arrearage of: $__________ for retroactive child support, as of *{date}* ____________________. $__________ for

previously ordered unpaid child support, as of *{date}* ________________________________.
The total of $______________________ in child support arrearage shall be repaid in the amount of $____________ per month, payable ( ) in accordance with Obligor's employer's payroll cycle, and in any event, at least once a month ( ) other *{explain}* ______________________________

____

beginning *{date}* __________________________, until paid in full including statutory interest.

4. **Insurance.**
[√ **all** that apply]

____ a. **Health/Dental Insurance.** ( ) Mother ( ) Father shall be required to maintain ( ) health ( ) dental insurance coverage for the parties' minor child(ren), so long as reasonably available. The party providing coverage shall be required to convey insurance cards demonstrating said coverage to the other party. **OR** ( ) Health ( ) dental insurance is not reasonably available at this time.

____ b. Reasonable and necessary **uninsured medical/dental/prescription drug costs** for the minor child(ren) shall be assessed as follows:
( ) Shared equally by both parents.
( ) Prorated according to the child support guideline percentages.
( ) Other *{explain}*: ____

____

As to these uninsured medical/dental/prescription drug expenses, the party who incurs the expense shall submit a request for reimbursement to the other party within 30 days, and the other party, within 30 days of receipt, shall submit the applicable reimbursement for that expense, according to the schedule of reimbursement set out in this paragraph.

5. **Life Insurance (to secure payment of support).** To secure the child support obligations in this judgment, ( ) Petitioner ( ) Respondent ( ) Each party shall maintain life insurance coverage, in an amount of at least $______________, on ( ) his life ( ) her life ( ) his/her life naming the ( ) minor child(ren) as the beneficiary(ies) ( ) primary residential parent as the beneficiary as Trustee for the minor child(ren). The obligation to maintain the life insurance coverage shall continue until the youngest child turns 18, becomes emancipated, marries, dies, or otherwise becomes self-supporting.

6. **IRS Income Tax Exemption(s).** Petitioner shall have the benefit of any tax exemption(s) for the child(ren), **OR**, if checked here, ( ) assignment of any tax exemption(s) for the child(ren) shall be as follows: ____

____.

Further, each party shall execute any and all IRS forms necessary to effectuate the provisions of this paragraph.

7. **Other provisions relating to child support:** ______________________________________

____

____

SECTION III. METHOD OF PAYMENT

Obligor shall pay court-ordered child support/alimony and arrears, if any, as follows:

1. **Central Governmental Depository.**
[√ **if** applies]

___ a. Obligor shall pay court-ordered support directly to the Central Governmental Depository in *{name}*

_____________________ County, along with any depository service charge.

____ b. Both parties have requested and the court finds that it is in the best interests of the child(ren) that support payments need not be directed through the Central Governmental Depository. However, either party may subsequently apply to the depository pursuant to section 61.08 or 61.13, Florida Statutes, to require payments through the Central Governmental Depository.

2. **Income Deduction.**

[√ if applies]

____ a. **Immediate.** Obligor shall pay through income deduction, pursuant to a separate Income Deduction Order which shall be effective immediately. Obligor is individually responsible for paying this support obligation until all of said support is deducted from Obligor's income. Until support payments are deducted from Obligor's paycheck, Obligor is responsible for making timely payments directly to the Central Governmental Depository or the Obligee, as previously set forth in this order.

____ b. **Deferred.** Income deduction is ordered this day, but it shall not be effective until a delinquency of $____________, or, if not specified, an amount equal to one month's obligation occurs. Income deduction is not being implemented immediately based on the following findings: Income deduction is **not** in the best interests of the child(ren) because: *{explain}* ______________________________
____
____,

AND

there is proof of timely payment of a previously ordered obligation without an income deduction order in cases of modification,

AND

( ) there is an agreement by the Obligor to advise the central governmental depository of any change in payor and health insurance **OR** ( ) there is a signed written agreement providing an alternative arrangement between the Obligor and the Obligee.

3. **Bonus/one-time payments.** ( ) All ( ) _________% ( ) No income paid in the form of a bonus or other similar one-time payment, up to the amount of any arrearage or the remaining balance thereof owed pursuant to this order, shall be forwarded to Obligee pursuant to the payment method prescribed above.

4. **Other provisions relating to method of payment.** ______________________________
____
____

SECTION IV. ATTORNEY FEES, COSTS, AND SUIT MONEY

____ 1. ( ) Petitioner's ( ) Respondent's request(s) for attorney fees, costs, and suit money is (are) denied because ____
____.

____ 2. The Court finds there is a need for and an ability to pay attorney fees, costs, and suit money. ( ) Petitioner ( ) Respondent is hereby ordered to pay to the other party $________ in attorney fees, and $________ in costs. The Court further finds that the attorney fees awarded are based on the reasonable rate of $_______ per hour and ____________ reasonable hours. Other provisions relating to attorney fees, costs, and suit money are as follows: ______________________________
____
____

SECTION V. OTHER PROVISIONS

1. **Other Provisions:** ____

____
____
____
____
____

2. The Court reserves jurisdiction to modify and enforce this Final Judgment.

ORDERED on ________________________.

____
CIRCUIT JUDGE

COPIES TO:
Petitioner (or his or her attorney)
Respondent (or his or her attorney)
Central Governmental Depository
Other: __________________________________

INDEX